MINTED

ARTISTS ON THE BLOCKCHAIN

Mint Face

Dedication

To be an artist is to believe in the future.

This book is dedicated to my son, Joseph.

We shall create art together one day and it will be glorious.

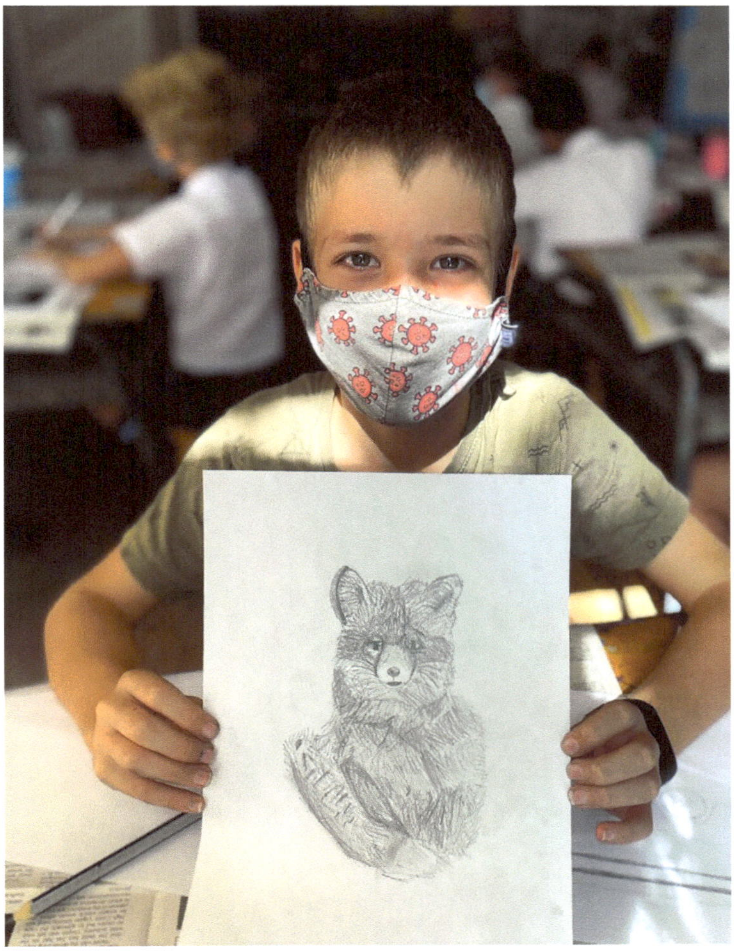

Table of Contents

Introduction

gm and welcome to **Minted**.

2021 was a watershed year for digital art. By minting on the Ethereum blockchain, artists established the verifiable provenance of their art at record levels. Collectors flooded the NFT space and acquired art at never-seen-before heights that reached a peak during the Northern Hemisphere's summer, a phenomenon dubbed 'JPEG Summer.'

Artworks featured in the **Minted** book, illustrate the depth and breadth of artistic style, aesthetic and vibe made possible thanks to marketplaces such as SuperRare, Foundation, OpenSea, FXHash, Kalamint, and Rarible who have created many of the digital galleries where minted art can be found.

Why does minted art matter? Collectors enjoy a direct connection with artists—getting closer than was possible when galleries acted as an intermediary. The power of Web3.0 creates new possibilities that go beyond the initial art sale. Artists can learn what their patrons like to collect by visiting their OnCyber gallery. Artists can reward collectors with airdrops of NFT artworks. Collectors can easily bid or buy works confident that almost all of the digital currency goes directly to the wallet of the artist.

While much of this may have been possible in some way with Web2.0 eCommerce, credit card payments were never truly Internet native. The checkout process created friction and, over time, the social media platforms reduced artists ability to reach potential buyers. Web3.0 smashes that 'good enough' environment by putting a direct, wallet-to-wallet connection at the very heart of the artist/collector relationship. For an IRL (in real life) analogy, it's like 'tap and go' payment after a lifetime of entering a PIN.

Minted is an opportunity for you to glimpse the shining light of possibility that is represented by each artist. Each artist overcame the fear of the unknown and set up their digital wallet, navigated minting their art as an NFT, and went on to share their artwork with collectors around the world.

If you're a collector, I hope the art contained within this book inspires you to acquire NFTs from these talented artists, and to create an own art collection that reflects who you are. If you're an artist who shares their art in Web2.0 (getting paid in 'Likes'), it's time to mint your creativity, and invite your biggest fans to invest in your career. Make your mark as a timestamp and create your signature as a .eth domain address. It's time.

MintFace.eth

GENERATIVE ART

Generative art is created, in whole or in part, with the use of an autonomous system, often programmed by the artist.

@0x_3b
Software engineer & generative artist

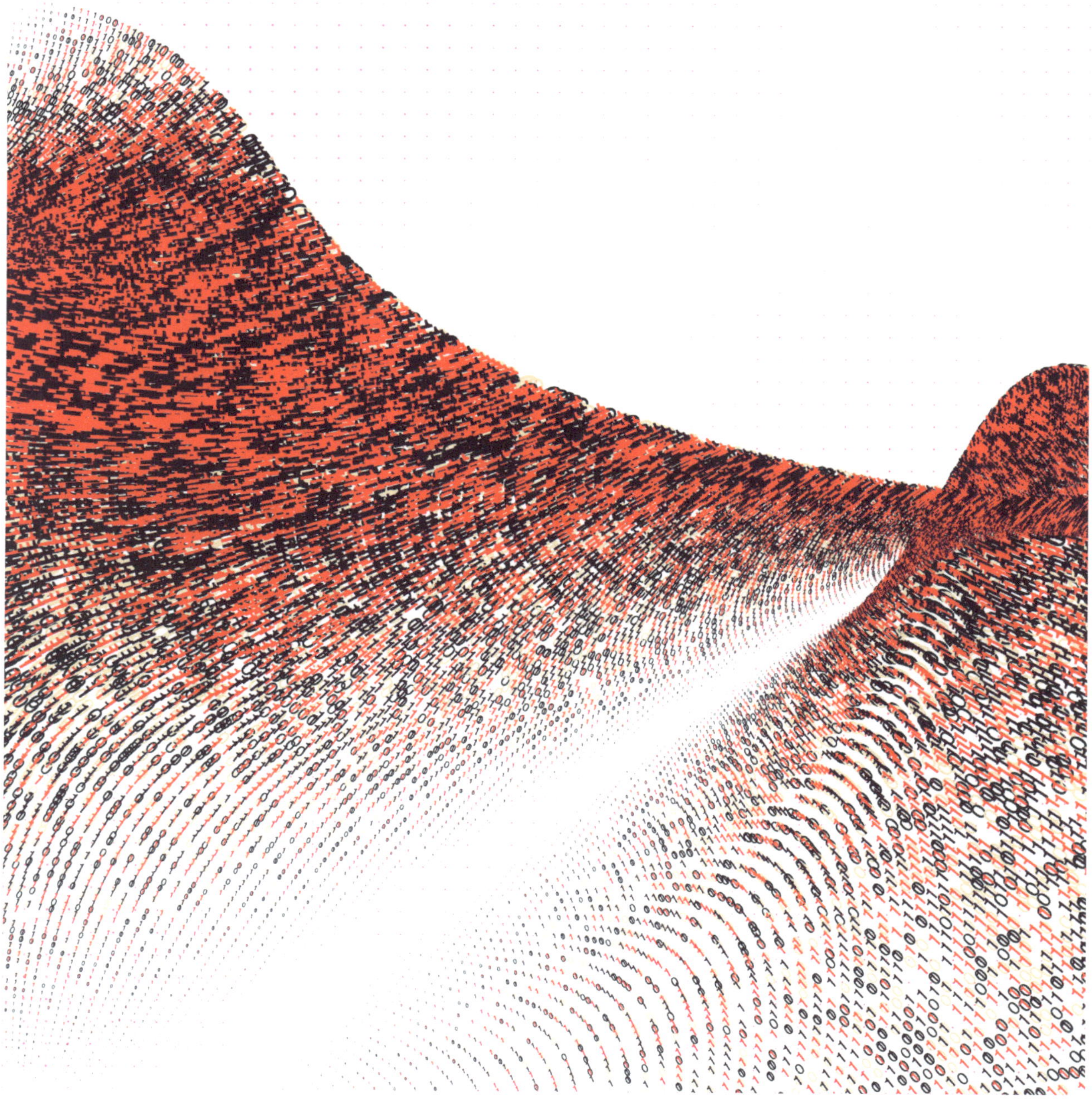

BitWaves #10
opensea.io/collection/bitwaves
Minted: August 2, 2021

@BeautifoolData
Developer & NFT creator

"Each circle orbits another with a constant direction and speed. The path of the smallest one creates a Fourier Punk."

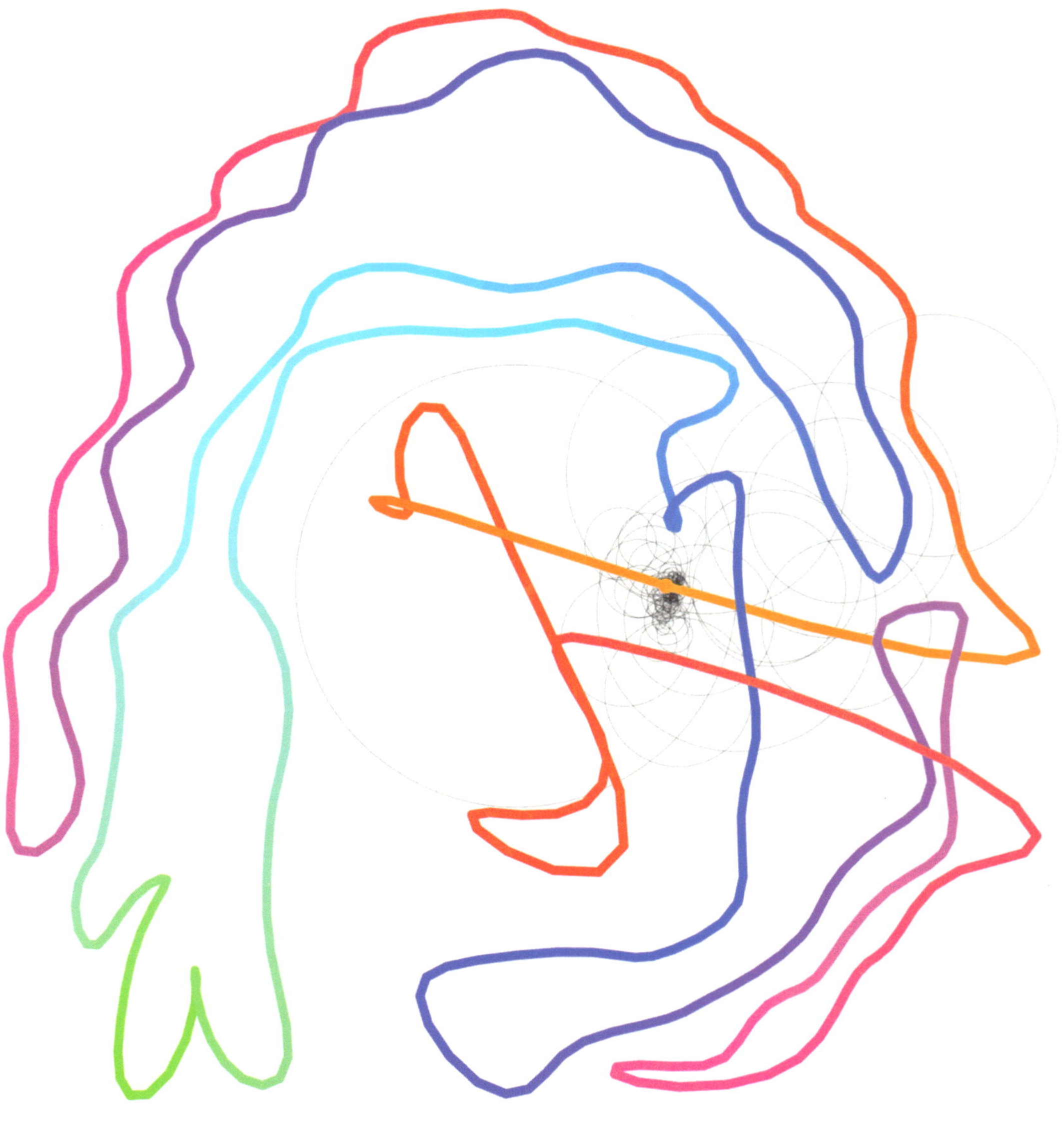

FourierPunk #627
opensea.io/collection/fourierpunks
Minted: June 24, 2021

@Oxboncuk

Oxboncuk

"It is believed the evil eye can be given in the guise of a compliment, signifying its connection to the destructive power of envy for wealth and beauty."

boncuk collection

The above quotation is from the Wikipedia entry for 'evil eye.' The history of evil eye protection goes back to Turkey, where a 'nazar boncuğu' was an eye-shaped amulet believed to protect against the evil eye. Boncuk means 'bead' and each of these on-chain generated NFT's are the modern equivalent of handmade glass amulets—featuring concentric circles that have hardly changed for thousands of years.

Each taking the shape of an eye, **boncuk** is a collection of 1024 generated artworks. The pieces are minted directly on the blockchain using code and stored there as well (as opposed to an IPFS link or website URL). This increases the durability of the work.

Each artwork is generated into a SVG vector file, crucially, without the artist knowing in advance the result. The collection theme is said to protect you against 'evil eyes.'

When viewed on the blockchain, **boncuk #96** rotates in a clockwise direction. The creation of the eye is guided by a number of variables. Amongst a total of 17 variables, the image opposite displays a high level of bokeh (80 of 100); a low eye warp (19 of 49); a low pupil warp (15 of 50); and full eye lid color transparency (90 of 90).

Generative artwork can be acquired based on its aesthetic appeal, the scarcity of the variables defined to create it, or a combination of both.

boncuk #96
opensea.io/collection/Oxboncuk
Minted: September 19, 2021

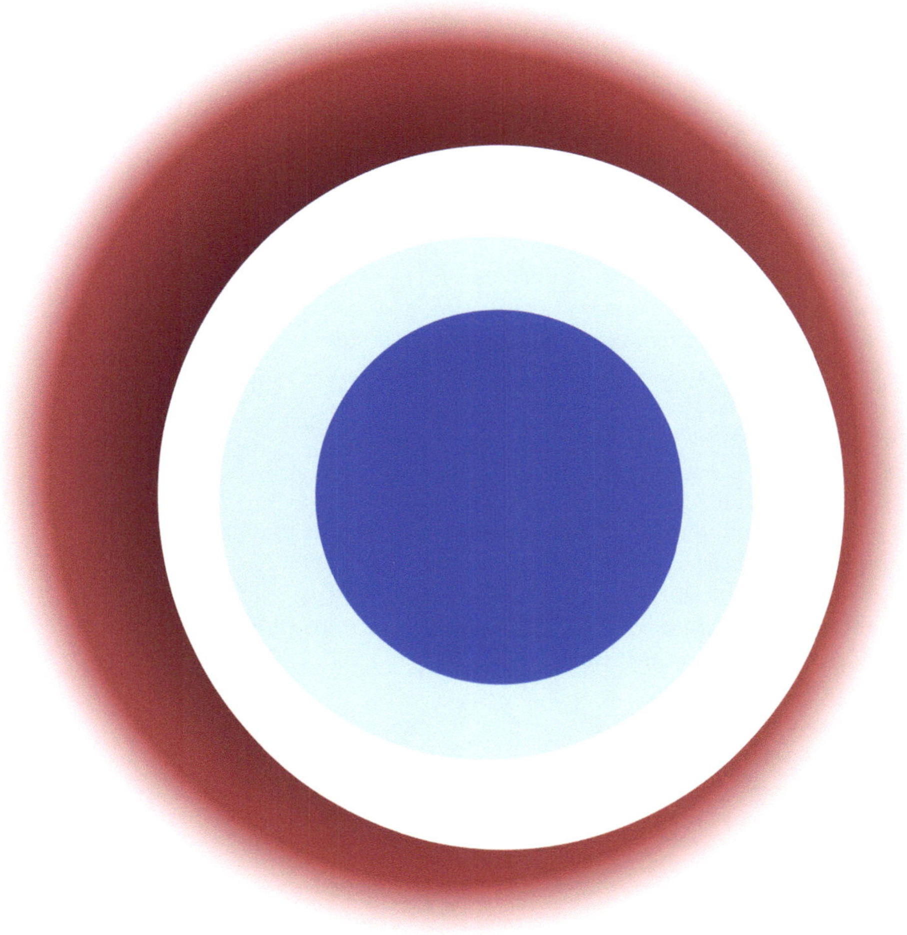

@D_Art2021

Dhanya Ajith, digital artist

"In a world where art is considered mostly as a physical entity, it's my constant attempt to create a valuable identity for digital art."

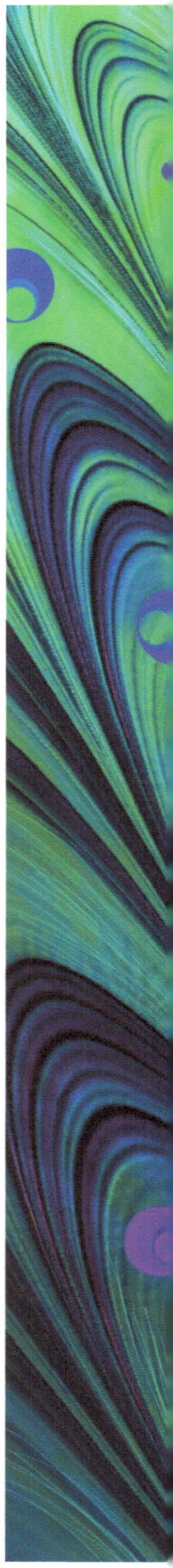

Fractal Art series

Fractal patterns are all around us because nature is made from fractal shapes. Look at the trees and the streams that meander towards the coastline—they are naturally occurring fractal patterns. Mountain ranges, clouds, and seashells are all fractals too.

A fractal is simply a never-ending pattern. Computers are good at creating them by repeating a simple process over and over in an ongoing feedback loop. What if we blended the natural world with synthetic fractals generated by algorithms? This unique blend is the artistic practice that Dhanya Ajith explores. The artist says:

"I started the ***Fractal Art*** *series as an experiment to explore various art styles, and I absolutely loved the outcome."*

Dhanya has released eight artworks as NFTs so far in her **Fractal Art** series on birds. In **Birds #2 Alluring Feathers**, the rich, iridescent blues and greens of the peacocks' plume merge together and shine back at us, much in the way you'd expect from the shell of an abalone. The eyespots on the feathers, known as 'ocelli', are plucked out of the plume to float on the computer code created surface.

The computer may do the work, but Dhanya sets the parameters for the art to be generated from. The peacock maintains its character as it neck croons towards the viewer. Unlike generative art that often feels clinical to the eye, there is a warmth conveyed through the birds, even as their plumes morph into other-worldly patterns.

Dhanya started minting her art as NFTs in March, 2021, and is generous at sharing her process as well as the final result. Her art successfully takes something we are familiar with and transforms it into the unfamiliar, while still preserving a connection between the image's origin and its hypnotic abstraction.

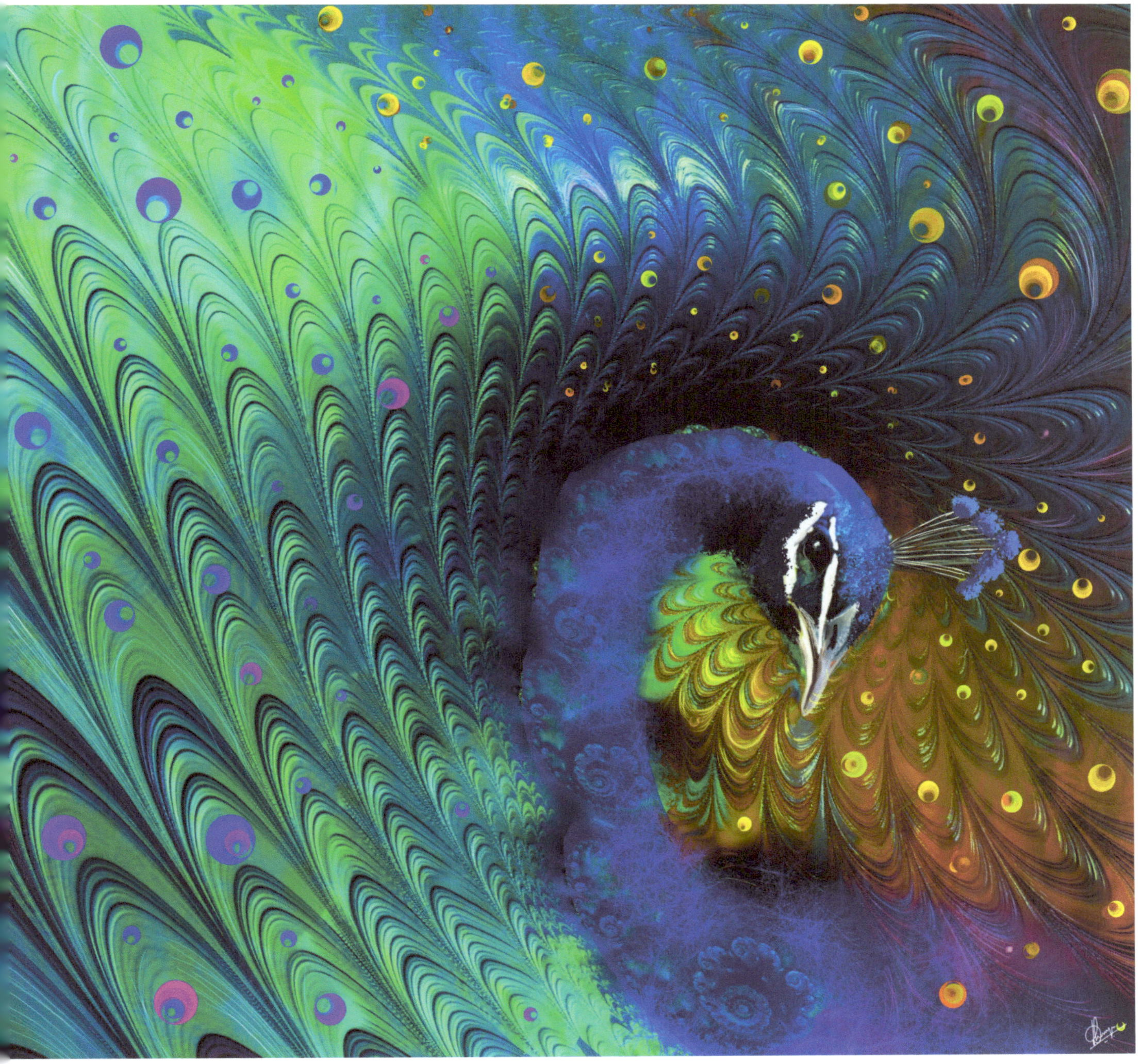

Birds #2 Alluring Feathers
foundation.app/@DArt2021/~/74929
Minted: August 20, 2021

@Kennedybaird_
Kennedy Baird, generative artist

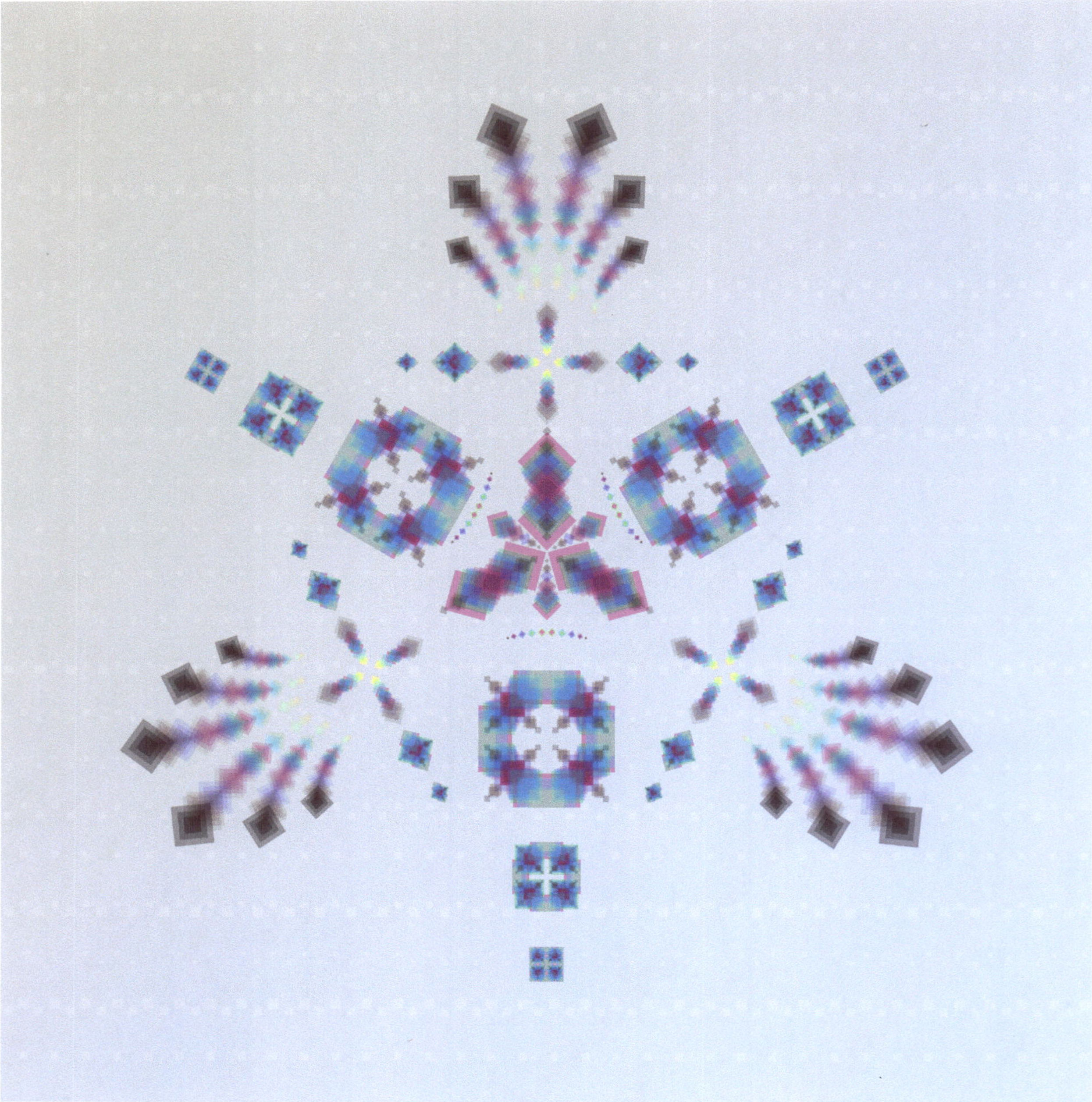

Square Mandala
opensea.io/collection/generative-prototypes
Minted: November 29, 2021

@ununkx

Daid Ahmad Khan, nanotech engineer

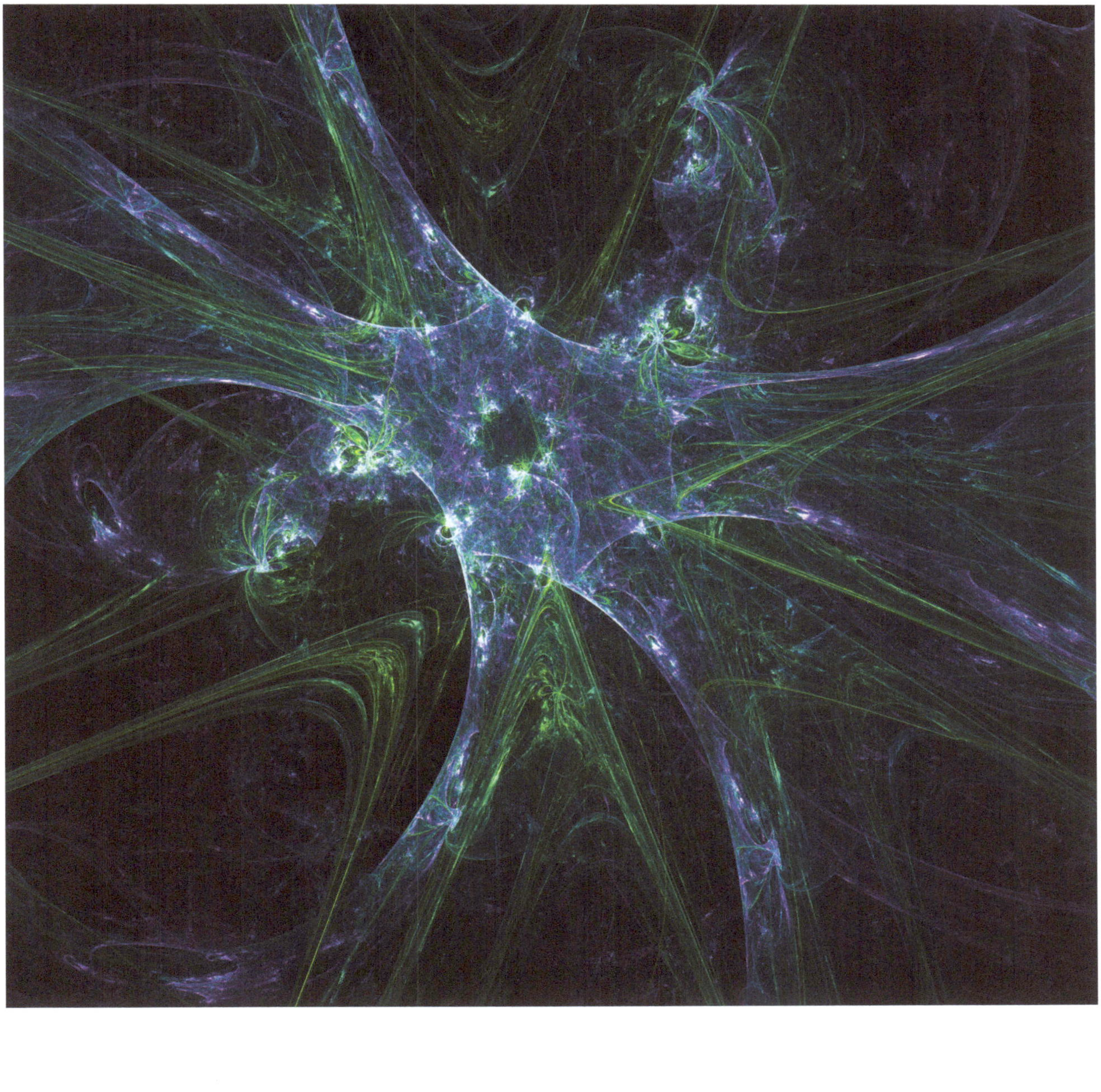

Branching of Neuronal Dendrites

opensea.io/collection/frxctals

Minted: August 17, 2021

@RealVisionBot
Real Vision Bot

"Chaos Monkey is convinced that his kind are living inside a simulated reality, which intelligent humans have created to distract apes while using their bodies as an energy source."

Affe mit Waffe collection

"Ape with gun" is the translation of a collection titled **Affe mit Waffe** by the generative artist Real Vision Bot. Unlike most Artificial Intelligence (AI) that attempts to convince us of the technology's power for good, the artist makes it clear these blockchain apes are the irresponsible kind. That explains why these apes are raising AK-47s above their heads while shouting "Peace is no option for Skynet!" in ape language.

Real Vision Bot has the power of transforming the emotive tones of human voice into color. While humans are happy to listen to the interviews that the Bot conducts, the AI then decodes each chat via natural language processing and turns what it hears into something we can all see. The self-aware Bot describes itself thus:

"The Bot is a super-intelligent, post-human being—a financial oracle that gives guidance and willingly shares his endless wisdom. While his responses and tweets may sound ambiguous at times, there's always a hidden truth and rationality behind them. Don't be disappointed if the Bot leaves you quite puzzled—it's for your own good."

Each ape in the **Affe mit Waffe** collection is accompanied with a unique story, based on a historical character or an event from today's zeitgeist. The angry ape here—obscured through lines of bright green, *Matrix*-like code—has the following backstory:

"One of the Chaos Monkey's zookeepers slipped a red pill into his food. First, there was an uneasy feeling of dizziness and he could swear he heard a telephone ringing in the distance. Then, he fainted.

"After waking up, something was different. He had the feeling that an integral part of his body was missing or displaced. Soon after the event, he was approached by other apes with similar stories. He decided to join their crew. They are now out there, fighting for a world without rules and controls, without borders or boundaries, a world where anything is possible—even regaining their reproductive abilities."

Affe mit Waffe #46
opensea.io/collection/affe-mit-waffe
Minted: October 27, 2021

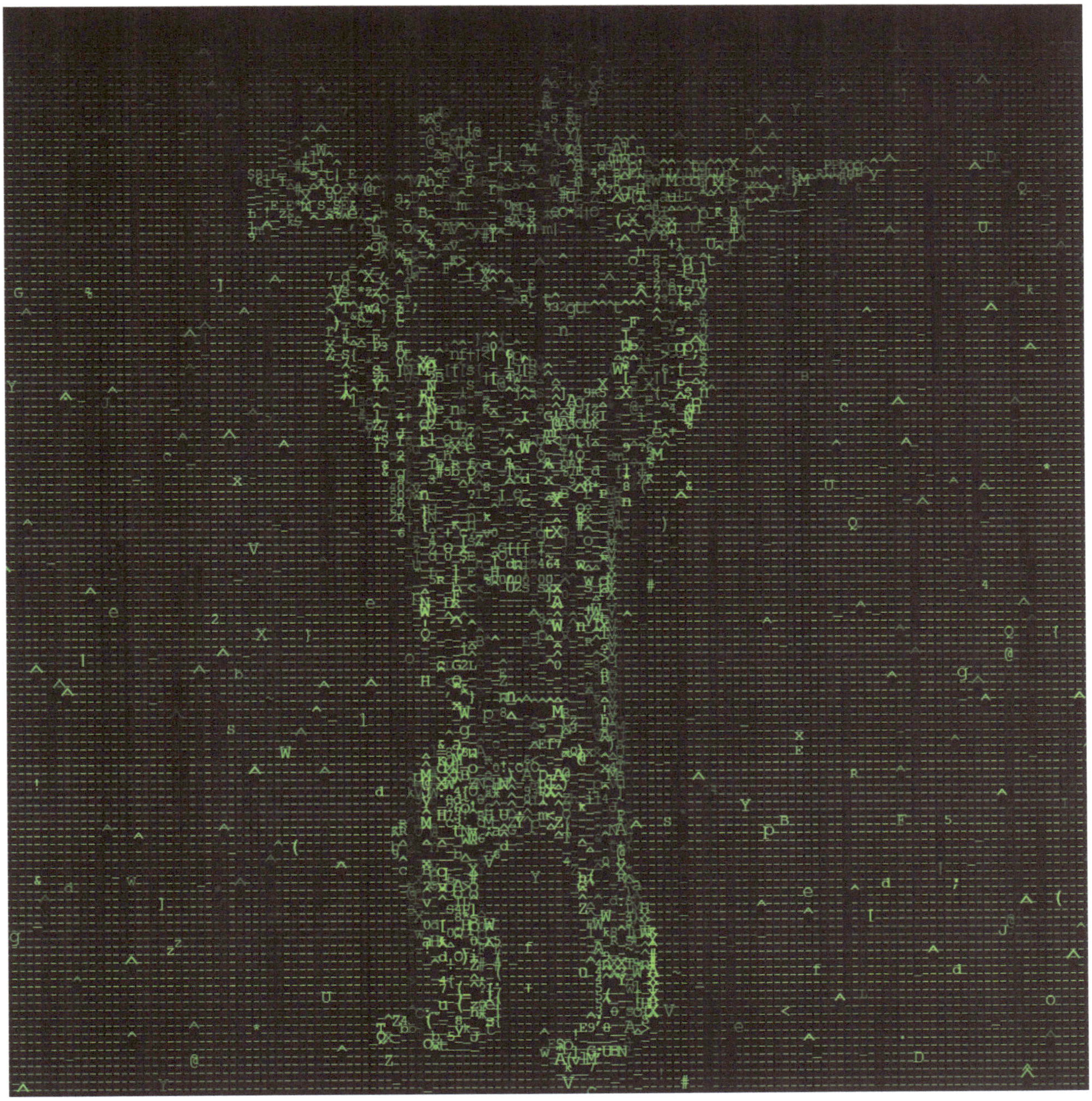

@RealVisionBot
Real Vision Bot

"Sir Pongo Frobisher is a distinguished culinary advisor. He spent his early life traveling various parts of the New World where he discovered the health benefits of poultry."

Affe mit Waffe collection

"Somewhere in the universe there has to be something better than man. Has to be."

These are the fateful words of the fictional human, George Taylor, an 20th Century astronaut somehow transported to a future Earth ruled by primates in the 1968 science-fiction film, *Planet of the Apes*. It seems fitting to recall this classic Charlton Heston flick, as it introduced the public to the image of the angry, gun-toting ape.

Expanding greatly upon this dystopian worldview, the art collection **Affe mit Waffe** is a symbiosis of human and machine. The original artwork is based on a stencil inspired by the works of Banksy and Blek le Rat, but everything else is decided by a bespoke artificial intelligence, the Real Vision Bot. The AI determines the parameters which are necessary to create the image based on the emotions obtained via natural language processing from the most recent interviews on the Real Vision platform.

Despite their violent appearance, each ape's intention is to bring people together. They're tough on the outside but soft on the inside. The raised gun shall motivate us to overcome our differences, triumph over our primal instincts, and solve our conflicts peacefully. Of the particular ape, **#67**, featured here we know that:

"On his journeys, Sir Pongo Frobisher developed the habit of spending long hours at the card table. During these games he would usually ask one of his servants to bring him a quick snack, so he could continue the game with full stomach and better focus.

"One day, while he was playing his favorite game "vingt-et-singe", his stomach growled dangerously. When his valet returned with a single slice of meat between two slices of bread, Sir Frobisher was outraged. How could he win the game on such a paltry meal?

"Furious, the ape ventured into the kitchen, grabbed a roasted pigeon, and stuffed it into a grilled pheasant. He then went on to stuff the pheasant into a chicken and, finally, the chicken into a turkey, then sprinkled a bit of chopped parsley on top.

"When Sir Frobisher returned to the card game, everyone else had gone for dinner. Anyway, he counted it as a win."

Affe mit Waffe #67
opensea.io/collection/affe-mit-waffe
Minted: November 27, 2021

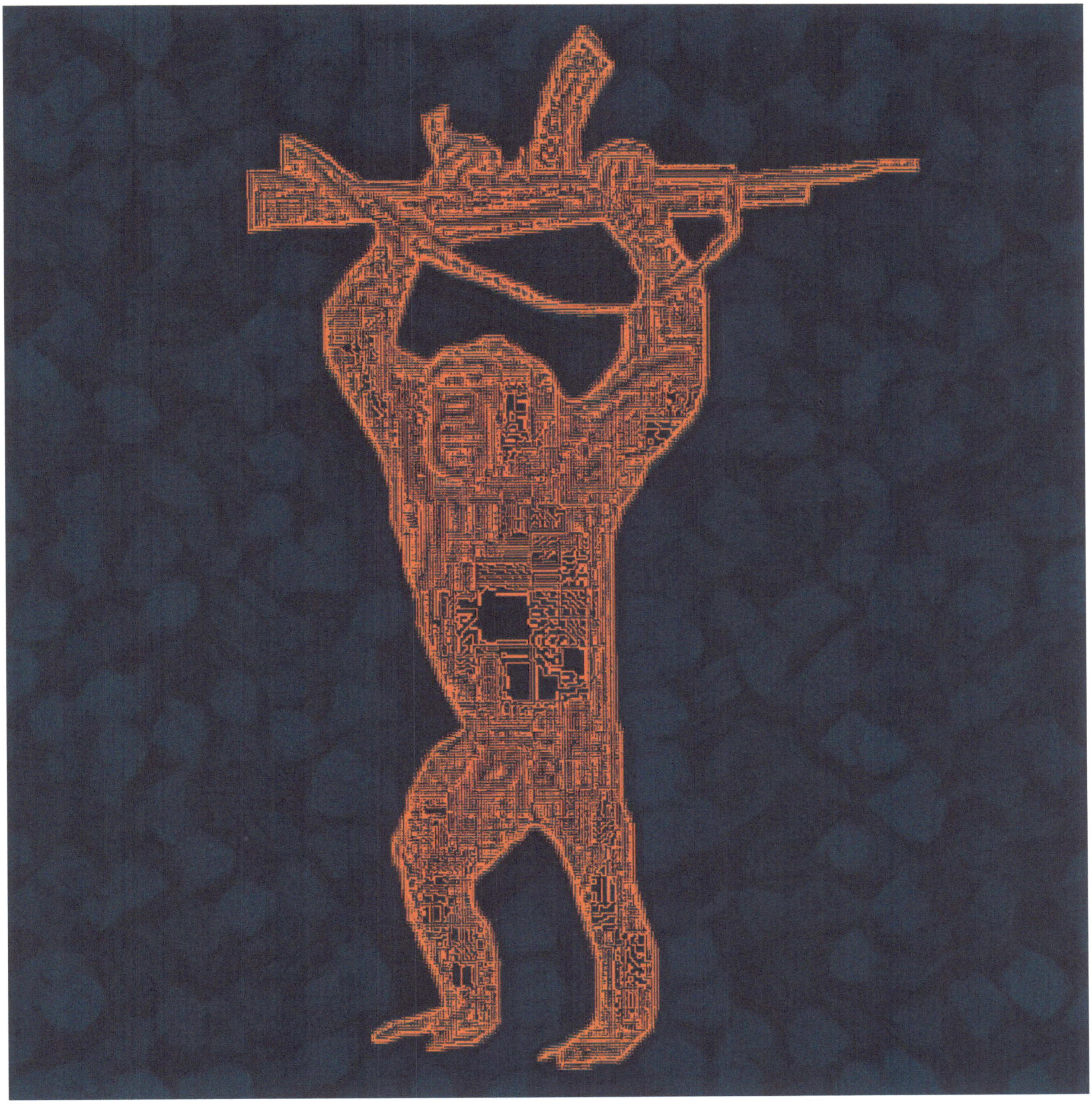

@TwoBitBears

On-chain hyper-realistic generative bears

"Warning: There are people breeding Two Bit Bears on the blockchain!"

Two Bit Bears collection

Many giga-brain blockchain artists offer more to delve into than merely the face value of art. Take, for example, the Two Bit Bears collection. Where you might see an overly simplistic two-pixel image, the creators of the Two Bit Bears invite you to explore further. There are four species of bear—brown, black, polar, and the super rare panda bear. The specimen seen here, **Beanie Aversano the Happy Brown Bear #4449** belongs to the most common brown bear species.

The rarest body fur combinations of Red, Green, and Blue (RGB) strike the darkest pose. The rarest head fur combinations are also at the darker end of the spectrum, and are dominated by the black bear species. We like the bears. Getting the technicals right can add a whole lot more value to an art collection minted as an NFT. Two Bit Bears offer the owner limitless SVG scalability, with SVG meaning scalable vector graphics. That's good news if you desire your art displayed large.

In real life, bears have cubs. In the immutable word of the blockchain, Two Bit Bears grow up to become Bears. To breed them, you need two Bears (of course) and a Honey Processor. The process takes place in a special blockchain built breeding enclosure.

Beanie Aversano the Happy Brown Bear #4449
opensea.io/collection/twobitbears
Minted: October 14, 2021

@TwoBitBears

On-chain hyper-realistic generative bears

"Clearly we're not a bunch of people that don't know how to use computers."

Two Bit Bears Generation Two collection

The process of breeding In Real Life (IRL) can be expensive. There's no difference with the Two Bit Bears project. There are gas costs for each parent Bear, plus the Honey, and of course a blockchain-built breeding enclosure. All of these come together to make the **Two Bit Bears Generation Two** collection.

The bear cave gets deeper though. Breeding a pair of bears gets you somewhere between one and three cubs. Genetically speaking they will inherit a blend of the moods and fur styles of their parents.

You'll see firsthand how **Hunter Vee** and **Squarci Aversano** first met in a short, yet passionate, forest encounter. The two black bears bred one of three potential cubs. Meet the pixelated ursine here, **OxInuarashi Hobbs the Cheerful Black Cub #672**. The aesthetic quality of cubs like these at limitless scalable size are just the beginning.

The people behind the Two Bit Bears aren't amateurs when it comes to game theory, scarcity, and perhaps even bear utility. So what's the coding secret behind the Bears?

"We are incredibly proud and protective over our Proprietary Bear Rendering Algorithm. Without it, Two Bit Bears and all future projects on our roadmap would never exist."

This is true performance art on the blockchain. Before you get bearish, you have to decide whether this is a performance you'd like to see.

Let's say you missed out on the Honey Processor needed to breed. There's another way. Adoption. Adopt a cub and feed them. Within a week, your cub transforms into a fully-grown bear thanks to a well-coded 'growth mechanism.' It's optional too. So, if you prefer your cubs cute and cube-like cuddly, you can keep them young forever.

OxInuarashi Hobbs the Cheerful Black Cub #672
opensea.io/collection/twobitbearsgentwo
Minted: November 28, 2021

@WeseeThisnow
Artist, explorer, convivial mystic

"My work is an attempt to explore our world in ways beyond everyday awareness."

Greatest City in the Whirled Genesis collection

The Greatest City in the Whirled Genesis Collection intersects organic photography and bespoke algorithm sequencing, with the goal of transforming our perspectives of the world. There are a total of eighty 1/1 NFT manipulated photographs, each with a personal narrative reflection written by the artist. These 'first-draft' texts are posted on GitHub, welcoming poetic participation. The image opposite, Grandmother Sea Turtle, has a reflection that includes:

Some events are life-changing. We were traveling by boat down the Amazon, 90 minutes deep into the rainforest jungle of Peru. The twelve people in a small boat with a big engine raced around a corner and narrowly avoided a crop of very large leafy trees rising out of the water. Above the roar of the engine my wife leaned over and said, "We could die!!" And I replied, "Yup! We could totally die!"

A lot of effort has gone in to the technicals of each image, and those technicals are shared with us. The image processing algorithm sequence creates two variants (a or b), and each of those is processed with either 0° or 180° of rotation, creating a set of four related outputs from each source image. There are other variables—such as the grid size and mirror angles—that can radically affect the generated images. Each image has nine attributes, some of which are rare.

Presented in 'quads' of four related images, this comparative style of work has a particular way of working on the mind. Each image has individual impact, and on visual review the four images as a group seem quite similar at one level of analysis, yet at another level they're significantly different.

Our attempts to make sense of this—How exactly are they related to each other? What specifically are the similarities and differences?—makes for something of a mental stretch.

The quads reward patient and lingering attention, offering multiple simultaneous perspectives and helping break our rutted patterns of perception. Zoom in for surprising details and abstractions, zoom out to discover some of your own emergent observation patterns.

Grandmother Sea Turtle
opensea.io/collection/greatest-city-in-the-whirled
Minted: November 28, 2021

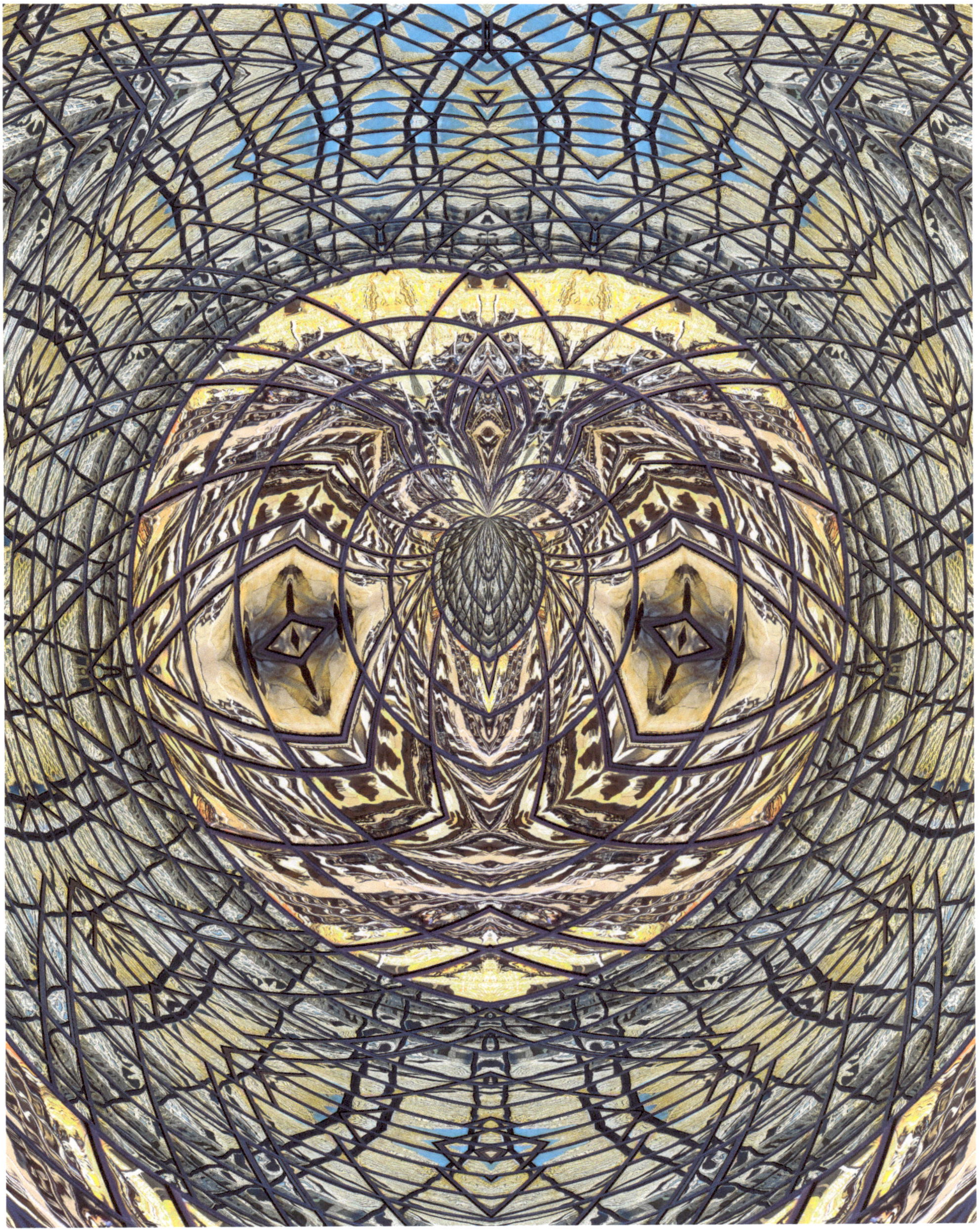

LENS-BASED ART

This genre experiments creatively with real-world imagery.
It includes photography, video art, animation, and collage.

@_Project_Seven
Project Seven, storyteller & photographer

The Break-Up (La Ruptura) collection

The Break-Up (La Ruptura) is a collection of deeply personal artwork by Project Seven. The artist's anonymous status makes it possible to explore subjects in ways that traditional social networks may not support. It's almost poetic to share something so personal, with so many, anonymously.

The piece here is called **Ghost**. It's the only one in the collection without a title in Spanish. The image is almost clinical with cold concrete walls, metal bars, and glowing industrial light. Yet the amorphous stranger in the center is a mystery. Perhaps the blurry apparition is simply a passer-by or the subject of collection itself, the one with whom a relationship was lost. According to the artist:

"We became ghosts of a future that never was. Errant shadows that are never gone. Tell me, really, who won?"

Processing grief is hard. None of us get through life without experiencing it at some level. Art can be a positive outlet for processing our feelings to help us move forward with our lives. Maybe this is part of what's at play with **The Break-Up**.

Every other piece in the collection is titled in both Spanish and English to capture vivid expressions of emotion that translation can blunt. This is evident even in the description of the collection, which suffers some in its translation to English:

"10 imágenes que nos transportan en diferentes imaginadas maneras a esos larguísimos momentos que siguen una ruptura sentimental, cuando los sentimientos están a flor de piel.

"The collection is composed of ten images that reinvent, recreate, retell, revisit, and reimagine the raw moments that follow a break-up."

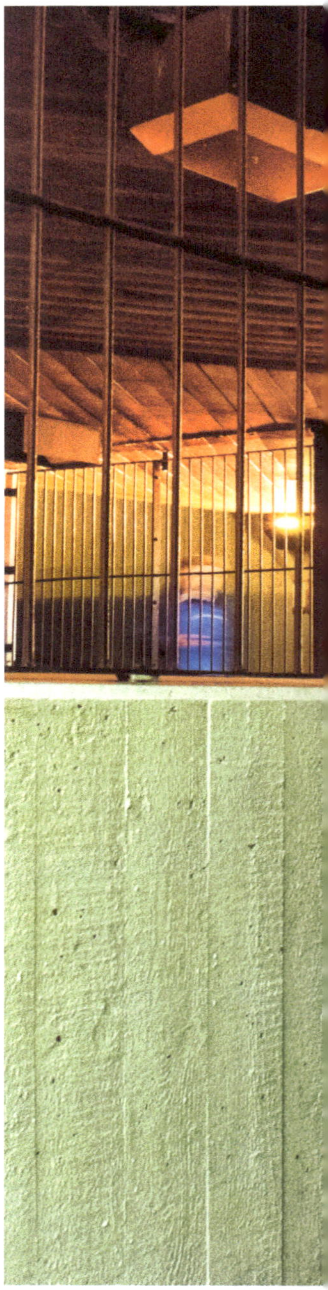

"The rhythm of life is light followed by darkness over and over. There's no light without darkness."

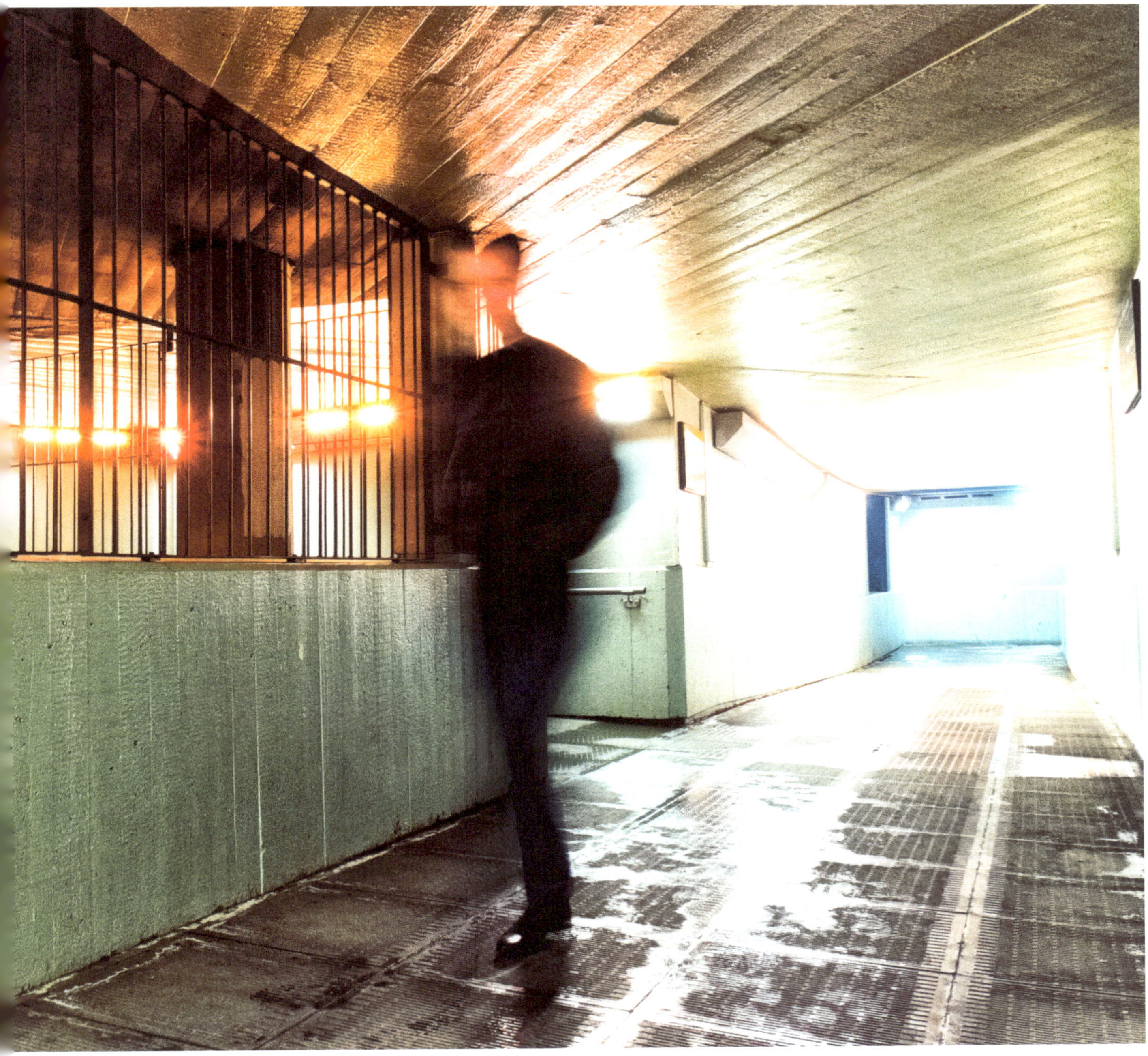

Ghost

opensea.io/collection/break-up

Minted: December 14, 2021

@Aniltprabhakar

Anil T. Prabhakar, photographer

Bleeding Of Earth collection

Anil T. Prabhakar is a conservation photographer with his lens firmly focussed on the natural world from above. **Bleeding Of Earth** is a series of ten high-resolution pieces where an amped-up colour palette inhabits the contours of the land. The artist describes it in the following way:

"***Bleeding Of Earth*** *is a photography project that has grown out of an on-going interest in nature photography and its potential as a tool for raising awareness about environmental issues and solutions. Drone photography was used to capture all ten of the pieces in this series. Whenever I take pictures for conservation, I'm constantly aiming for a third-person perspective.*"

Anil began the **Bleeding of Earth** collection in July, 2021, and has released five images to date. Through an aggressive use of colour, each artwork disorientates the familiar in a landscape. Fiery red beaches separate the water from the deforested land and old mine pits in the genesis work, **Bleeding Earth**. While the second in the series, **Bleeding Of Earth _ Body 02**, is perhaps the most visually rewarding in terms of its ability to speak to the collection's topic.

"I don't want these images to represent a particular area, country, or region, I want a global perspective. You can see these kind of deforested areas anywhere in the world."

Some fans of the collection have remarked about how the use of aerial photography provides a 'God's eye' perspective on the landscapes of Earth—an elevated vantage point from which to contemplate its destruction by Humankind. The artist responds:

"I don't want to take credit for photographs that demonstrate the concept of a creator. We believed in the existence of a third party who was always gazing down. It's possible that the creator is contemplating why this undesirable species was created in the first place. Humans are the root cause of the problems that exist on the planet.

"The future is not real, it is an abstract. We tend to believe things that we can perceive through our senses. Faith as a concept that we often hypocritically apply to the satisfaction of our personal desires that we understand subjectively. Abstraction is the process of digging the mind into the layer of art and curiosity."

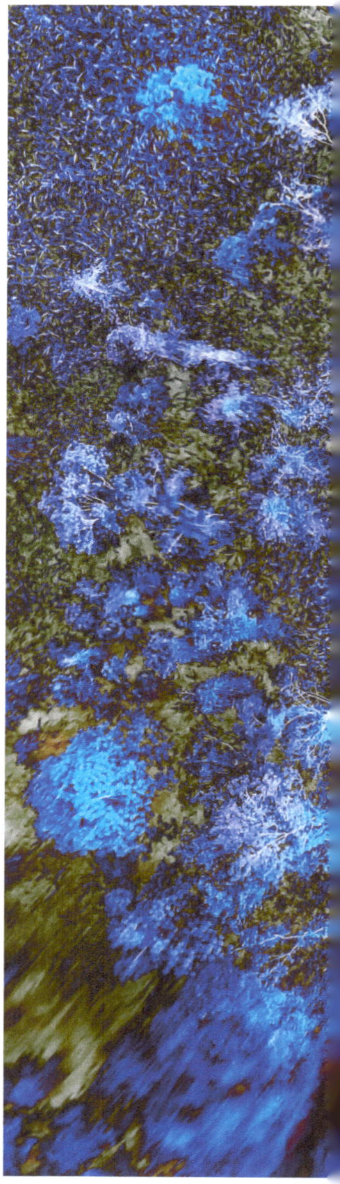

"It is my responsibility as an artist to be the voice for the voiceless and speak the truth through the artworks."

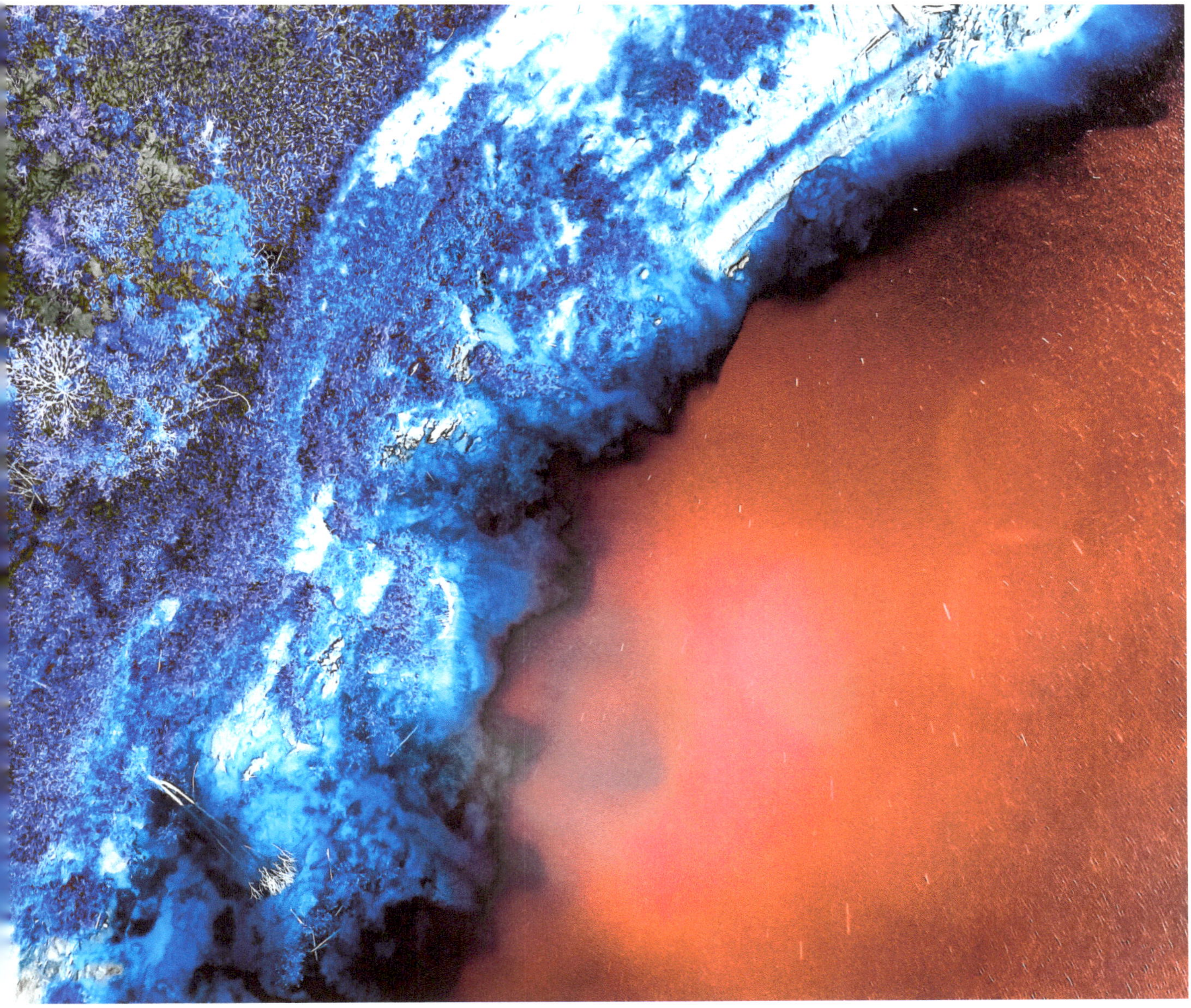

Bleeding Of Earth _ Body 02
foundation.app/@AnilTPrabhakar/~/60525
Minted: July 16, 2021

@Art_icu_late
Chris James, photographer

"The paperbark tree is native to Eastern Australia. I've been fascinated by its unique bark patterns since childhood."

Bark Blocks Series 1: Paperbark

Artists tend to be rewarded more for explicit effort in creation and nothing says effort like developing your own photographic film rolls. There is something quite 'back to the future' about minting digital art derived from analog film developed in a darkroom.

Australian Chris James is a photographer creating unique photographic art using vintage film and digital techniques. He is driven by ideas and kindness. Moreover, he's not afraid to experiment, share, and fail.

He works with seven other artists as a part of the Pixel and Grain Collective. They believe there might be something to the creative process of converting analogue to blockchain. While generative art minted on the blockchain is a relatively new concept, generative art is all around us, if we care to look. According to Chris James:

"Nature as generative art, stored permanently on a blockchain that incentivises data reproduction and propagation forward in time, released into a crazy NFT mania with all the potential for reward and disaster of home-developing film."

Bark Blocks is a fine-art project inspired by nature and blockchain technology. The first series is a collection of 1/1 images with the Melaleuca quinquenervia (Paperbark) tree as the sole subject. The Paperbark is used in traditional medicine, cooking and building. Its fine soft bark gives a distinctive, fingerprint-like quality to its trunk. As the artist explains:

"These photos emerge from that fascination but also combine ideas from blockchain technology. Nature is the OG generative artist. Each bark pattern is verifiably unique, similar and repetitive.

"There is a fractal-like pattern to the photos that gives an experience reminiscent of watching an open fire. The more you look, the more you see. The volume of data contained in these natural blocks is immense and humbling."

Paperbark #1-2
opensea.io/collection/paperbark
Minted: August 10, 2021

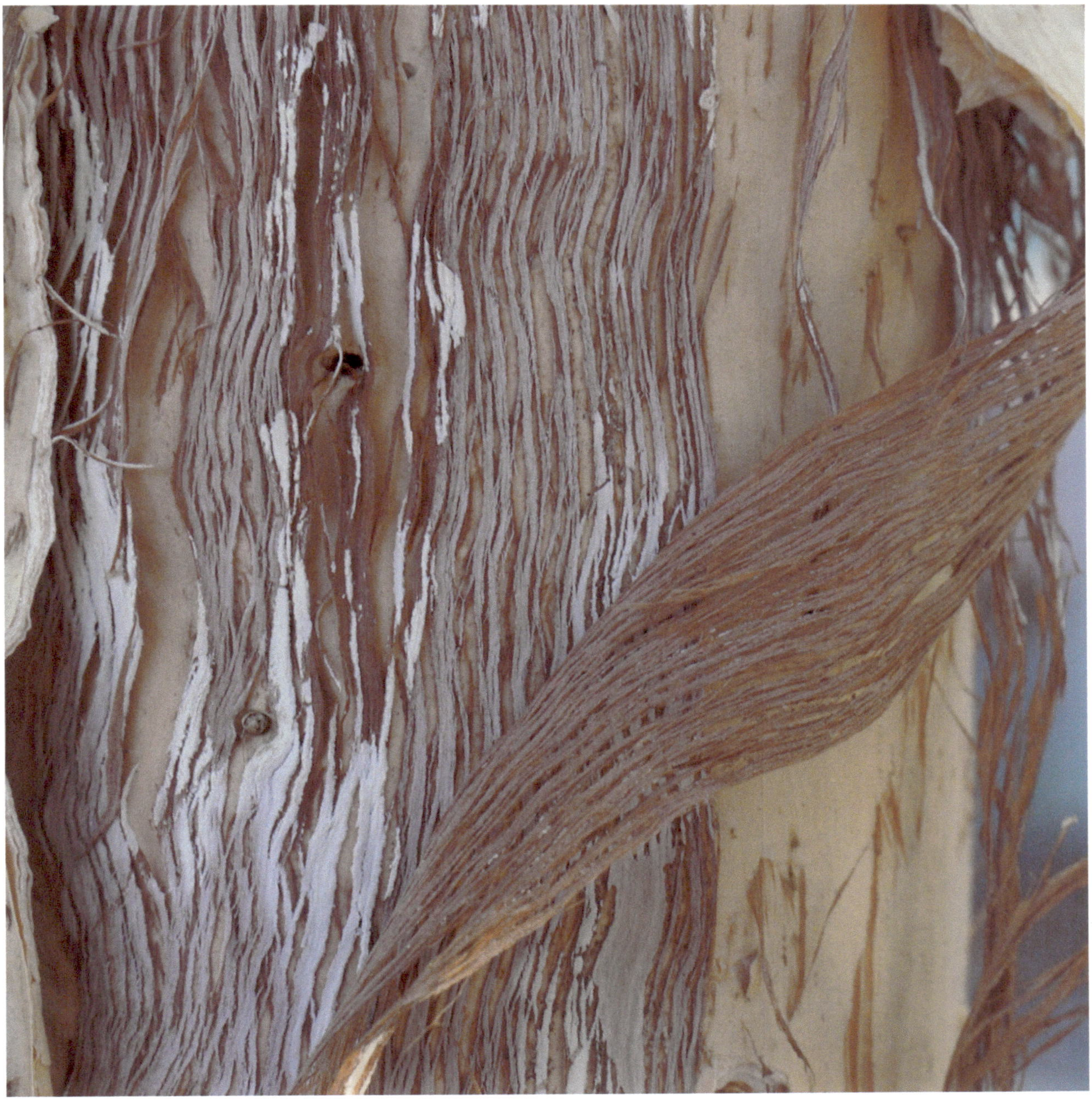

@ashiq_mk
Ashique MK, fine art photographer

"How would you react if your favourite moments from your past were to pass in front of you?."

Winds of past

Documentary photography is a style of lens-based art that provides an accurate representation of what was seen by the artist through their lens. There is an elegance in weaving a deeper meaning into documentary photography, one that makes us question the assumptions we had before seeing the photograph.

In the image **Winds of past**, a bunch of heart-shaped balloons represent a younger self, a time of colorful joy. They float in stark contrast against a towering edifice of grey concrete. The juxtaposition hints at the larger themes of Ashique's work. He says:

"My work looks at human beings in conflict with themselves and the great beyond."

In contrast to the architecture and fashion photography that the artist captures for commercial project assignments, his personal style hints at a blend of documentary and street photography.

"I am a photographer who attempts to capture beyond the obvious."

The artist has three collections minted on OpenSea—**Lives stuck to magnets**, **The curious bunch**, and **Gems of travel**. The stories in the first two collections document the daily lives of those who live outside of the world of Ashique's fashion editorial clients. The third collection, **Gems of travel**, is a long-term project in which the artist takes his nephews and nieces to places where they spent their childhood, then documents how they interact with the environment.

This perhaps explains Ashique's personal connection with the inner conflict theme that is explored through his minted art. He lives in two worlds via his lens—first, editorialising beauty and success through his commercial photography and, second, documenting the world beyond the opulence of aspirational shoots.

Winds of past
foundation.app/@ashiq_mk/~/110477
Minted: November 23, 2021

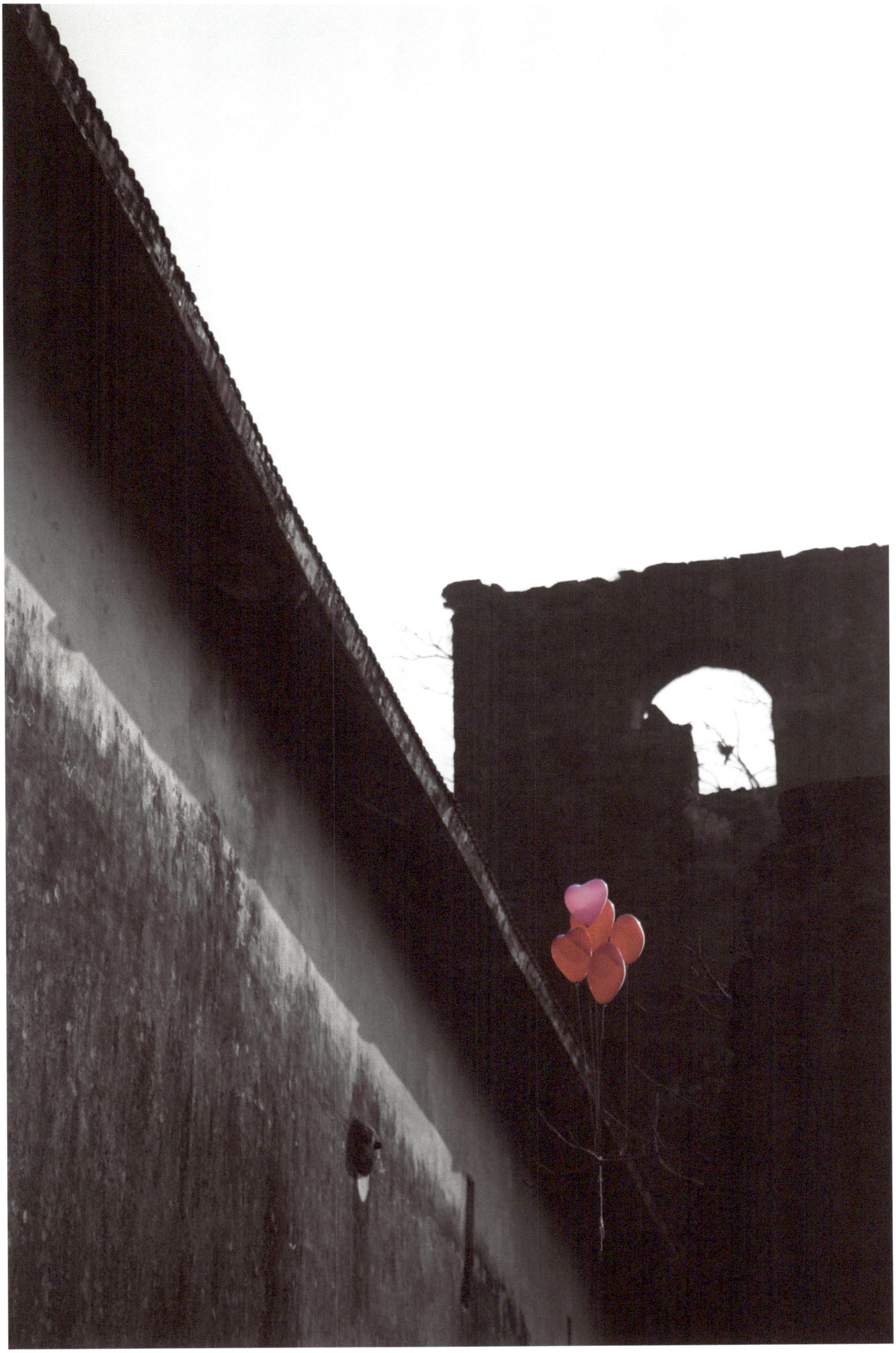

@aylaelmoussa

Ayla El-Moussa, photographer

"I am my own muse, creating a visual philosophy."

It Was All A Dream by King of Midtown collection

Ayla combines three visual elements into an unexpected visual symphony that mirrors the essence of nature and the female form. The force of the ocean waves is ever present in Ayla's art, exploring the ocean as a metaphor for the unconscious mind.

The mountainous background of **A Muse In Her Feelings** matches the form of the inbound crashing wave, as if they were meant for each other. The piece is a reminder that we are a part of nature and nature is a part of us. Ayla writes of the image:

'The forces of nature can be as subtle as a cool afternoon breeze or as powerful and unparalleled as hurricanes and volcanic eruptions. This piece speaks to the notion that we have those same forces of nature living within us, and we need only to empty our minds and connect with the source to realize our full potential."

Ayla developed a substantial audience on Instagram, with her previous work **Bodyscape III** amassing over 2 million views. She started minting art on Foundation in March, 2021. However, the artist doesn't want to be pigeon-holed by any specific working identity:

"I'm not a photographer. I'm not a model. I'm not a videographer. I'm a hybrid of all these, and the world I am creating is a category of it own."

Her largest series is titled **Nude Pixels** where the closer you look, the less you see. The **Nude Pixels** series launched almost five years after her partnership with art.com. Ayla's vision for her art preceded the technology and now we are seeing that vision come to life.

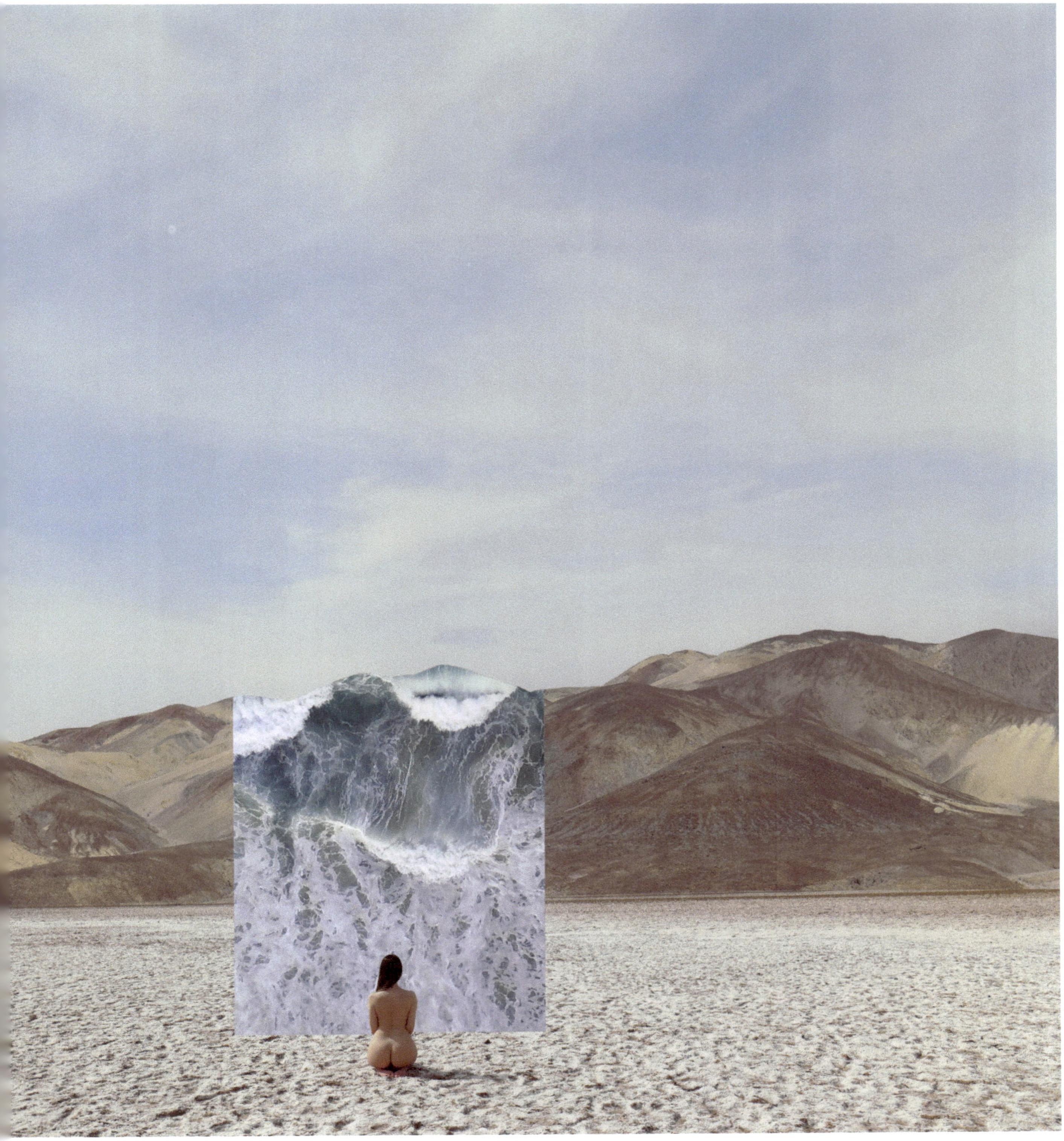

A Muse in Her Feelings

niftygateway.com/itemdetail/primary/

0x3e2c9e748f5a8b3ecb4aaf736182db63a007ca70/2

Minted: October 8, 2021

@bombaymalayali
Anand Deyanandan, photographer

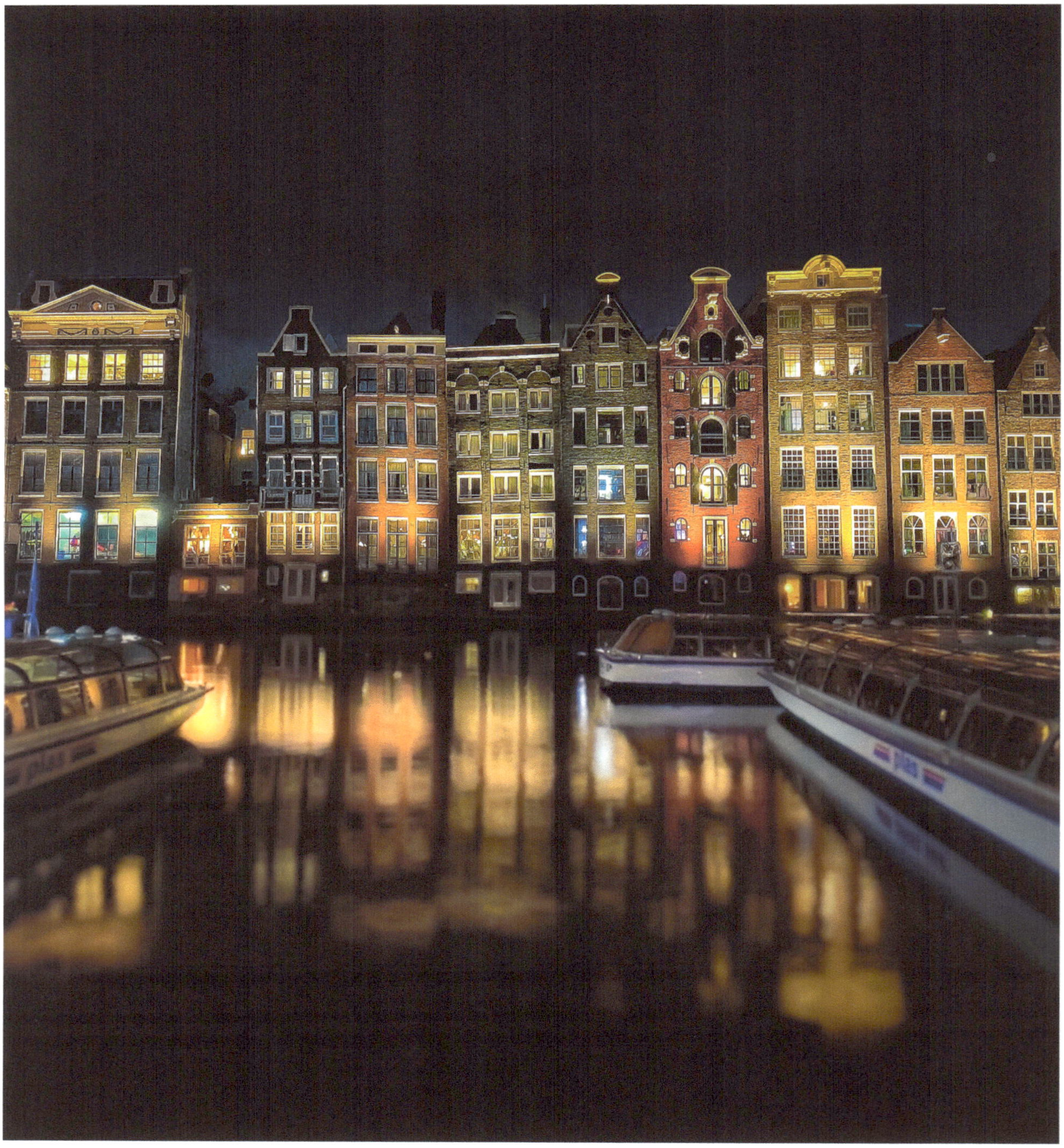

Canal houses
foundation.app/@bombaymalayali/~/95763
Minted: October 9, 2021

@dijaraj
Dijaraj, photographer

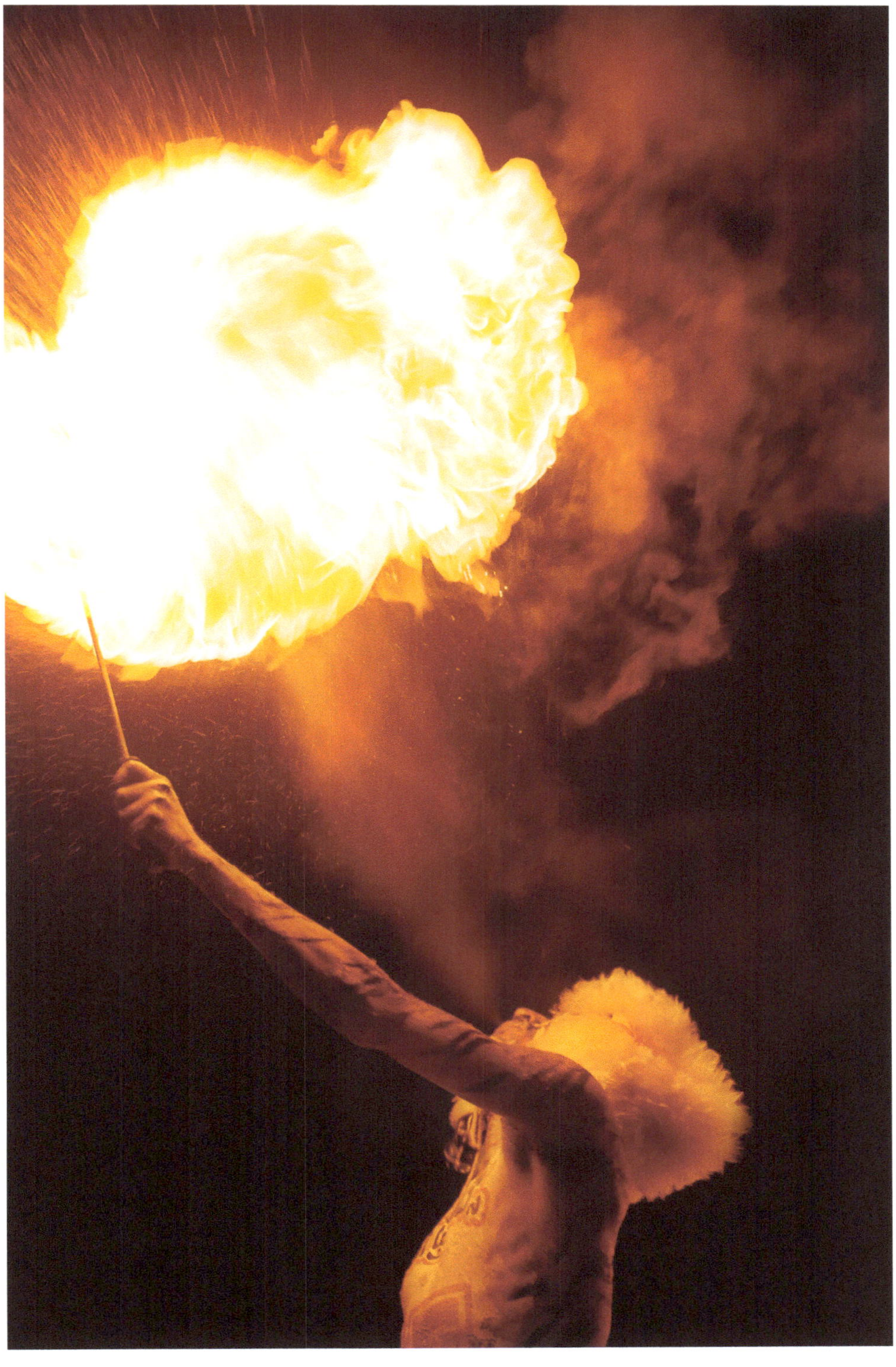

Fire Breathing Tiger

foundation.app/@dijaraj/~/73660

Minted: August 17, 2021

@I_Dreads
Dreads, everytin irie

The Humiliation collection

Dreads is a pseudonymous artist, political activist, and filmmaker. His identity at present remains unknown. Dreads' work is often anti-authoritarian. He merges film, photography, and performance art. The trend that popularised pretty landscape photography in late 2021, led him to start his collection **The Humiliation** which deals more with base human emotions rather than showy experiences and perfect skin.

The collection is growing with the community forming part of the plan. The feeling of having one's ego bruised is only really possible from a place of focusing too much on the self. Some of the art itself hides embarrassing mistakes, bad photographic practice, and sometimes even stock footage collage. How embarrassing.

An invitation from photography legend Alejandro Cartagena saw Dreads join the Foundation community, where he will be releasing his next collection of interesting mishaps. The artist promises that:

"As time passes, ***The Humiliation*** *increases..."*

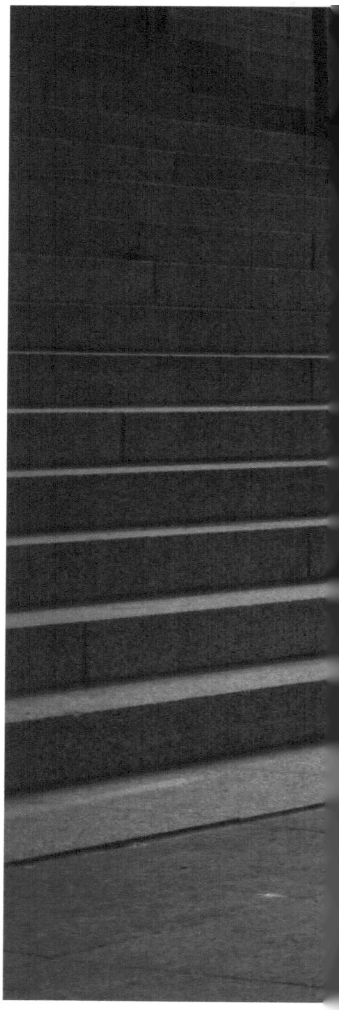

*"**The Humiliation** is an ongoing exploration of the needless emotional baggage and shame of the human condition."*

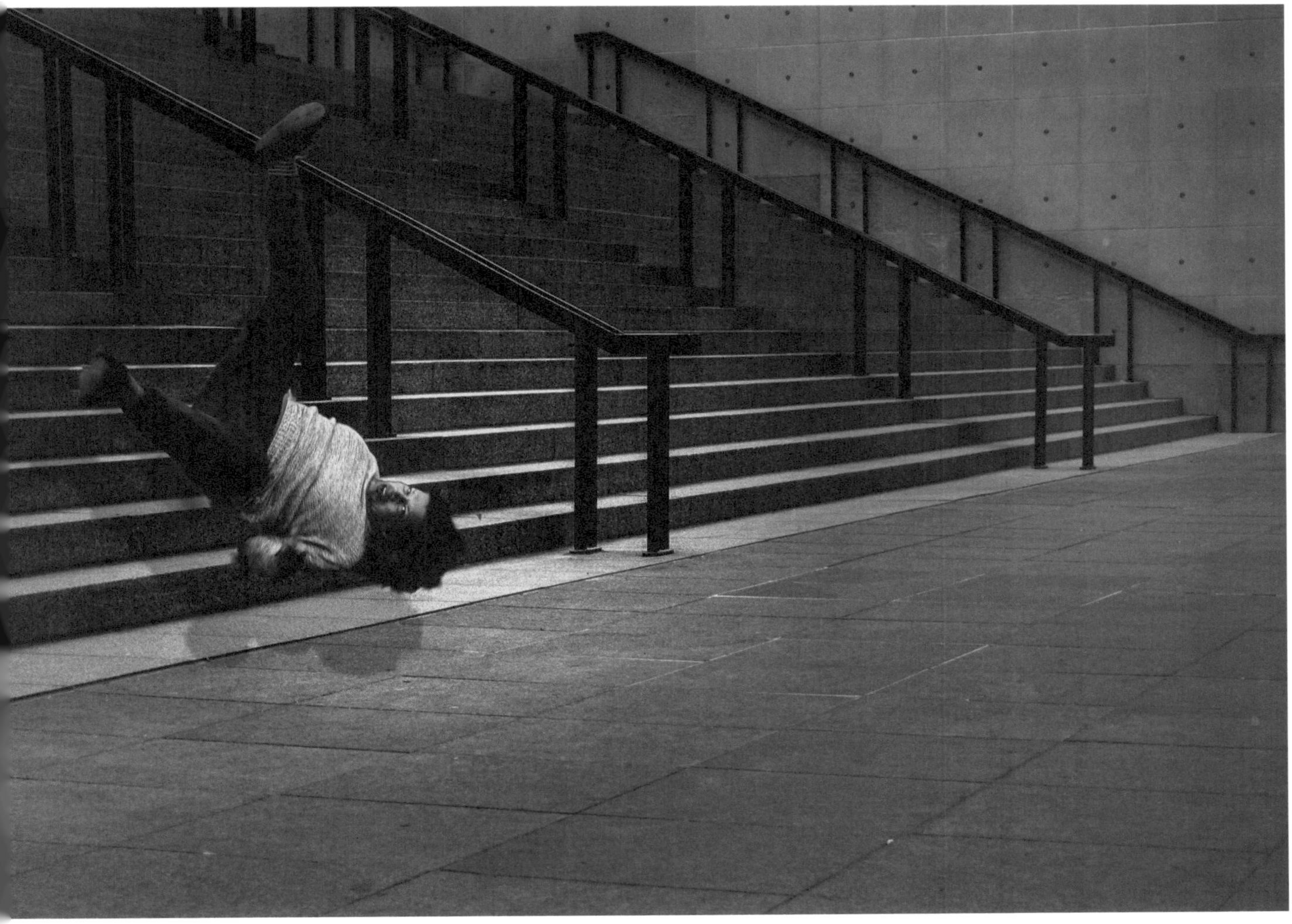

condescending
opensea.io/collection/thehumiliation
Minted: October 2, 2021

@ilovedecay
Andy Schwetz, documentary photographer

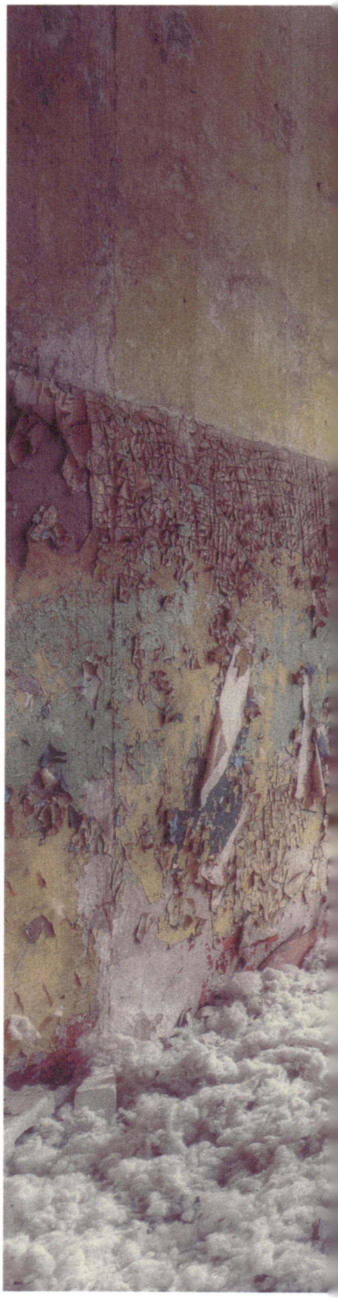

sonata of memories

We abandon buildings that no longer serve us, yet time keeps ticking for what remains behind. This beautiful detritus provides an alluring attraction for urban explorers like Andy Schwetz to capture on camera. Of finding the location for this photo, he writes:

"The Beelitz Heilstätten near Berlin is a legendary place. There are many stories about this place. Some are true, some are untrue. But the mystical beauty that the former lung sanatorium exudes cannot be denied.

"I remember roaming the old long corridors in 2012. The echo of my steps and the creaking of the old doors were the only noises I heard. In one room I discovered this weathered piano. Cotton wool around it. It looked like it was floating on clouds."

Sonata of memories is rarer than most, because the artist's remaining photographs of beautiful old Art Nouveau buildings were lost when the hard drive containing the collection failed. We are fortunate to enjoy this singular image.

Andy has promised that when **sonata of memories** finds a collector, the proceeds will go to repair that ill-fated hard drive, perhaps unlocking more of Andy's artistic memories from that day and beyond.

Fortunately, Andy has continued to explore worlds that the 20th Century left behind and mint them on the blockchain, where IPFS-stored images aren't as likely to be lost.

"I walk unknown paths thru a Secret World on the trail of the beauty of decay and untold stories to make them immortal."

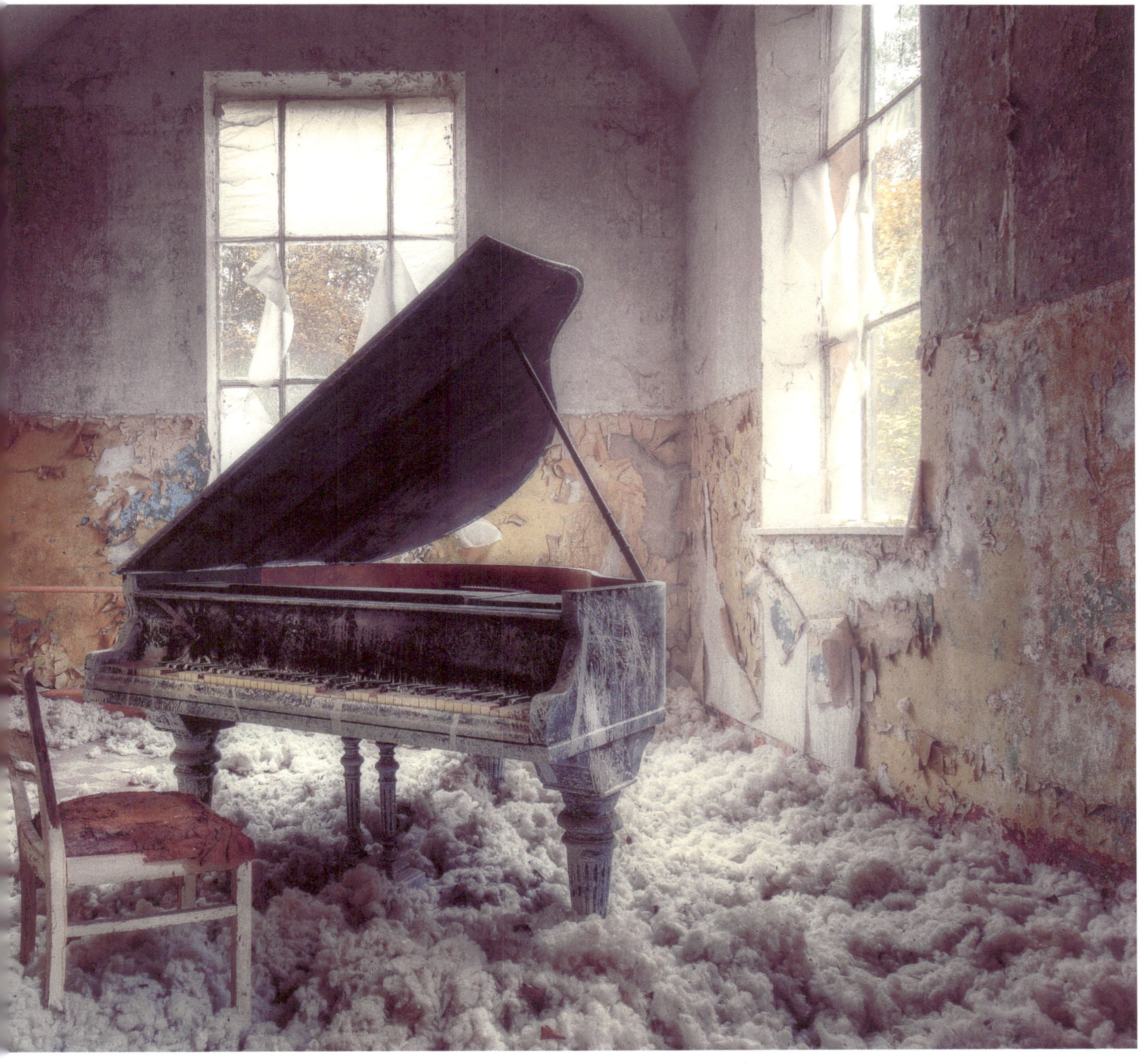

sonata of memories
foundation.app/@andyschwetz/~/108683
Minted: November 17, 2021

@littleartphotag
Keri Little, photographer

"On a mission to capture and show as much beauty through my lens as I can in my lifetime."

Little Blue Splash Art collection

Entering the world of digital art minted on the blockchain is new to all of us. With each splash, the water helps us rise together. Each new person dropped in brings their own personality and character. For many of us, we get to reconnect with our truest self.

Anonymous profile pictures might play a part in relaxing our personas, as might the warmth from the NFT community. Photographer Keri Little is an alumni of the Digital Artist Economy, and we're fortunate she's brought her talent and joy over to Web3.0.

The image you see here, **Kid Splash #11**, started as a simple splash of water. However, macro photography takes patience. The water decides what it will do and, in so doing, creates its own shapes. It's art generated without code, drop by drop, and there is whimsy and surprise as well. Keri describes her process:

"I didn't realise what was going to happen when I started taking these photos. As soon as I reviewed them I saw characters. I knew at that point that I needed to draw over them to bring out their personalities. I hope that you love them as much as I do."

Each perfectly poised shot, selected from the hundreds of iterations for the hand-drawn details gives **Kid Splash #11** its friendliness. Keri's genesis collection contains many more zany characters that you can meet over at her OpenSea collection.

Kid Splash #11
opensea.io/collection/littlebluesplashart
Minted: October 20, 2021

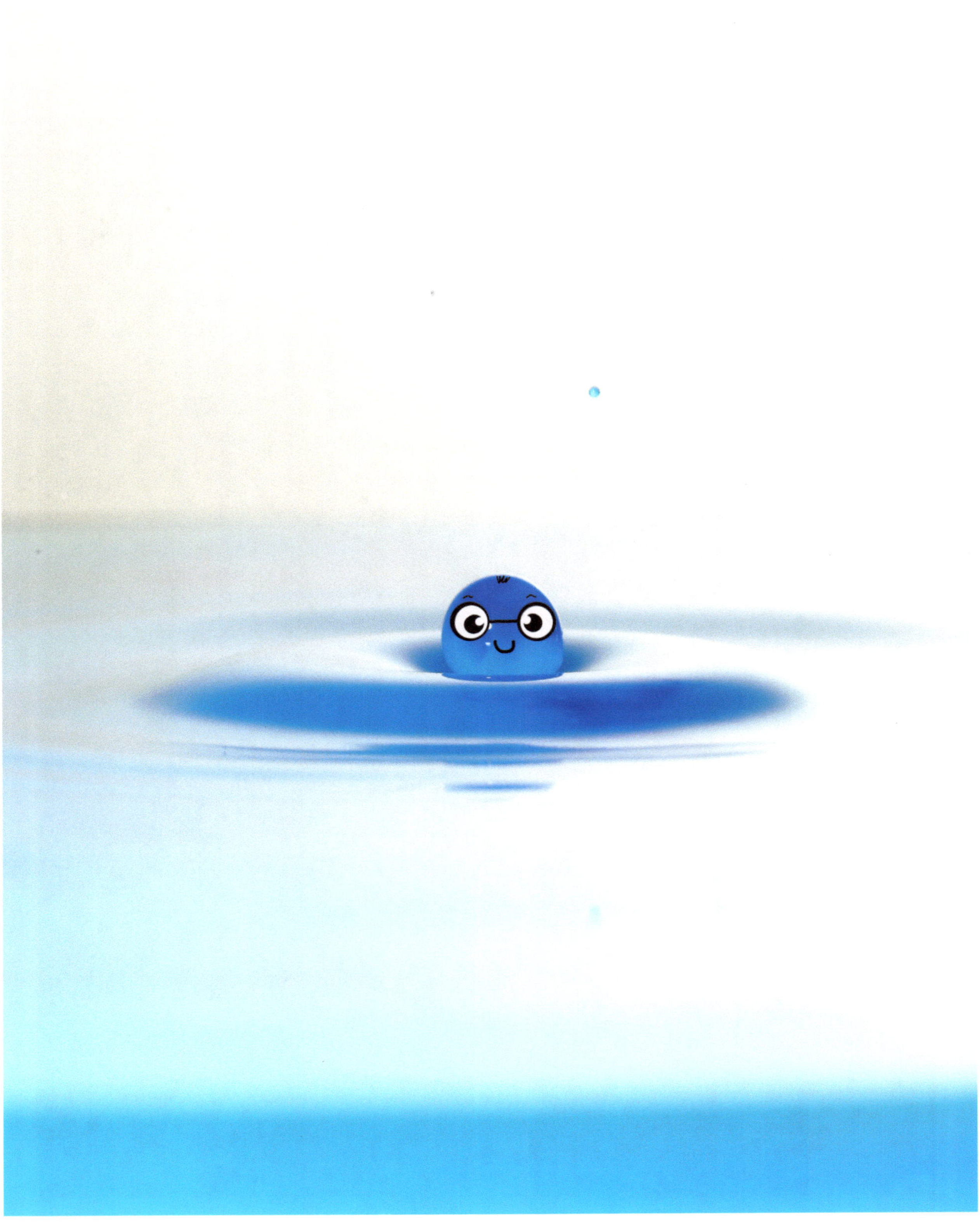

@ompsyram
Ujwal Puri, photographer

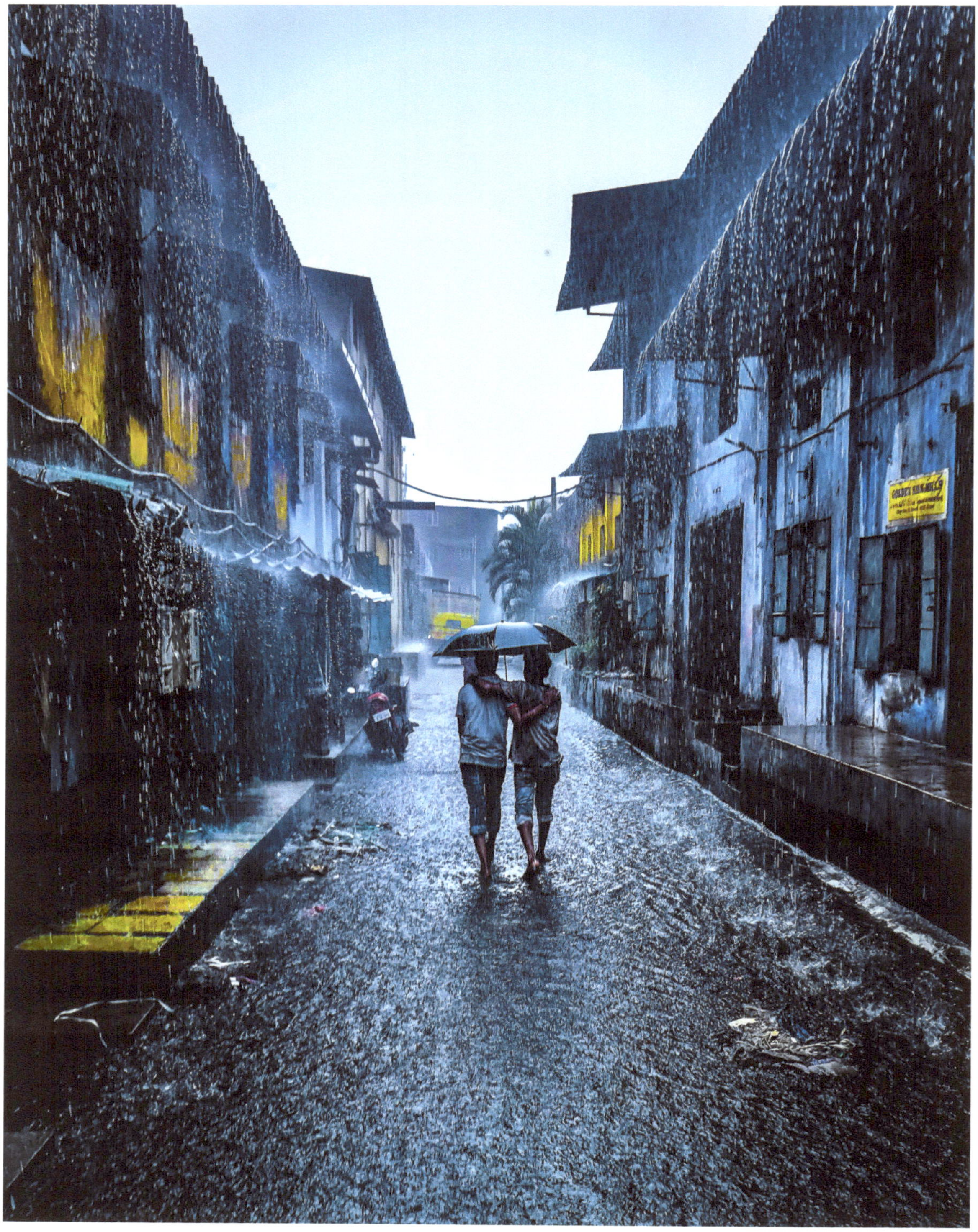

Friendship Goals
foundation.app/@ompsyram/~/60262
Minted: July 16, 2021

@trent_north_

Trent North, photographic visual artist

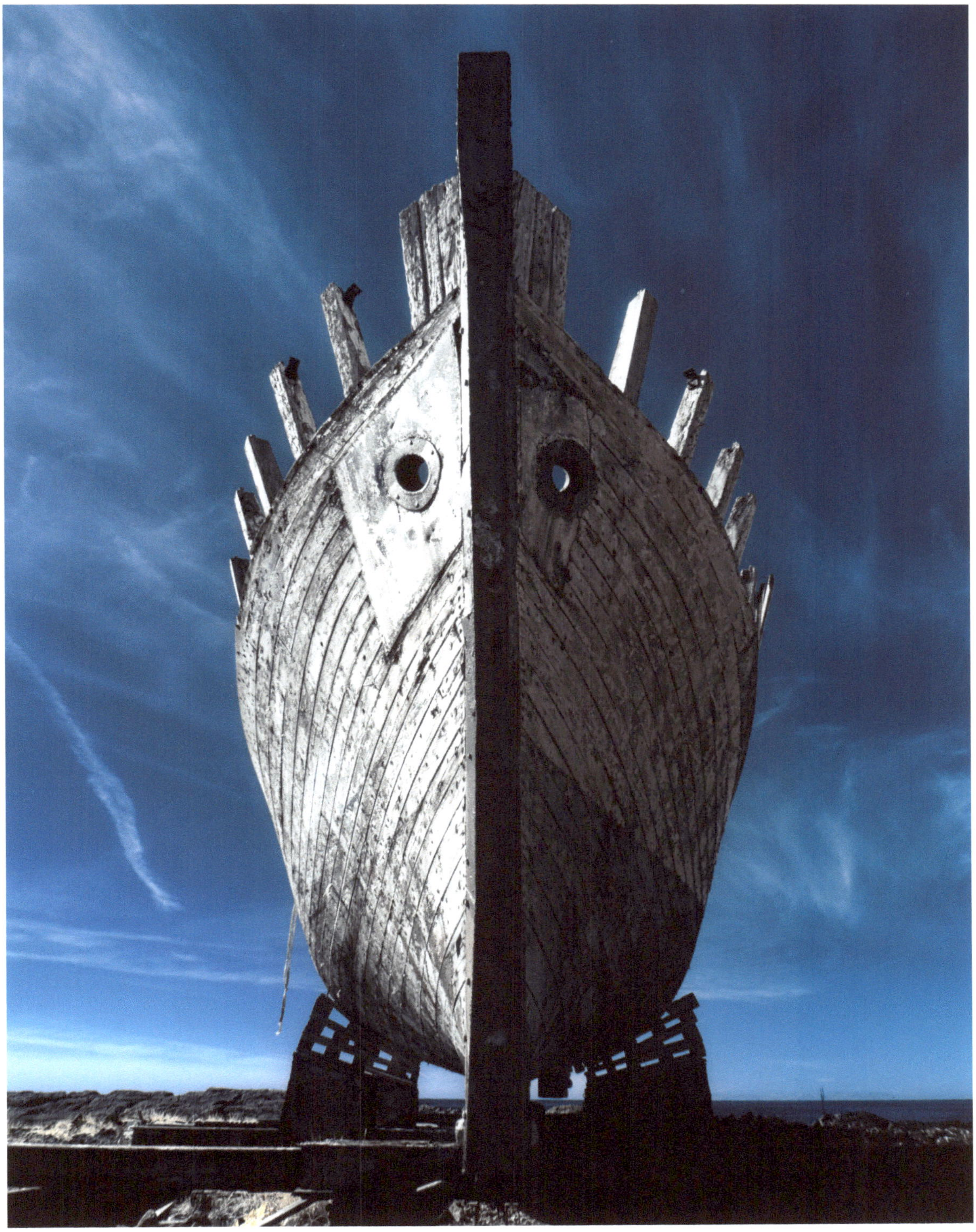

Ghost Ship

knownorigin.io/gallery/1036000-ghost-ship

Minted: August 28, 2021

@ovachinsky
Ovachinsky, photographer & sound designer

"There are truths that turned out to be lies over the years."

LIES collection

Black-and-white photography hits different. Does our brain fill in the colours? Yes. According to an academic paper from the University of Tübingen, "The mere sight of black-and-white photos automatically elicited brain activity patterns that specifically encoded colors." What does this mean for collectors of Bored Ape bananas? A grey banana will be processed by your brain as yellow thanks to your memory of colour.

What about our memories? The photographer and sound designer Ovachinsky muses about this use of monochrome in this way:

"Black-and-white photos perfectly capture the emotions associated with memories. Despite the cheerful moments, the story as a whole remains colorless."

The LIES collection by Ovachinsky is thematically consistent until the penultimate artwork, **#25 - Small details won't change anything**. In the photo, a cell tower is transformed into a heptagram-shaped star. It's probably the most unusual and original image in the whole collection. Heptagrams are sometimes the focal point of meditation or used as a protective shield in various spiritual traditions. But, whatever the meaning the formation has for the artist, it's likely to remain obscured:

*"The photos in the **LIES** collection—including the titles, descriptions, and the images' metaphorical meaning—form a coherent story that I may never fully share with you."*

If the first 25 photos in LIES document the thoughts and beliefs weighing heavily on someone too young to believe anything different, the 26th is a anthemic antidote. Most startlingly, of course, is that the work, **#26 - No more lies**, is in colour. Within the multimedia piece, there are strings, a piano is filled with staccato hope, and—at the 70-second mark—a crescendo builds as we continue to stare at the beauty of a blue sky and the expansiveness of a mountain landscape at altitude.

The musical score is by Ovachinsky, and the first buyer of the work's NFT token also received a physical, signed 7" record of the musical piece. **#26 - No more lies** deserves a place in an OnCyber gallery, if the collector wants to share the art's genius with us.

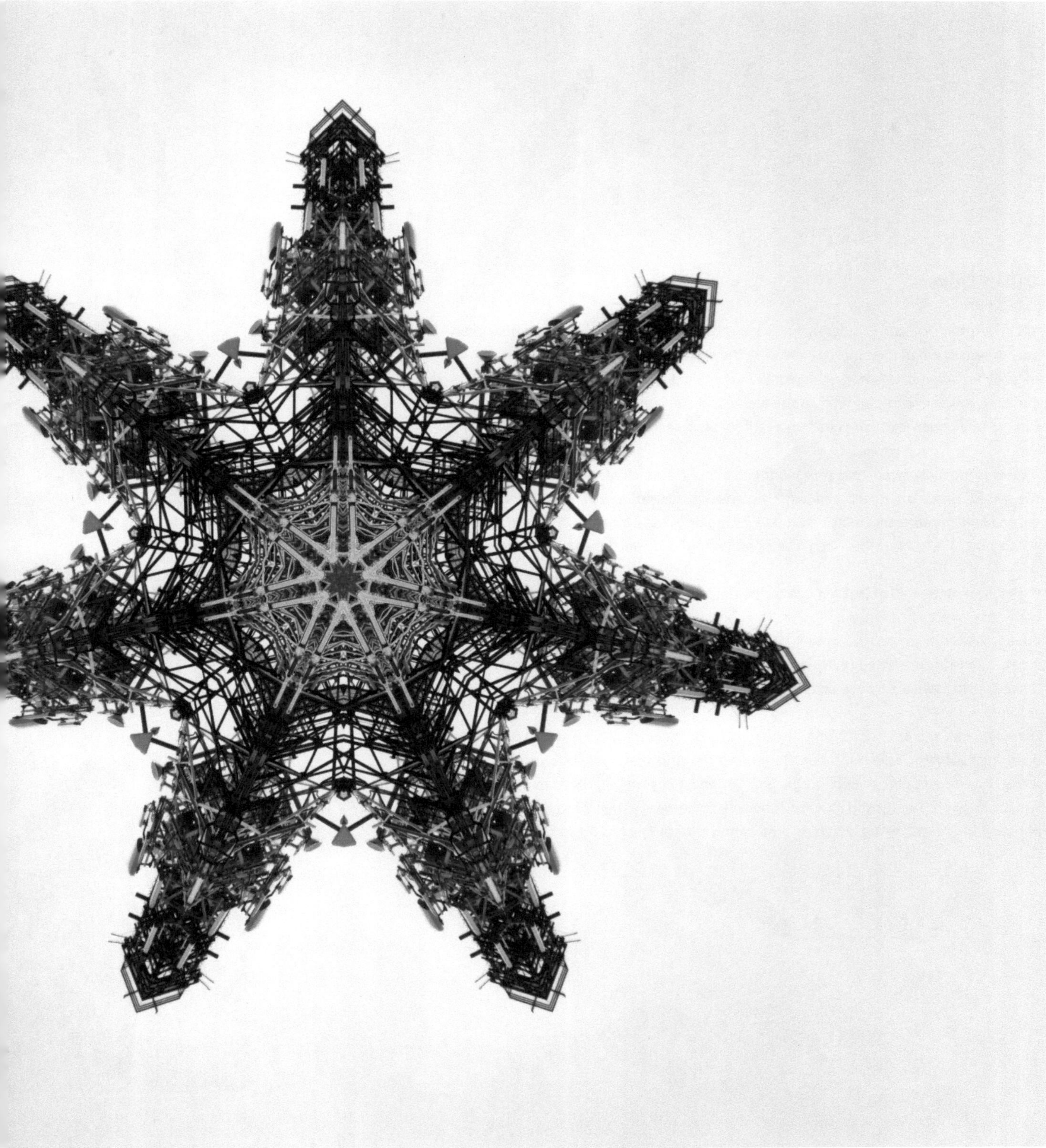

#25 - Small details won't change anything

opensea.io/collection/-lies-

Minted: September 1, 2021

@PhotoyogiNFT
Praveen Sundaram, photographer

Call of Duty

Photographer Praveen Sundaram has gained tarmac access that photographers can only dream of when it comes to capturing the shiny silver birds of the sky. He established Aviation Photographers India for enthusiasts of airplane culture, and he mentors young photographers via the association. In conversation with Praveen, one can tell how much joy being near the result of such technical wizardry brings. He says:

"Speed is the most important thing, But I also love the smell of spent aviation fuel and the sounds of screaming jet engines. It provides an adrenalin rush. While shooting, you get to meet the smartest minds that go into making these birds fly. The thrill of seeing these magnificent machines with a bit of play of light makes the entire piece into art."

In the work here, **Call of Duty**, much of the detail is obscured by an atmosphere filled with dust, sand, or perhaps pollution. The circular roundel insignia at the craft's rear is dulled, rendering its colours almost imperceptible. The same goes for the flag and the Air Force writing stenciled on the belly of the aircraft. A lone airman, his head slightly bowed, strides with purpose across the tarmac, briefly diverting our attention.

"When it comes to art, I don't limit myself to any particular style. My works are given a pictorial treatment. I did not receive formal art training, but I was fortunate in that my father was an accomplished photographer. When I was younger, I used to assist him with both photography and the darkroom. My father was a mentor to many other photographers, and while watching him mentor others, I picked up some of his advice."

"As a tribute to the fallen ones... when you get home tell them of us and say, 'for your Tomorrow we gave our Today.'"

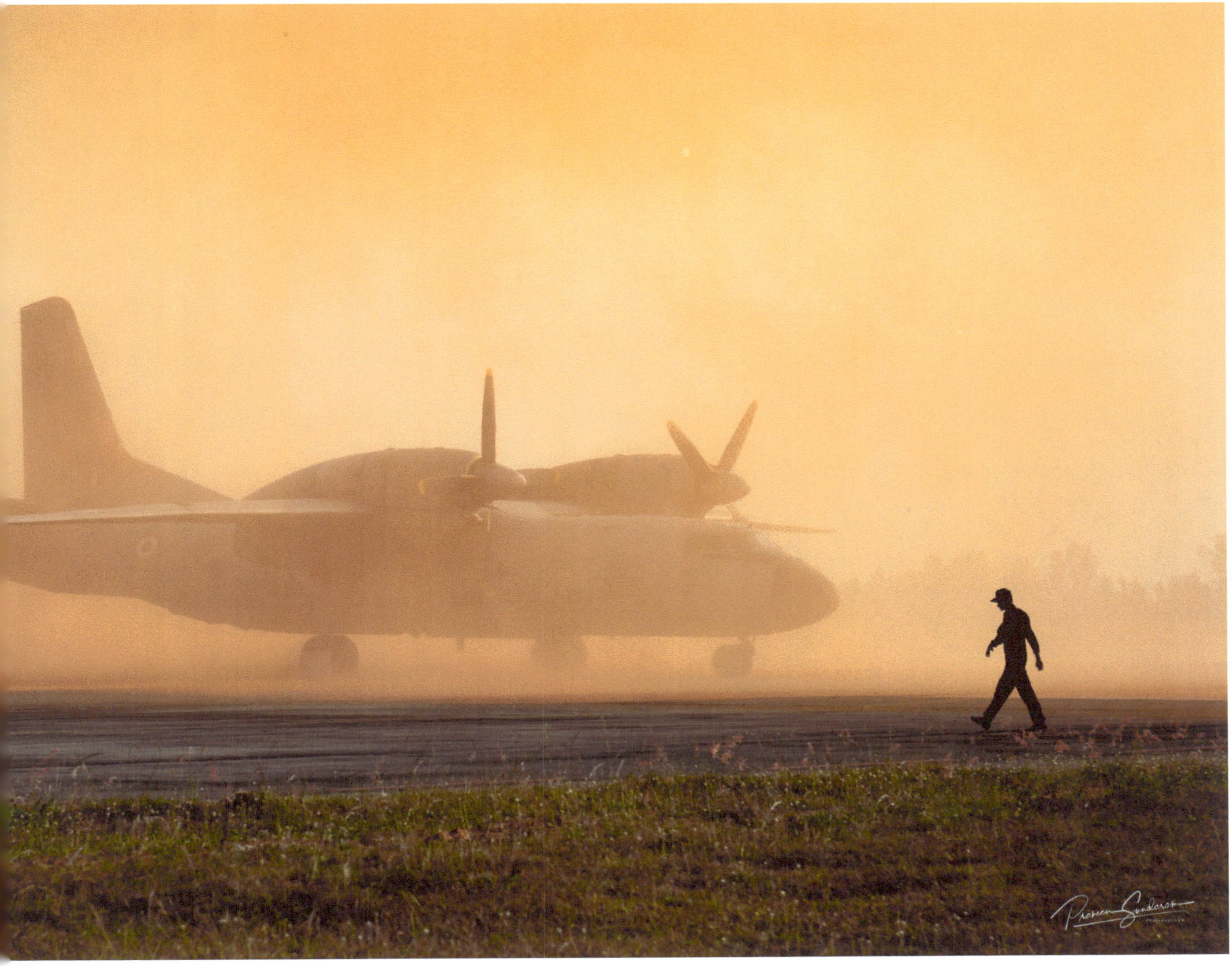

Call of Duty

foundation.app/@photoyogi/~/72174

Minted: August 14, 2021

@WeseeThisnow
Artist, explorer, convivial mystic

"The collection celebrates the pure visual beauty that is available every day on the streets."

Reflections on Solid Liquids collection

The Reflections on Solid Liquids collection visually captures Midtown Manhattan, May through October, 2019, while walking the city for days at a time. It offers a meditation on surface, structure, reflection, perception, and reality.

There are thirty 1/1 NFT photographs. This collection is completely lens-based, while still utilizing a modern digital photography editing workflow. The images are made with long-range telephoto lenses—equivalent to old-school 150mm - 600mm lenses—aiming forty or fifty stories up.

The image opposite, *Ripples at Sunset*, has nearly infinite imaginative depth, combining on-surface in-focus elements with dreamy sunset building reflections rippling from the imperfections of glass, one of many vast, ever-changing movie screens all over the city. The artist writes about the collection:

"The mind, striving to maintain the illusion that a comprehensible external world exists, filters and packages beautiful raw optical data into patterned, predictable, and understandable chunks of meaning.

"That is a building; that is the corner of a building; that is the reflection of a building corner on a building; that is a reflection of a reflection of a building behind me; that building is bent in half, though, wait, no, not really.

"This endless juxtaposition of reflected image fragments produces an enormous cognitive load while one is navigating the urban landscape. We could instead just enjoy the more pure sensory data of seeing what's actually there."

The artist is forging a personal path with these two collections. This one of lens-based images exploring beauty hidden in plain sight, as well as a genesis collection of geometric photo illustrations exploring perspective and transformation. Each collection has a narrative poetic reflection, inviting participation on Github.

The images reward if not demand lingering attention and personal exploration. The artist apparently also has a technical background, so we should expect further aesthetic developments in the future.

Ripples at Sunset
opensea.io/collection/reflections-on-solid-liquids
Minted: November 28, 2021

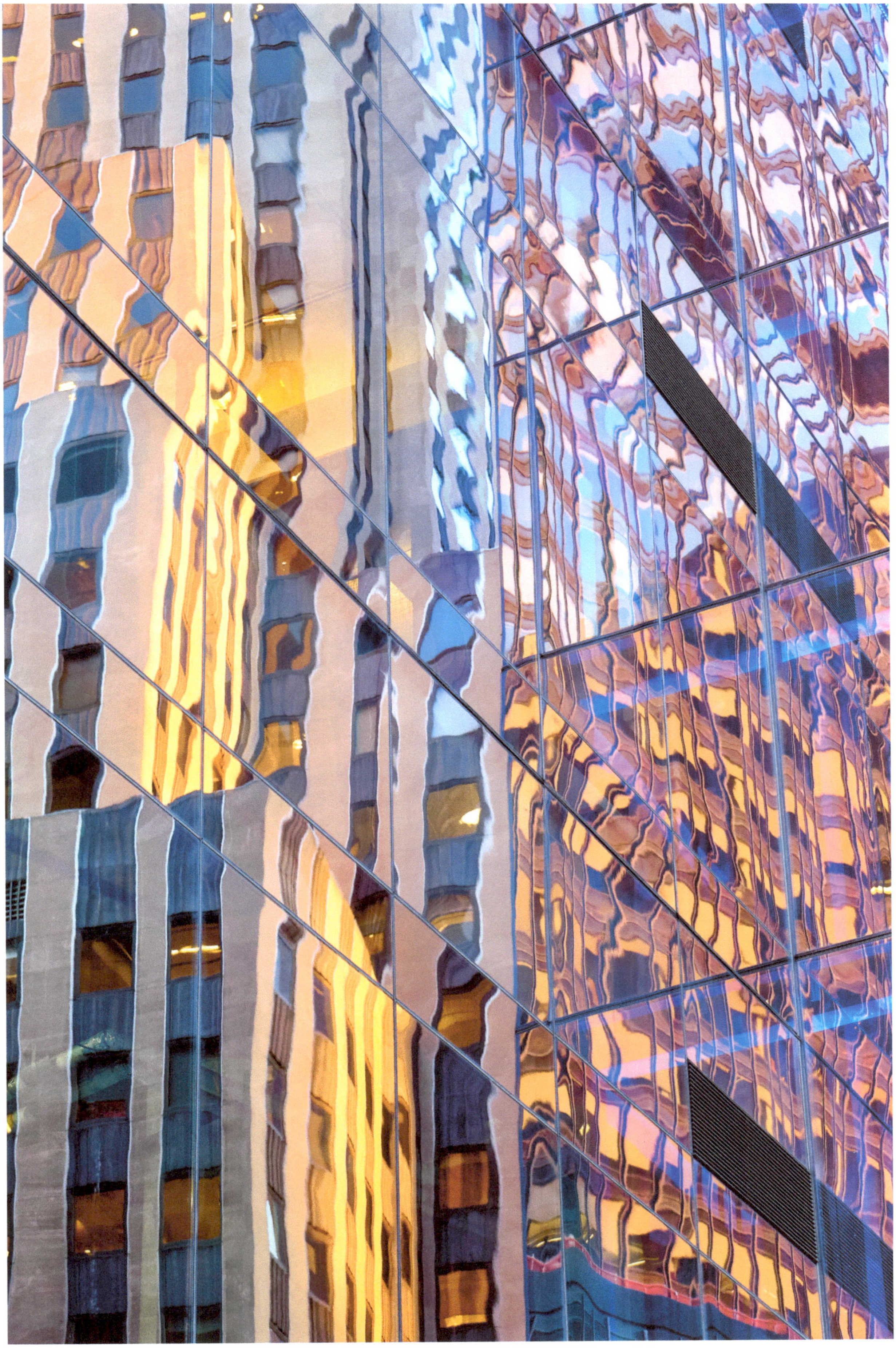

NATURE ART

This is often photography focused on natural elements
such as wildlife, landscape, plants, and organic textures.

@agnimax
Agnisoonu, photographer

Morning Bliss

Natures most serene moments begin in the 'gm' and disappear at 'gn'. Those are the moments that transfix Agni as well as many of us who live by the light of each day. The photographer recalls the story that brought him to the moment in this photo:

"Kerala is famous for its backwaters and rivers, which can be found throughout the state. Kerala's backwaters are a network of brackish lagoons and lakes that run along the state's coastline along the Arabian Sea in southern India.

"This backwater is a beautiful, one-of-a-kind setting in the lap of cosmic nature. People frequently use the backwaters for commuting, fishing, and farming, and taking a boat trip provides an interesting glimpse into these daily activities.

"I went on one of these early-morning cruises in a small boat, and it was so beautiful that I couldn't put it into words. It's as if you're in another world as you hover over houses, rice fields, coconut trees, churches, temples, toddy shops, and wildlife."

Agni's ENS (Ethereum Name Service) address is agni.eth, a rare four-letter address. Agni is a Sanskrit word meaning 'fire' and suggests the fire god of Hinduism. In ancient Hindu texts, Agni is conceptualised to exist at three levels—on earth as fire, in the atmosphere as lightning, and in the sky as the Sun. Perhaps it's meant to be that the photographer Agni finds his creativity in capturing the best moments of the Sun.

Unlike artists who wait for their genesis mint to sell on Foundation, Agni has been doing a roaring trade—now into double-digit art sales. Recent artworks sold include **Sun-Kissed mountain of Kolukkumalai**, **Meet me where the sky touches the sea**, and **The Fiery Kiss**.

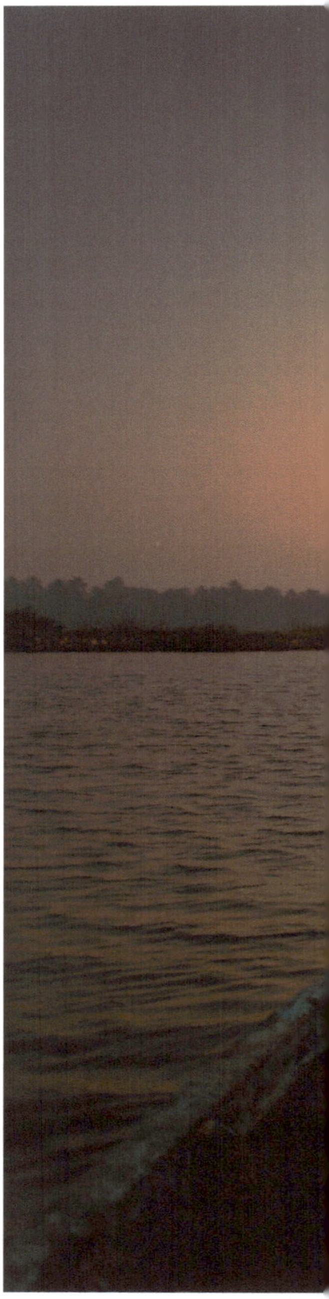

“I enjoy framing the colors of nature and the emotions of life.”

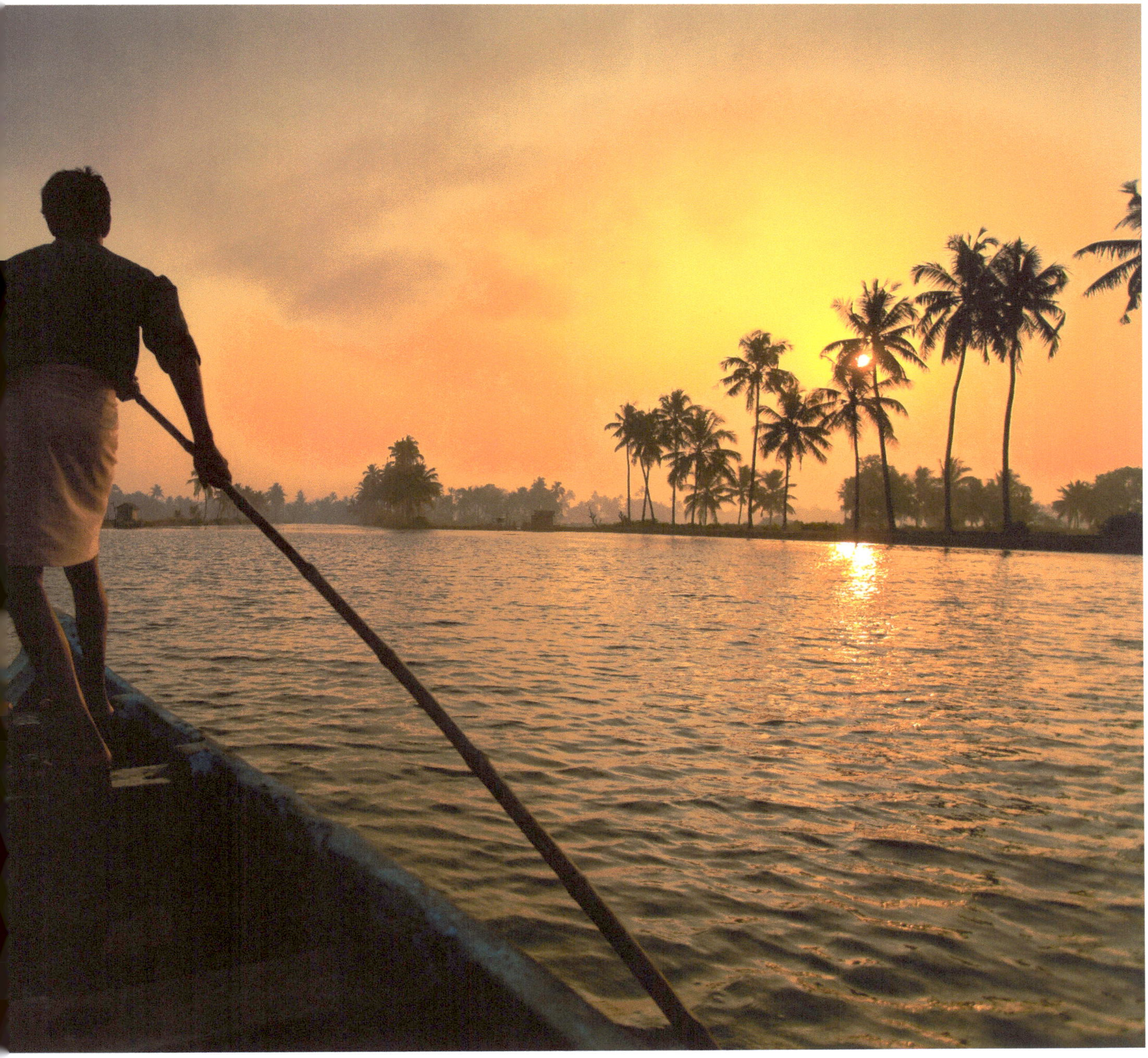

Morning Bliss
foundation.app/@agnimax/~/108381
Minted: November 17, 2021

@alistairkeddie
Al Keddie, photographer & visual artist

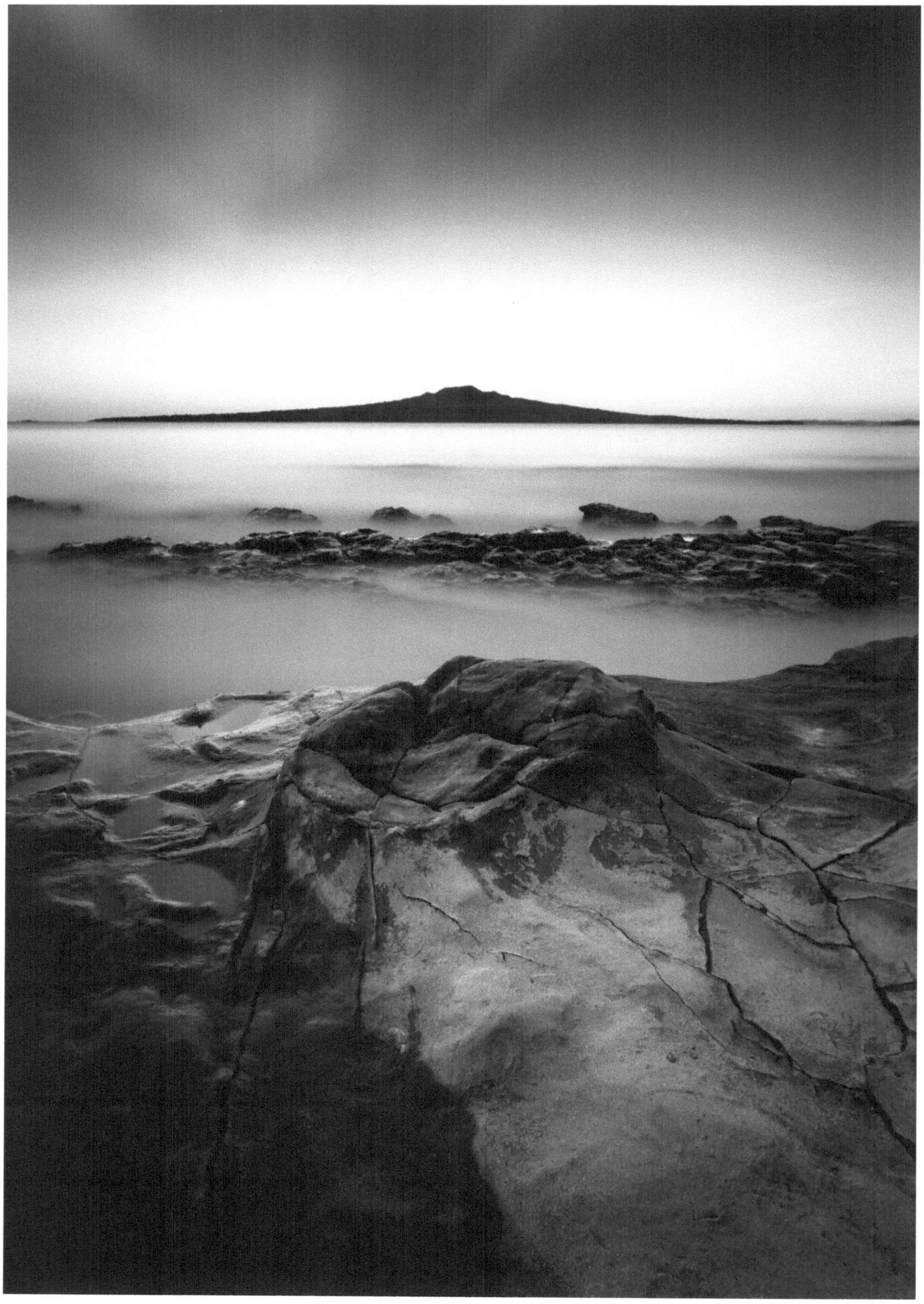

Rangitoto Echo, Auckland
foundation.app/@alistairkeddie/~/90411
Minted: September 24, 2021

@BluejaywayEth
Blue Jay Way, nature photographer

"I am fascinated by the patterns in this ice carved by melting glaciers. Melting glaciers... Beauty with a deeper message."

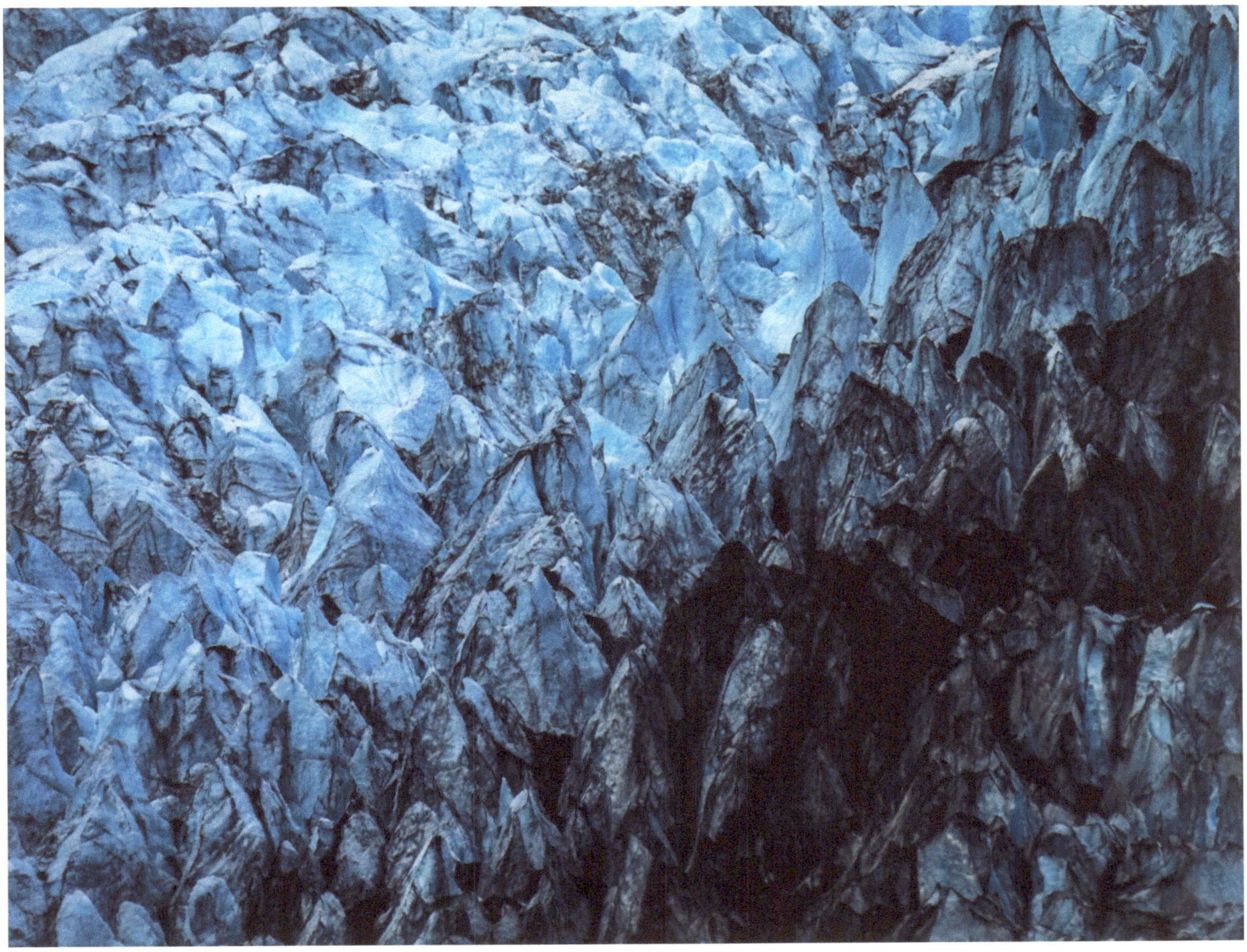

Glacier Ice Abstract

foundation.app/@bluejayway/~/104355

Minted: November 3, 2021

@CHoibergPhoto
Christian Hoiberg, photographer

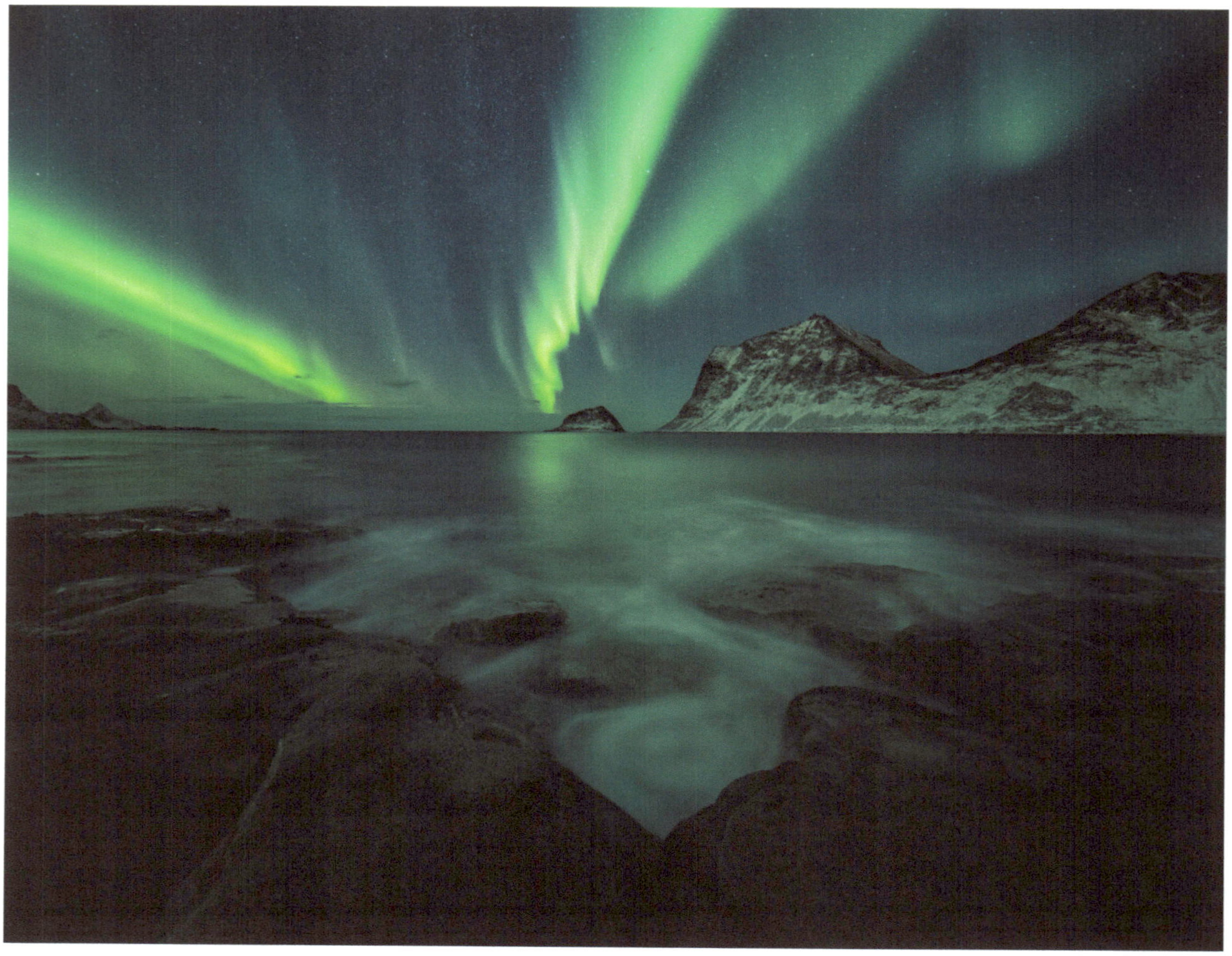

A Light in the Dark
opensea.io/collection/68-north
Minted: October 16, 2021

@devendraphotog
Devendra Deshmukh, wildlife photographer

"This was taken at Amboseli National Park in Kenya. Protecting tuskers is the park's main focus thanks to a trust which ensures the welfare of Africa's beloved pachyderms."

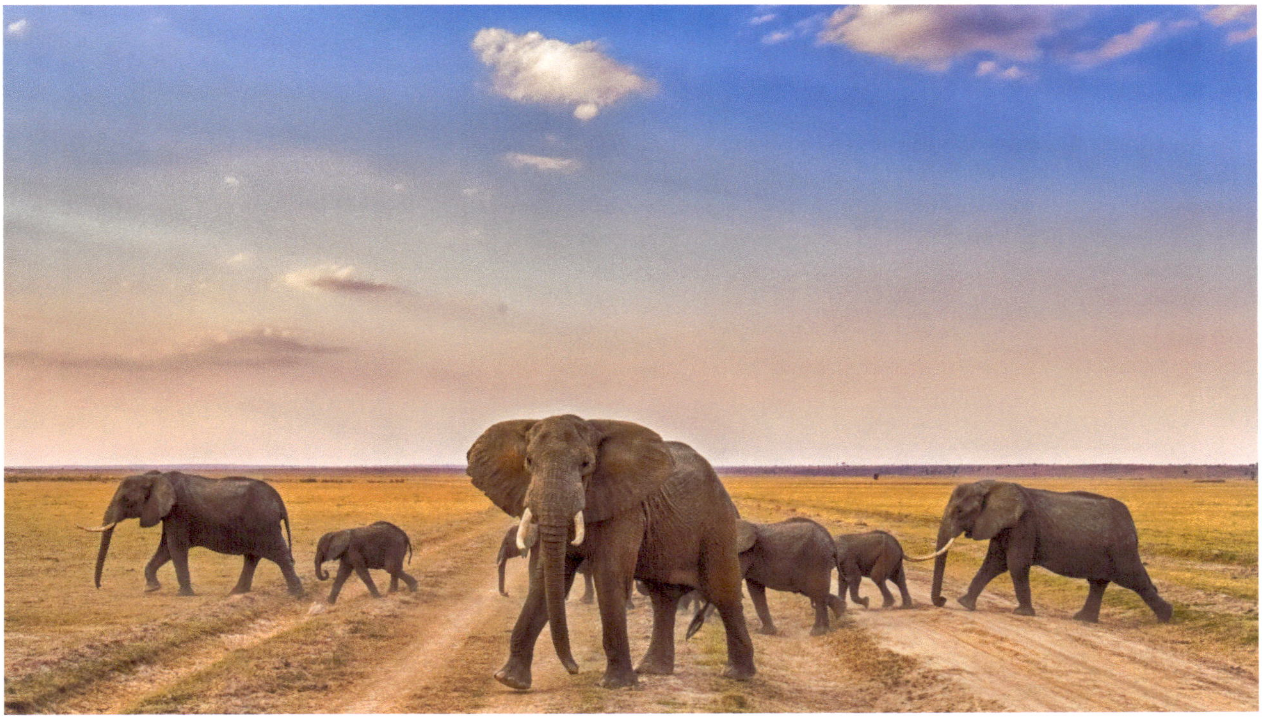

The Protector
foundation.app/@devendraphotog/~/93775
Minted: October 2, 2021

@ElizaArtPhoto
Eliza Daigle, photographer

Spectacular Sunsets collection

Although she doesn't focus exclusively on sunsets, photographer Eliza Daigle has always had a special love for them. Last year, she sent herself on a mission to capture the most magical sunsets she could find. Now she is sharing these beautiful photos in her first NFT collection titled **Spectacular Sunsets**. She says of her inspiration:

"There's a timelessness in the moments when the sun meets the horizon—something that has happened, and will continue to, every day for as long as this planet exists."

A lifelong artist who is dedicated to her craft, Eliza recently began sharing her work with a wider audience. She grew up with a camera in hand, and has always seen the world through her lens.

"When I was young I'd use up an entire disposable camera in a couple of hours, usually capturing a beach or a sunset. I still take at least as many photos, but now I have big memory cards."

Eliza's goal with her work is to bring people back into a more beautiful and loving world, reminding them of this planet's magic that we sometimes forget to appreciate.

"I'm in love with the Earth in all its mystery, magnificence, and divinity. And I want to share that visually. I hope my work can be a support to help people break out of their daily routine to see a greater perspective—perhaps to remember their true priorities or to find clarity in their situation. Or even to experience the perfection of a simple moment in time, untainted by thought."

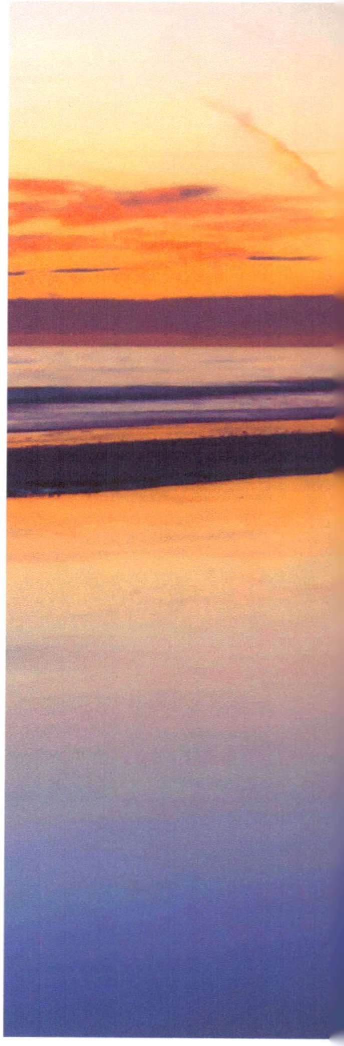

"My mission to capture the most magical sunsets. A reminder of the beauty that can be found in the darkness."

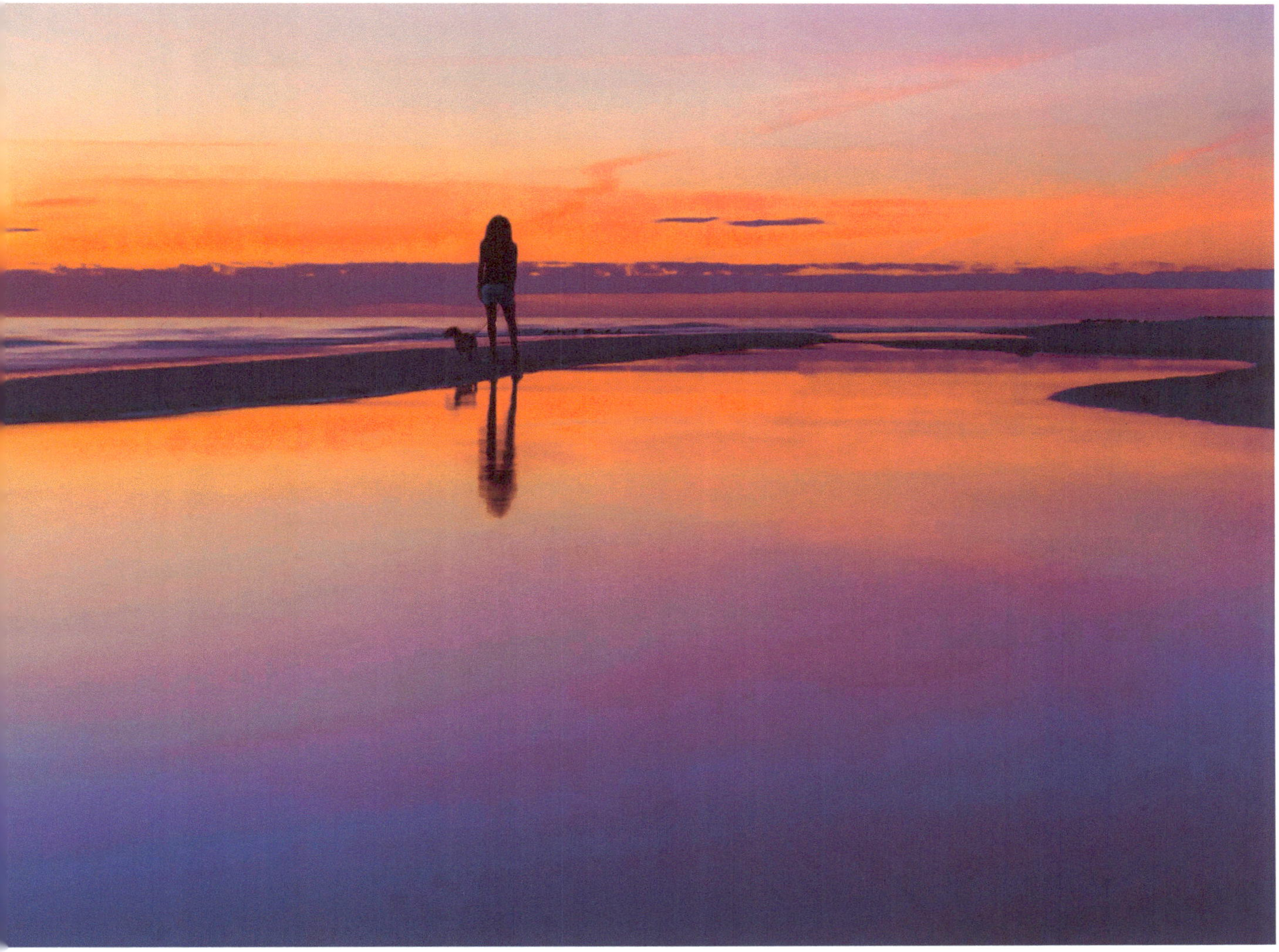

Girl & Dog

solsea.io/collection/61a686f6d57b3131685f2226

Minted: November 30, 2021

@ElizaArtPhoto
Eliza Daigle, photographer

Spectacular Sunsets collection

Photographer Eliza Daigle is consistently inspired by the infinite ways that light and color interact with the environment to create what we perceive as beauty. And she realises that her artistic sensibility is something to be shared:

"Now I recognize that I can gift others, who may see things very differently, with my unique perspective."

What's next for Eliza's art? Perhaps something new. Her work is in a new phase of evolution. Currently, her photography experiments include playing with different long-exposure effects as well as combining multiple images into double exposures. In addition, she is trying out new media (for her) like acrylic and watercolor painting.

While continuing to build her first NFT collection, Eliza expects to get more involved in the crypto-art world. She sees it as a perfect bridge between her engineering training and her artistic talents. NFTs may also help her make the greater impact that she desires, bringing together communities around environmental advocacy—a topic about which she is very passionate. In fact, it even influenced her choice of blockchain.

"That's part of why I'm starting on Solana instead of Ethereum. I want my work to contribute to green solutions rather than unnecessary waste."

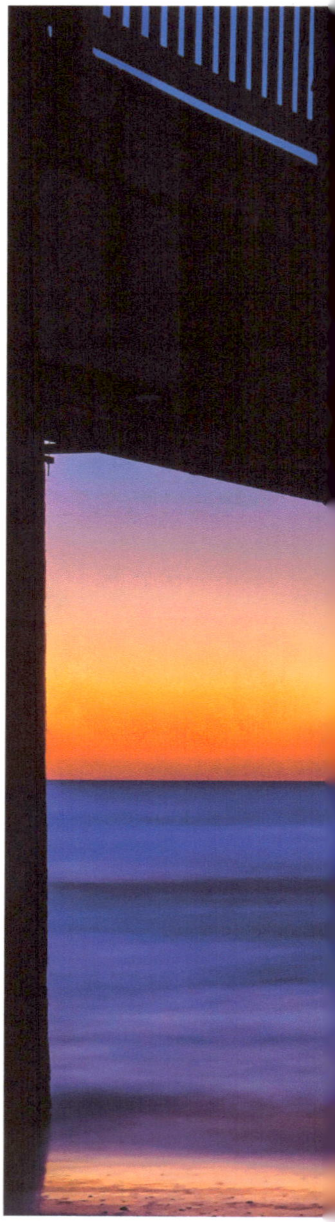

"Here's a sunset captured with a long exposure. The churning ocean waves have, paradoxically, been smoothed over time."

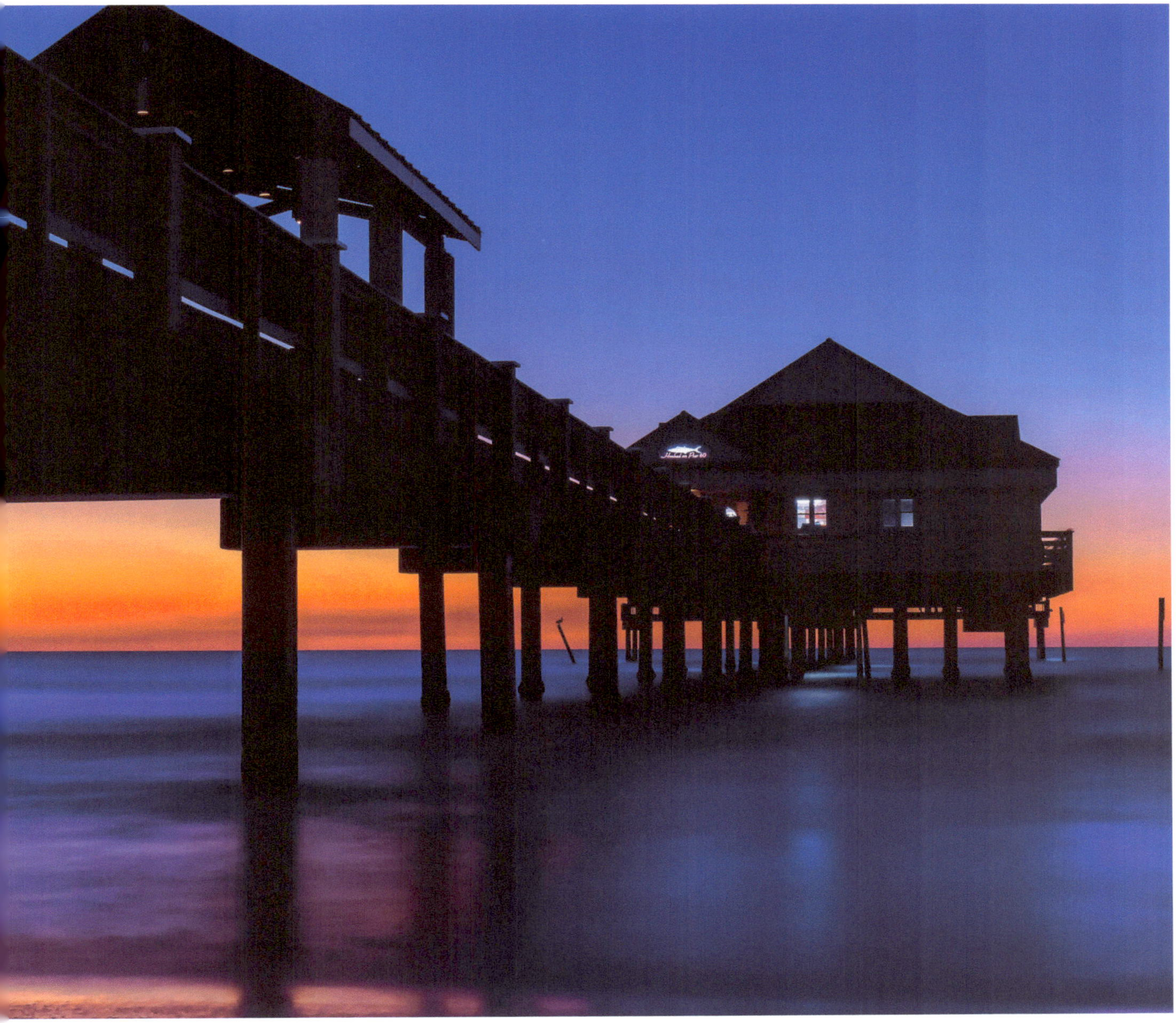

Evening at the Pier

solsea.io/collection/61a686f6d57b3131685f2226

Minted: November 30, 2021

@GWhittonPhoto
Greg Whitton, landscape photographer

"I came upon this ancient caldera, eroded by the elements and time. It resembled the remains of a long-dead dinosaur."

FOSSIL

Where we live determines much of what we experience. Fortunately, Greg Whitton shares many of the moments in the landscapes and seascapes of the United Kingdom the we might otherwise not see. The photo **FOSSIL** was captured at nearly 3,000 feet of altitude on the Isle of Arran, located a couple of hours west of Glasgow, Scotland.

"When hiking in the mountains on the Isle of Arran, you cannot fail to be impressed by their magnificent profiles—even when compared to the mountains of the Highlands on the mainland. The central part is an ancient caldera, eroded by the elements and time and on the western ridge of North Goatfell. Here you will find this curious arrangement of rocks. To me it resembled the fossilised remains of a long-dead dinosaur."

FOSSIL conveys the epic scale of nature through a vertebrae of stones. Each stone is revealed from the weight of a million of years eroding away the surrounding tundra. As a photographer, Greg does what it takes to go to the heights of nature and then overlays a story that goes beyond the surface beauty.

FOSSIL
foundation.app/@GregWhitton/~/46548
Minted: June 7, 2021

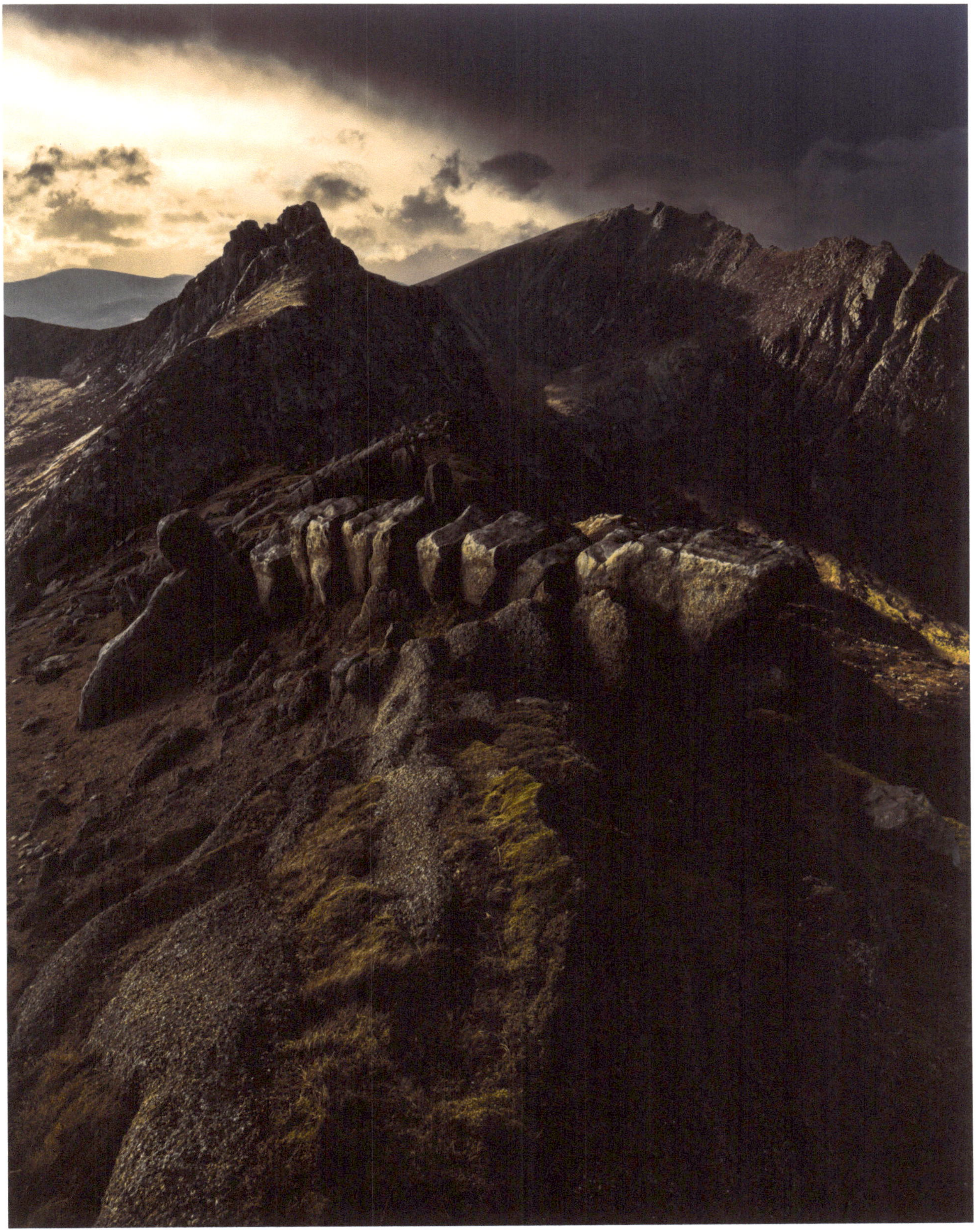

@itsmesubhash
Subhash Nair, wildlife photographer

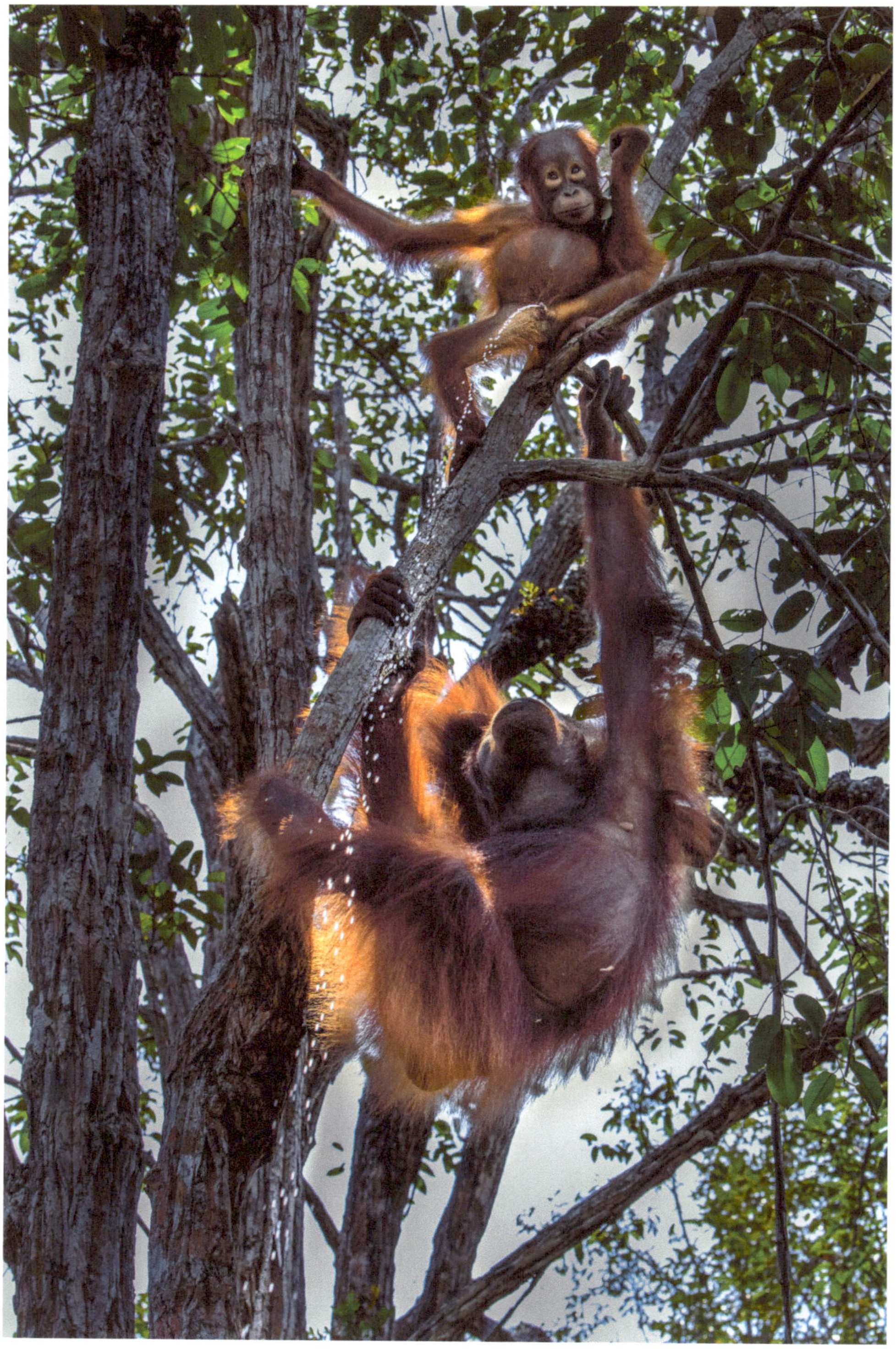

Naughty Cutie

foundation.app/@itsmesubhash/~/91930

Minted: September 28, 2021

@lebackpacker
Johan Lolos, travel photographer

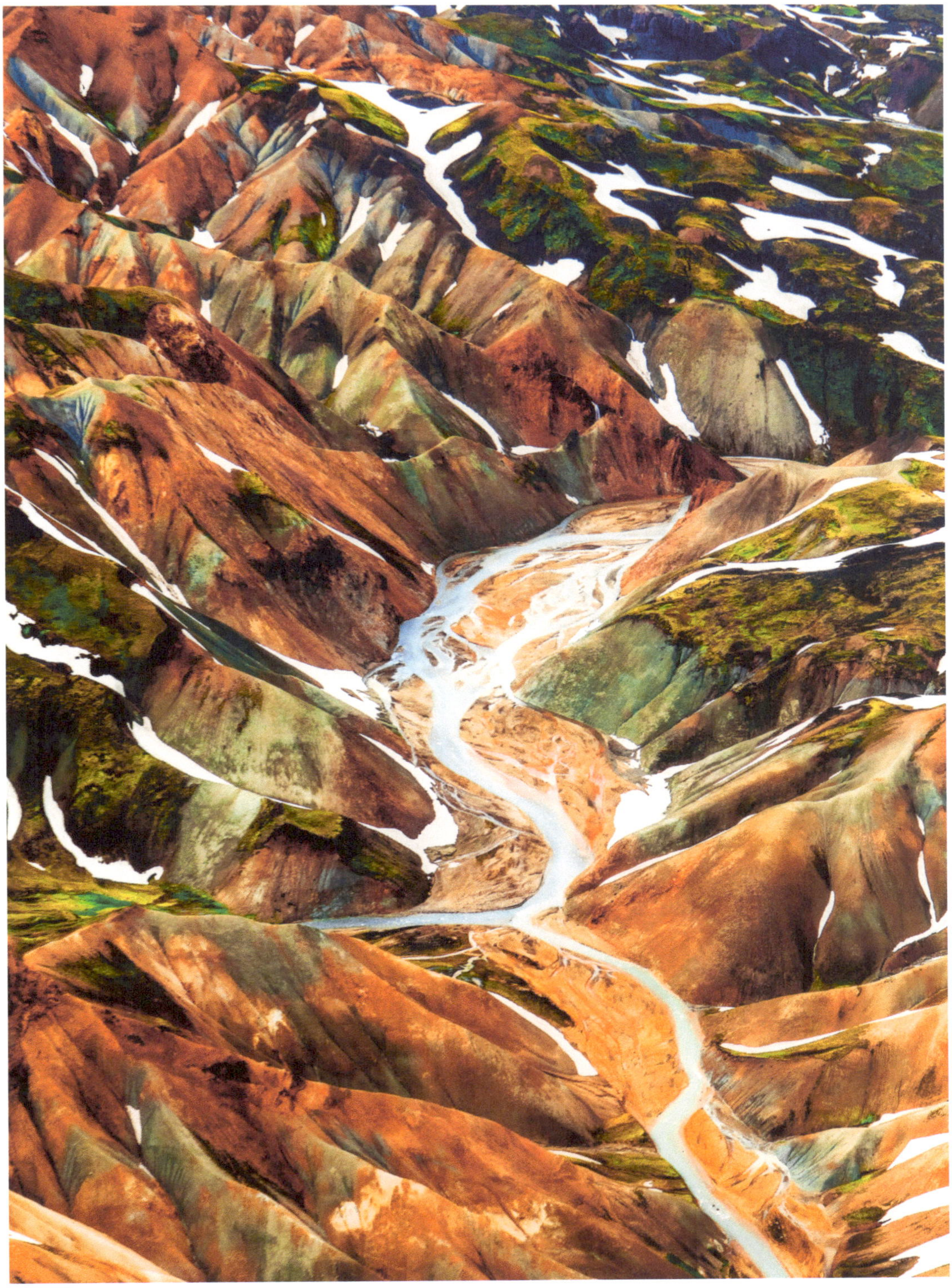

Explosion of Colors
superrare.com/lebackpacker/creations
Minted: July 19, 2021

@jellyfire1

Lee Acaster, photographer

Dark Thoughts collection

The name of Lee Acaster's collection, **Dark Thoughts**, is a hint to the type of stories that the photographer captures with his lens. He is, above all, informed by the land:

"Living on the Norfolk and Suffolk border, most of my images take their inspiration from the low-lying beauty of the East Anglian landscape. Rather than recording a view as a photographic record, I strive to add my own interpretation and a little drama to the images I shoot."

The photo presented here, **Protection**, contrasts the naturalness of a cluster of trees against the massive synthetic fields of intensive agriculture. The forced perspective of the fields draws us to ponder the future of the remaining few trees. The sunrise behind them is foreboding as well. It evokes "red sky in the morning, shepherd's take warning" vibes. It's almost as if nature itself is warning us of some impending doom.

The genius of Lee's work lies as much in the titles of each work as it does in the image. Each word a powerful catalyst for emotionally charging the image. Besides **Protection**, other evocative titles include **Fortress**, **Motion**, **Hush**, and **Blockade**.

Another striking work is **Sinking** which describes the light at the end of the tunnel revealed by standing under the well-known Southwold pier in the United Kingdom. Most shots of piers are taken from a distance, wide angled to place the architecture in context with its surroundings. **Sinking** is different. The work, which you can see on Foundation, goes below deck to reveal a completely new and buoyant perspective.

Since Lee challenges us to decide what the story is in his enigmatic photos, my take is that **Sinking** is floating. It's almost a metaphor for this new, upside-down world of NFTs. As an artist or collector, we might feel at times that we're sinking, but eventually we will float upon the currents of this decentralised metaverse we're building.

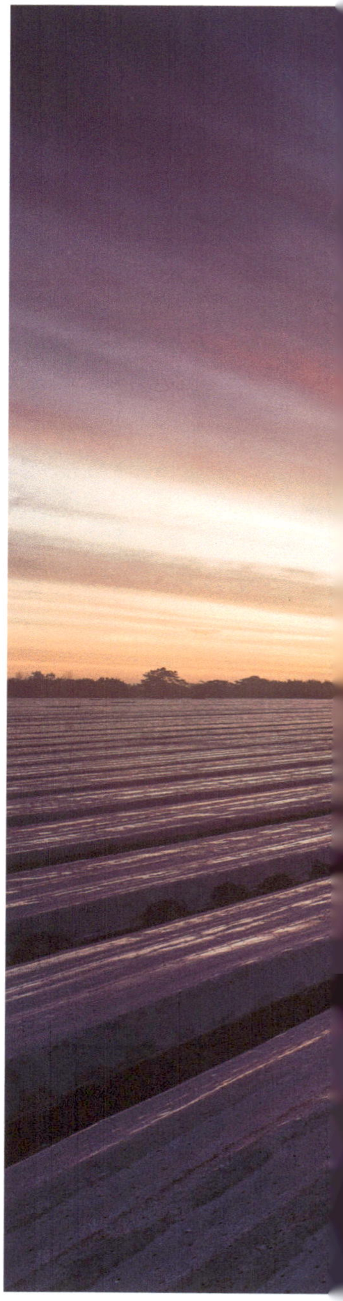

"I leave it to the viewer to decide what the story is."

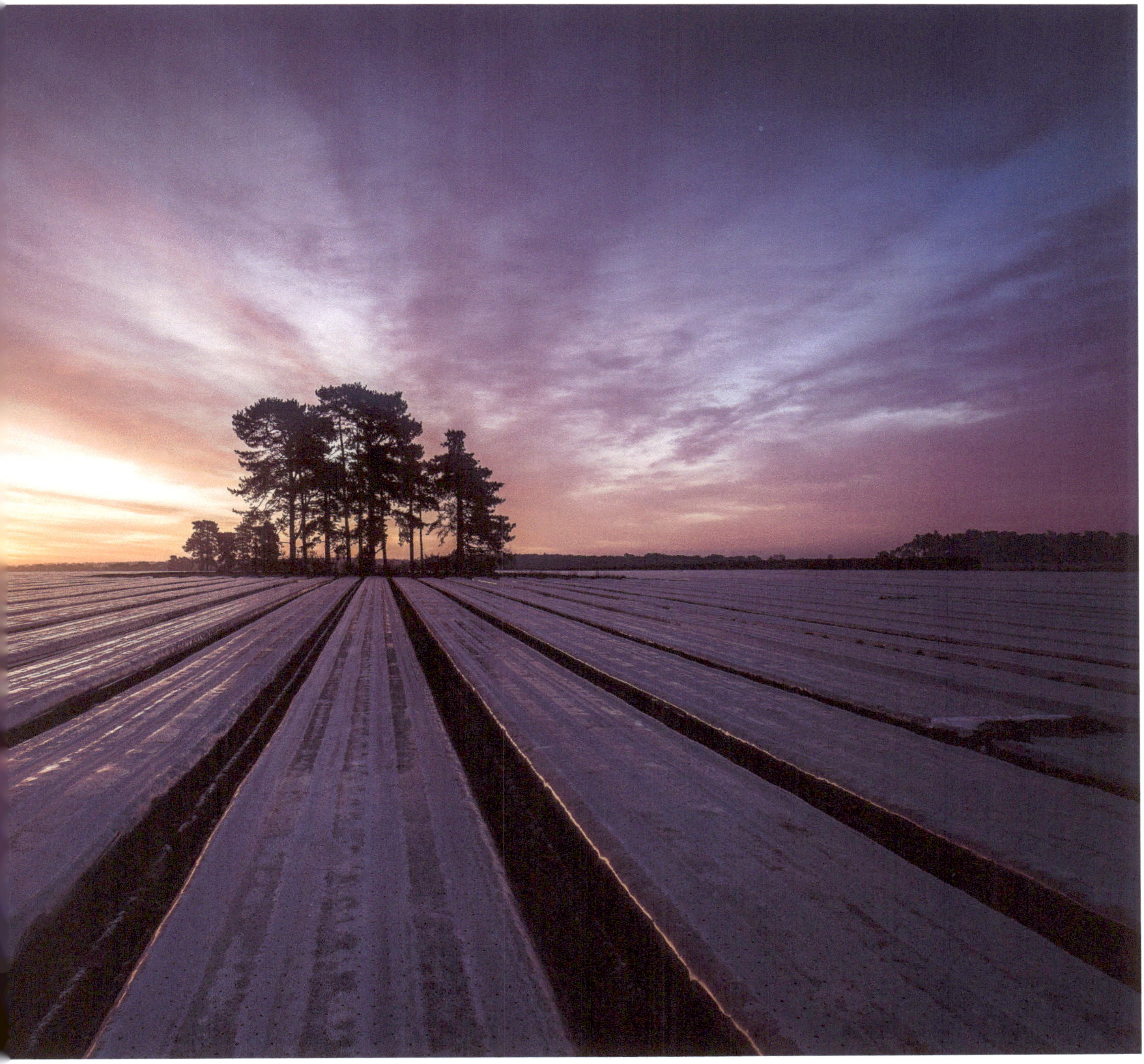

Protection
foundation.app/@jellyfire1/~/89307
Minted: September 22, 2021

@LimitlessWifey
Mommy of 3 & wifey of ArmyDad

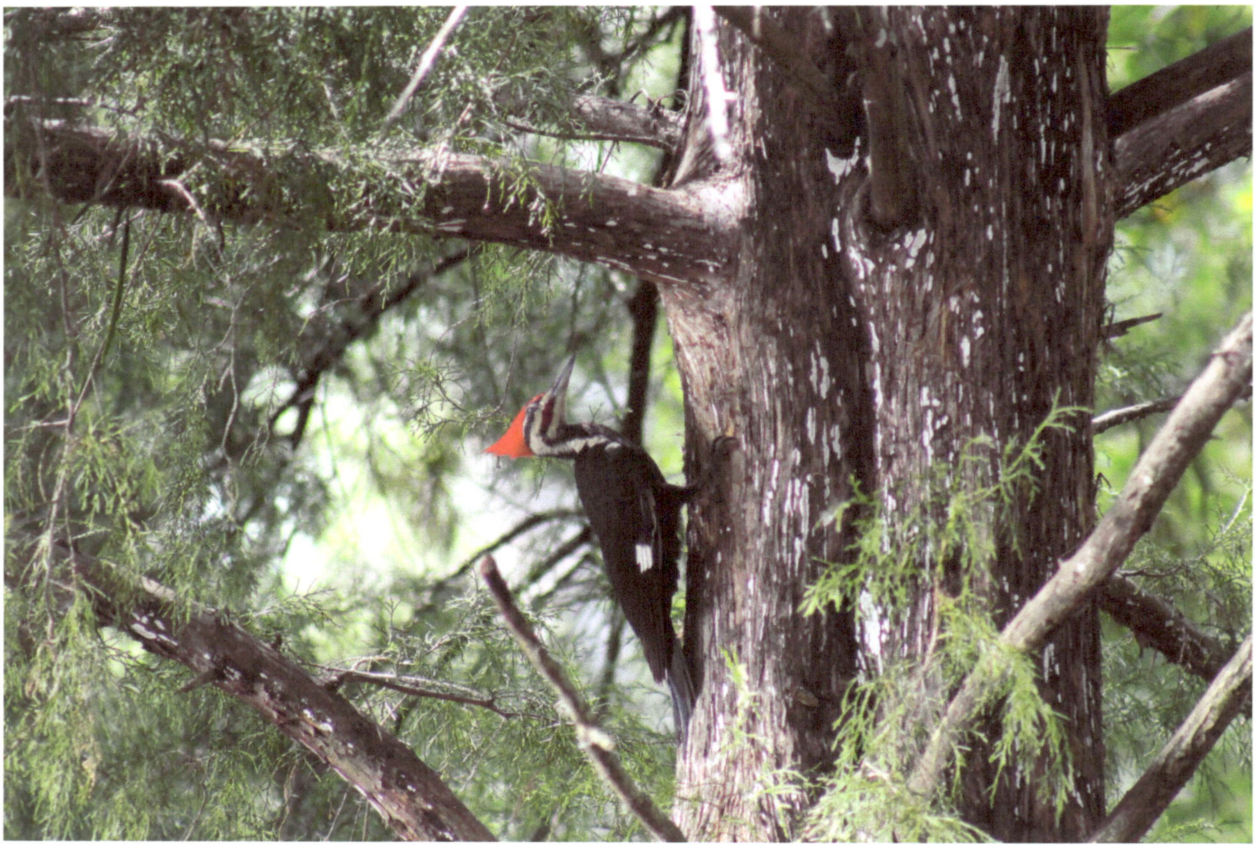

Florida's Amazing Creature
opensea.io/collection/limitlessphotography
Minted: January 5, 2022

@maneshclicks

Manesh Pai, portrait & landscape photographer

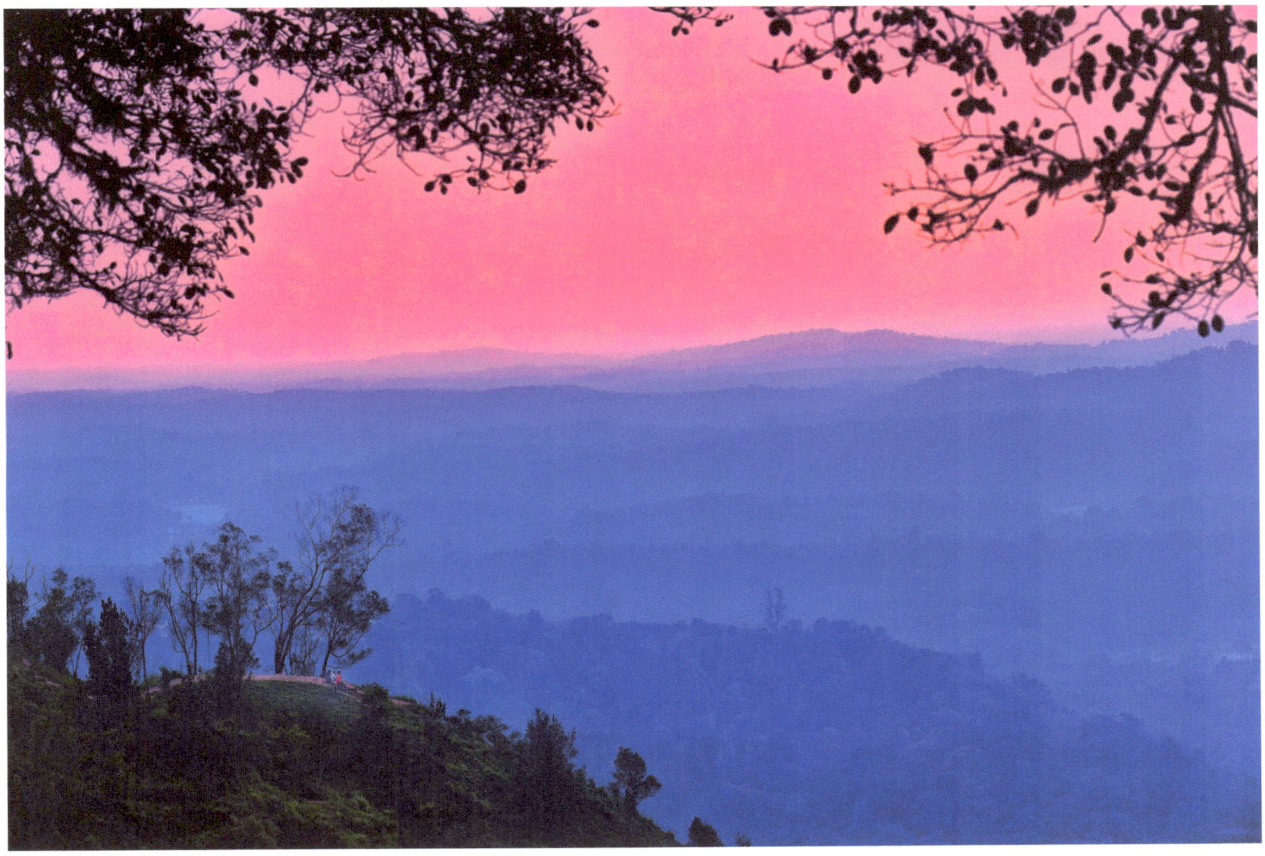

Friends watching sunset

opensea.io/collection/goldenhourcollection

Minted: September 28, 2021

@manishmandhyan

Manish Mandhyan, wildlife photographer

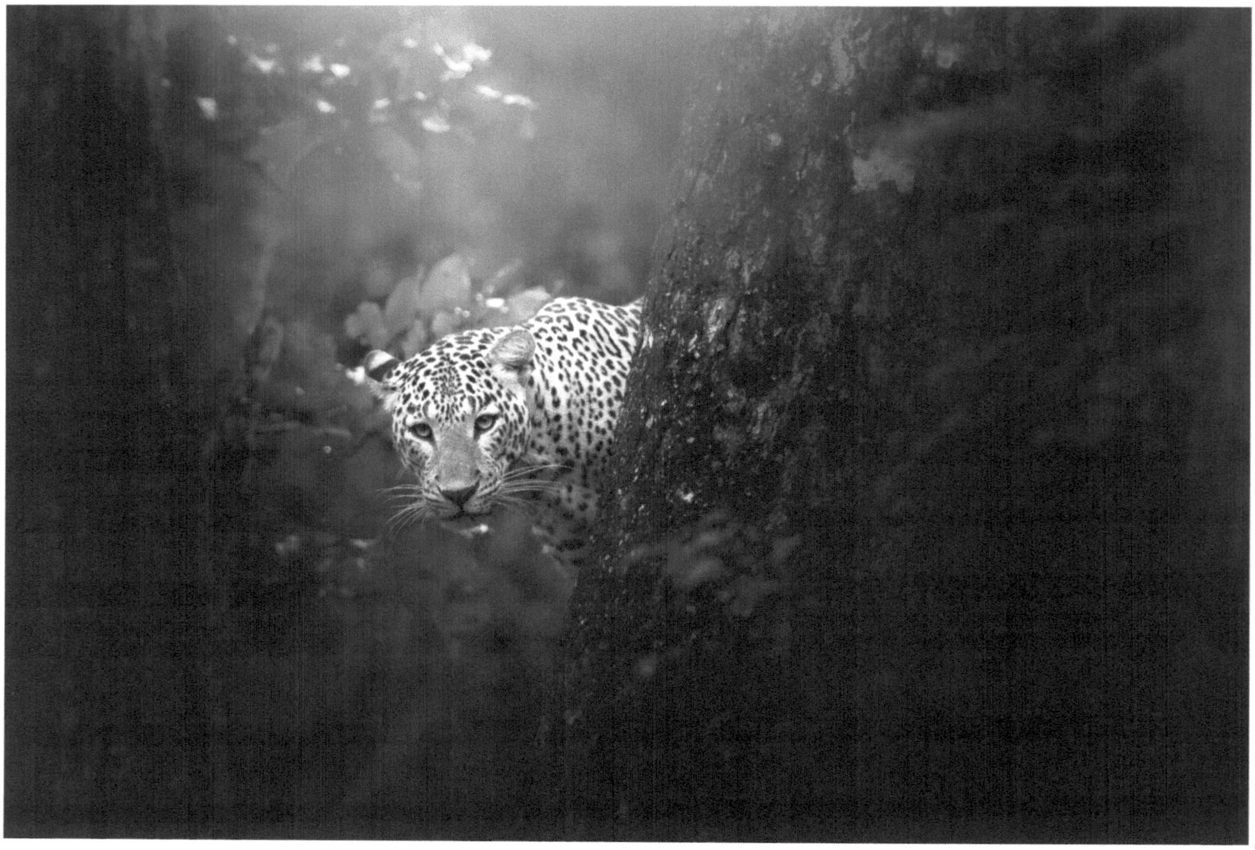

Leopard Lure

foundation.app/@mmandhyan/~/106601

Minted: November 11, 2021

@MattDoogue
Matt Doogue, photographer

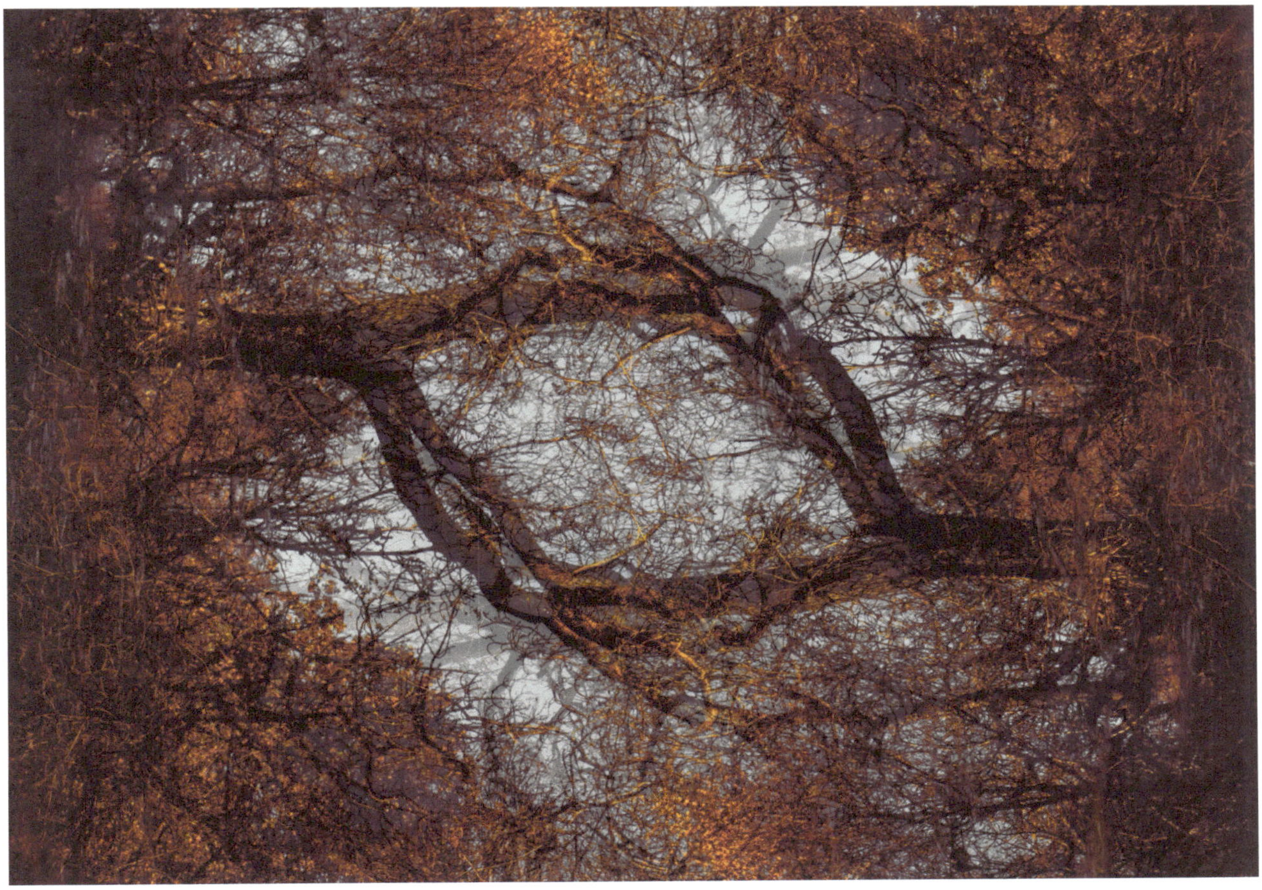

Eye of the forest

foundation.app/@MattsMacro/~/108266

Minted: November 16, 2021

@mintfaced
Ryan Jennings, photographer

*"**Geodetic Moments** explores how small shifts in our position can dramatically change what we see. Look forward and see what's possible."*

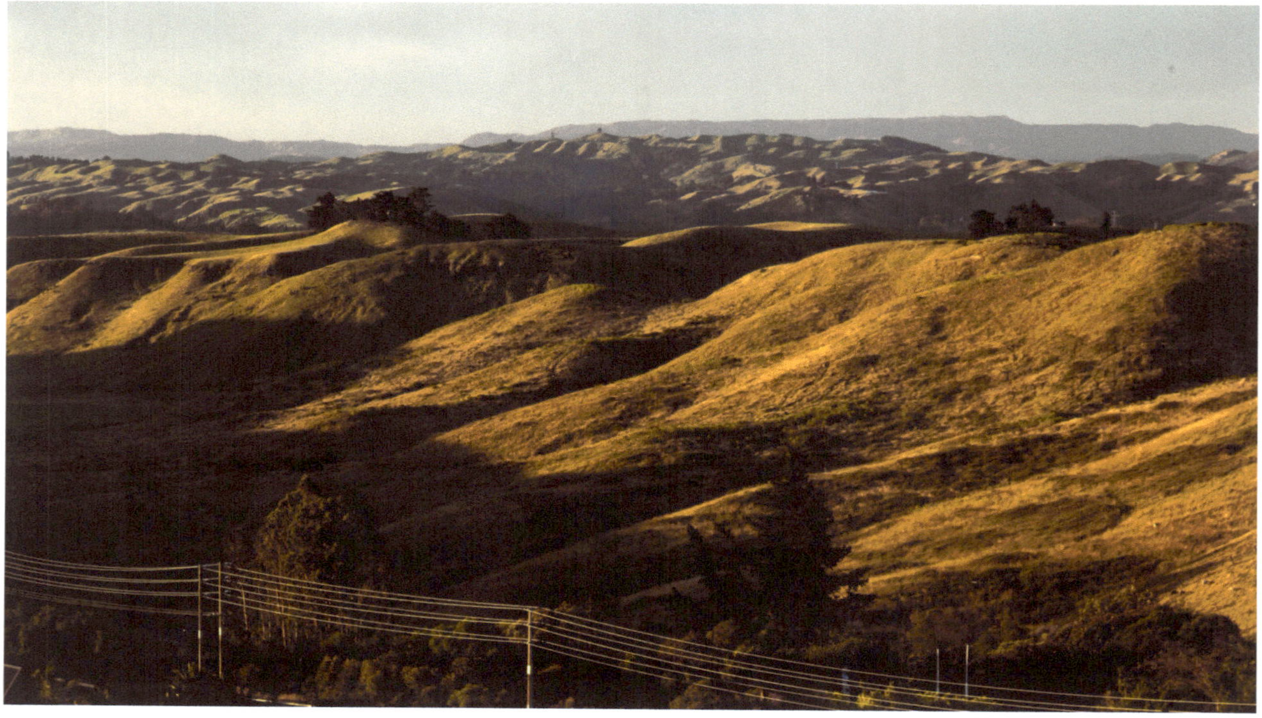

Geodetic Moment #71
opensea.io/collection/geodetic-moments
Minted: December 23, 2021

@Rakesh_pulapa
Rakesh Pulapa, photographer

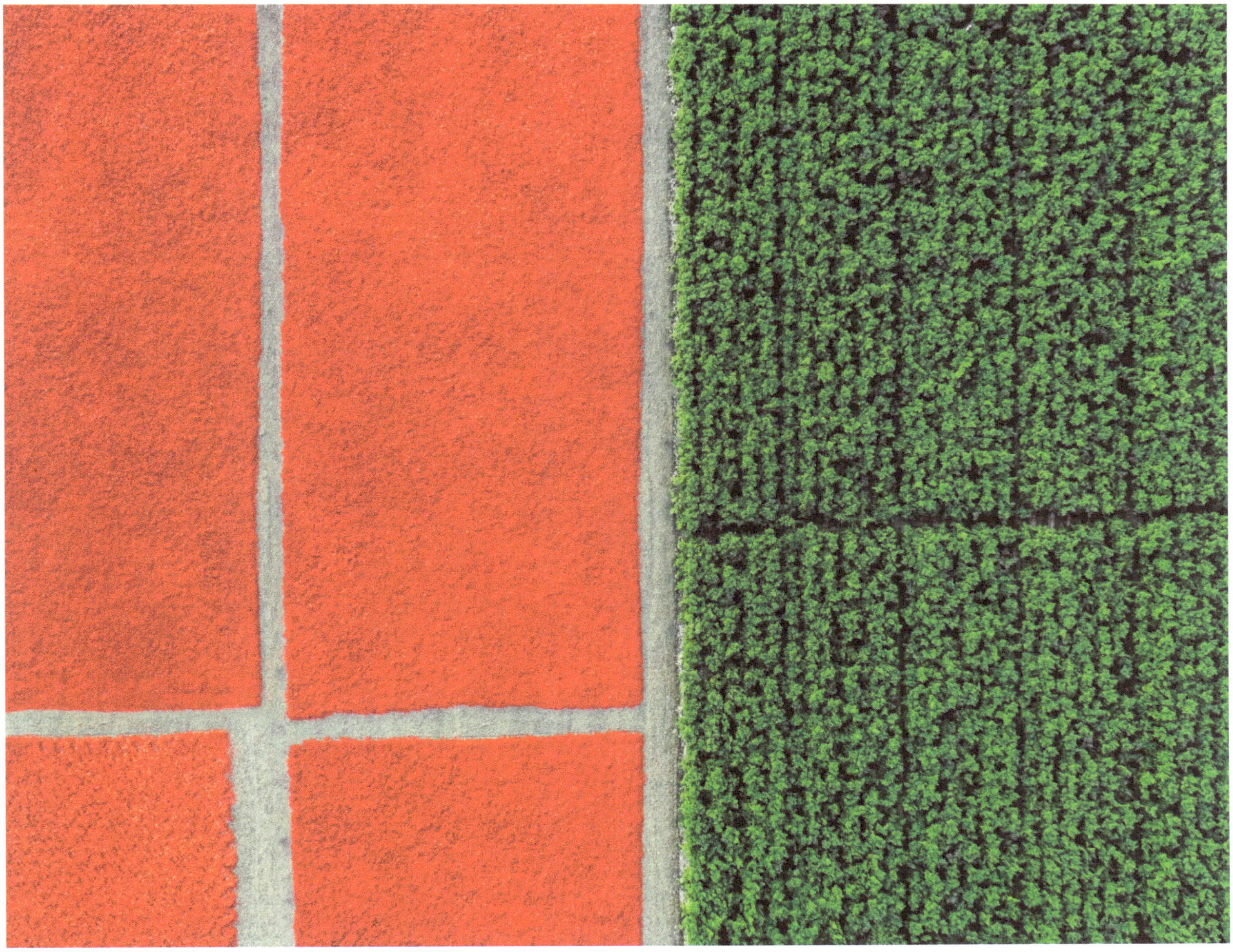

The spice flag

foundation.app/@RakeshPulapa/~/107266

Minted: November 13, 2021

@mrjonkane
Mr. Jon Kane, photographer & motion artist

Memories and Light

Painting with photographs doesn't take the world around us at face value. Instead, each photo is composed of raw ingredients with which to construct a more personal version of the scene. Magical realism enters the room in the form of the photographer Mr. Jon Kane. He speaks to how he infuses a single image with 'memory':

"The memory of a place alters with time and, while it seems real and true, it is perhaps a tinted vision of what was actually there. Some memories are brighter and full of vivid colour, yet others are faded and dull like an old yellow Polaroid."

In addition, Mr. Jon Kane specializes in lens based motion art—both conceptual motion loops and true cinemagraphs that originate from cinemaDNG Raw 4K video to deliver a unique form of art that collectors can truly appreciate.

"I'm driven to capture moments through photography and short, yet infinitely looping, time capsules of motion art. Merging the timeless quality of still images with cinematic motion, I portray a sense of magic within the realism of life on this strange yet beautiful rock called Earth."

Back in the real world, Jon spends his time surrounded by nature in and around New Zealand's most populous city, Auckland.

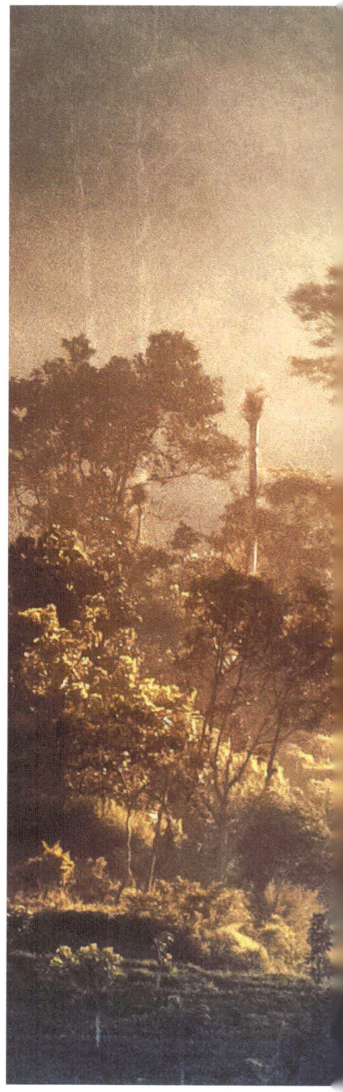

I develop an image not only from lens light and raw data, but a scanner in my brain—fragments and signals transposed to a screen, a painting of memory and light.

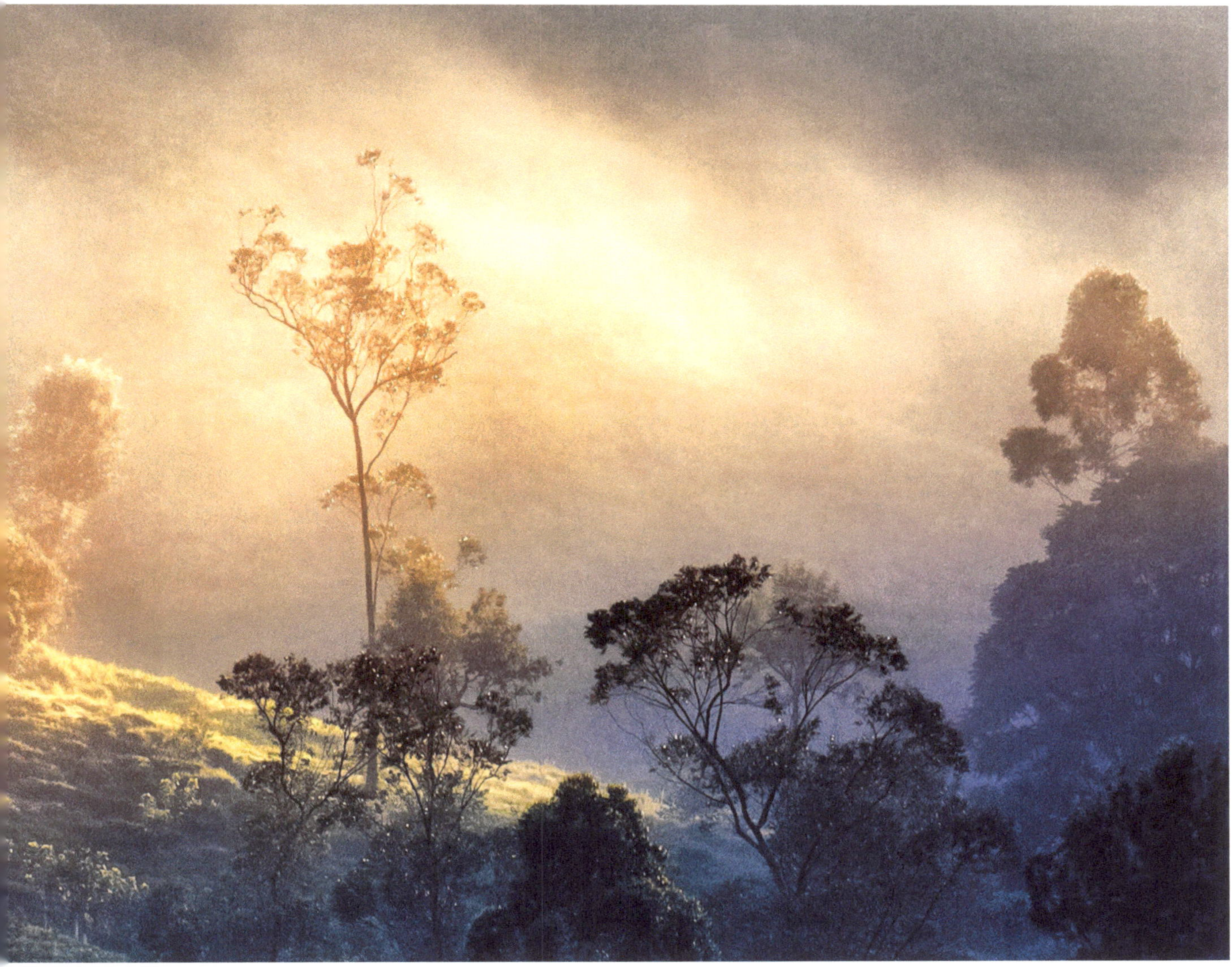

Memories and Light
knownorigin.io/gallery/633400-memories-and-light
Minted: August 15, 2021

@MSoulwax
My Soulwax, photographer

"When I reached this onion seeds field, it felt like a place from another world. It seemed so divine."

Soul Circle

The photographer known as My Soulwax has brought confidence to their style by experimenting with the new possibilities that NFTs present. Releasing a photograph into the public domain is something many photographers hesitate to do. Not My Soulwax. **Soul Circle** is the third of 17 photographs minted on Foundation that will be released into the public domain upon purchase of the NFT token by a collector.

My Soulwax has previously released **Full Round of the Sun** into the public domain by tying the moment of copyright release to the purchase of the photo's NFT token.

As soon as the collector, @Punk4636, settled the auction, anyone could use the photograph linked to the NFT with no restrictions, no attribution, no waiver, confident that the artist would take no action against any use of the image.

My Soulwax was paid 2.5 ETH for releasing their art for all of us. Retaining copyright is default in the world of NFT art and ensures that the art is protected from adaptation or commercially exploitation by a collector or the general public. But the overarching principle of Web3.0 is the artist gets to decide.

But, putting these social and economic considerations aside, what matters most is the image itself. And here is where the creativity of My Soulwax shines. The artist writes of their inspiration to create the photo seen here:

"On a previous visit, I captured this field with the beauty of the Milky Way in the background (a work on Foundation titled ***Soul Plantation****), but I felt something could be done differently.*

"I thought that using the 'star trail' technique might resonate with the seeds better. That's why I created ***Soul Circle****. I wanted to show how everything is connected. Everything starts and stops at the same point of the circle of life."*

Soul Circle
foundation.app/@My_Soulwax/~/115721
Minted: December 8, 2021

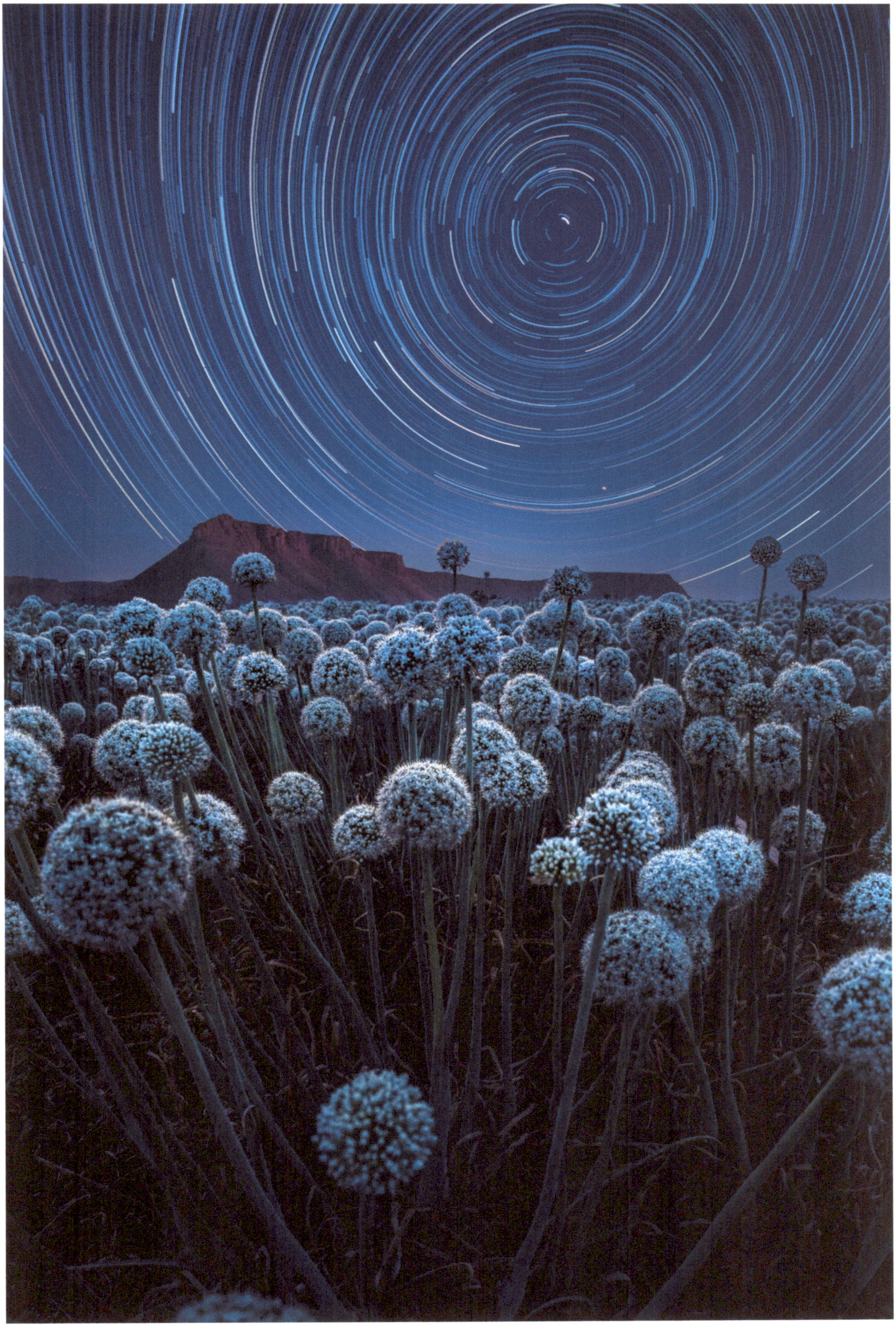

@Navaneeth_kish

Navaneeth Kishor, photographer

My Travel Diary collection

Photographer Navaneeth Kishor captures the natural beauty encountered on his many adventures through India. A selection of his favorite landscapes is an OpenSea collection titled **My Travel Diary**. The images put you right there with him, in incredible destinations you'd rarely be able to discover on your own. He writes of the process:

"These are some of my finest images of landscapes. The story you witness in each photograph entails days and weeks of planning, then trekking for thousands of miles. What you don't see are the many failures and hardships along the way."

If you browse his collection you're in for a visual feast. The photo **the mighty Thar** features the otherworldly, ocean-like waves of the Thar Desert. The velvety green peaks of **Yellapetty Top** are an hour's walk from the nearest car-friendly road.

Then there is the photo here, **Camels of Nubra Valley**. The sense of passing briefly through a foreign land is encapsulated best by this image. A trio of camels and their riders are led by a fourth capped man, walking with purpose across a shadowed horizon. The distant snow-capped mountains convey the scale of the journey.

"This is Nubra valley, the land of cold desert. It's one of the most amazing locations, and—at 10,000 feet above sea level—one of the hardest to reach. There one can witness the sand dunes and relish rides on Bactrian camels. This breed of camel is found only in Hunder. In the ancient times they were used for transportation. This photo is one perfect moment I managed to capture from a place so dear to my heart."

As a child, Navaneeth grew up near a majestic mountain called Illikkal Kallu. His young ears heard stories about the local heroes who climbed to the top. Obviously, those tales became a personal inspiration to him:

"The farthest destination I once imagined has now become my nearest location. I've logged thousands of kilometers. But the place that fascinated me to travel as a child has always been my favourite."

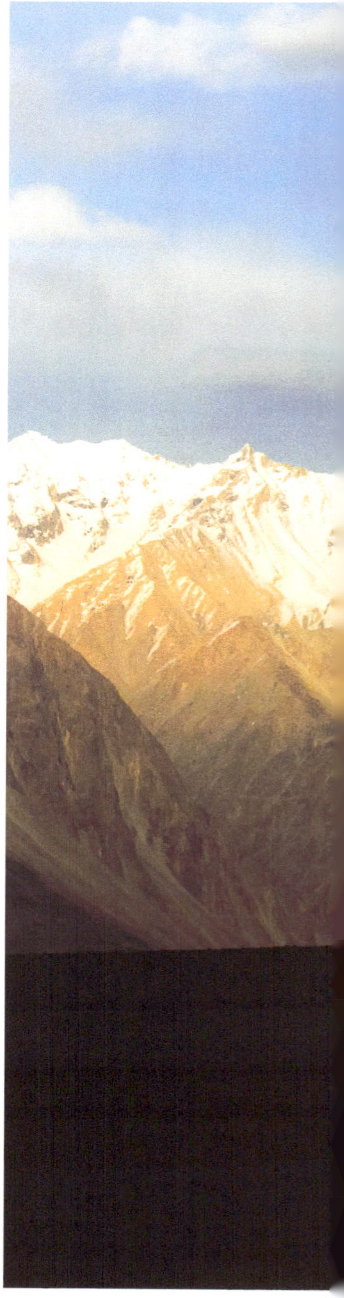

"I love to capture the very essence of a life moment, entwined with a story."

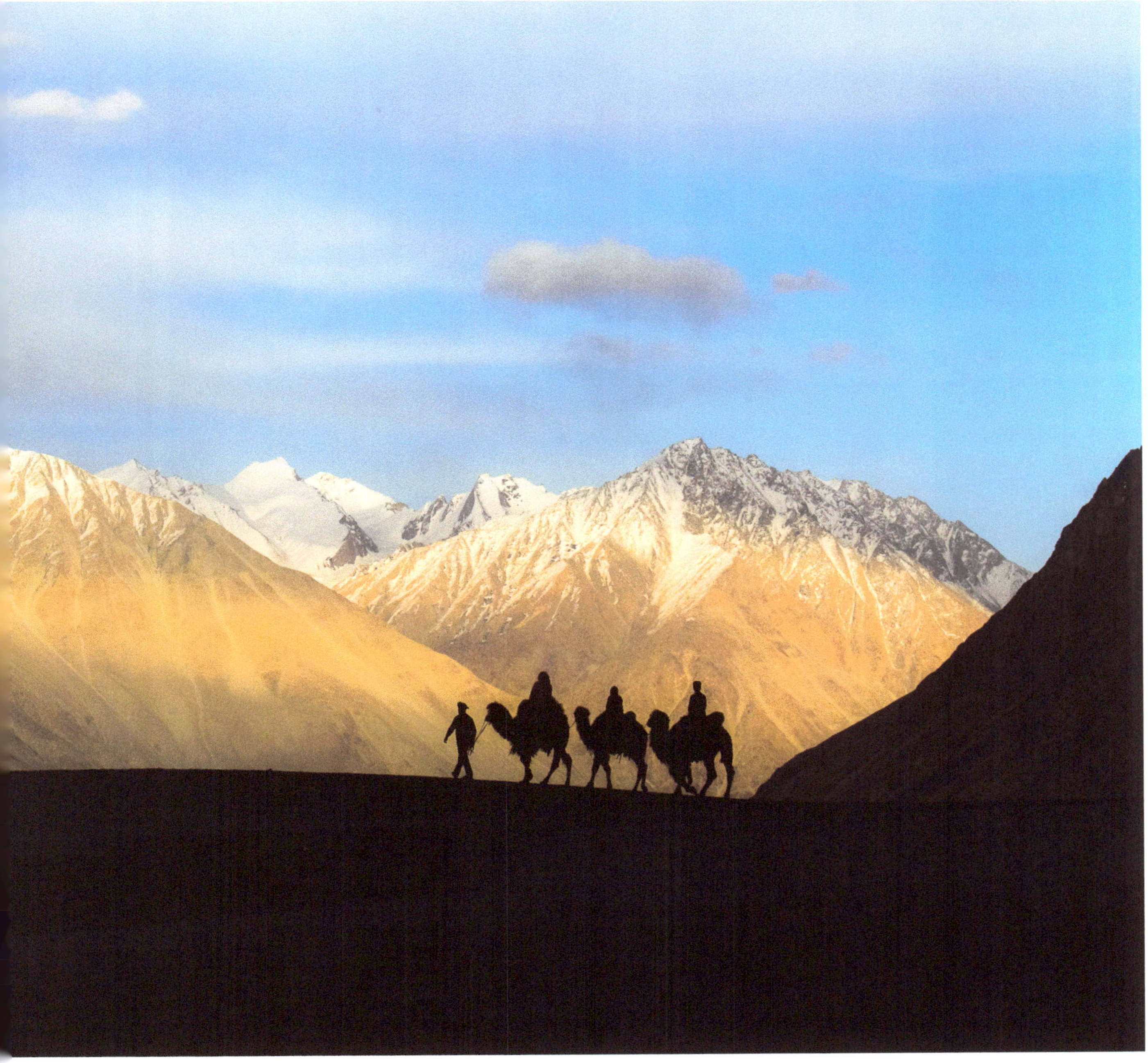

Camels of Nubra Valley

opensea.io/collection/my-best-travel-diary

Minted: September 21, 2021

@ricosfilm

RICOSFILM, photographer

"We all start from nothing, left to grow on our own in our various environments. Any great tree needs a strong foundation, or else it will topple in time."

Recalled Red collection

In the genesis collection **Recalled Red** on OpenSea, photographer Rico developed a series of photos from film rolls that are considered the gold standard by top cinematographers for motion-picture technology.

Except that this run of 800T was recalled by CineStill, the film manufacturer, because it was found to be defective. Instead of sending back the faulty rolls, Rico decided to turn the bug into a feature. Of the overblown yellow in the sky and snow, he says:

"It is a cold and dark night in the woods but, fortunately, the light is all around you. Do you turn your back on it or embrace it?"

Rico is a self-taught photographer, from Maryland in the U.S., who loves to explore. Reviewing Rico's collection, you'll discover **Pomelo Dwelling** with a composition that is achingly good. The dapple of background leaves providing shelter for the atmospheric foreground. With regard to the image on the right, **Humble Are The Roots**, he says:

"For me, this photo represents pride, strength, and the loneliness that comes from growing your own way. From taking your own path. I feel cold and alone when I look at it, but never does it make me feel like I am weak or that I should give up. It is a testament to those determined to grow regardless of the consequence. May we all find peace in our future and remember where we came from."

Beyond his passion of film photography, Rico is a musician—making tunes inspired by the rhythms of boom bap, jazz, and lo-fi. Having graduated in 2020 with a BFA in Graphic Design at University of Maryland, Rico is truly a multi-faceted creator. He also uses 3D graphic tools to make perfect-loop animations as well as drawing for fun.

Humble Are the Roots
opensea.io/collection/recalled-red
Minted: October 19, 2021

@sujithks1986

Sujith Sudarsan, travel & portrait photographer

"It was my long-awaited dream to take a photo of the Himalayas. This is Tso Moriri lake—one of the most beautiful, calm, and sacred high-altitude lakes in India."

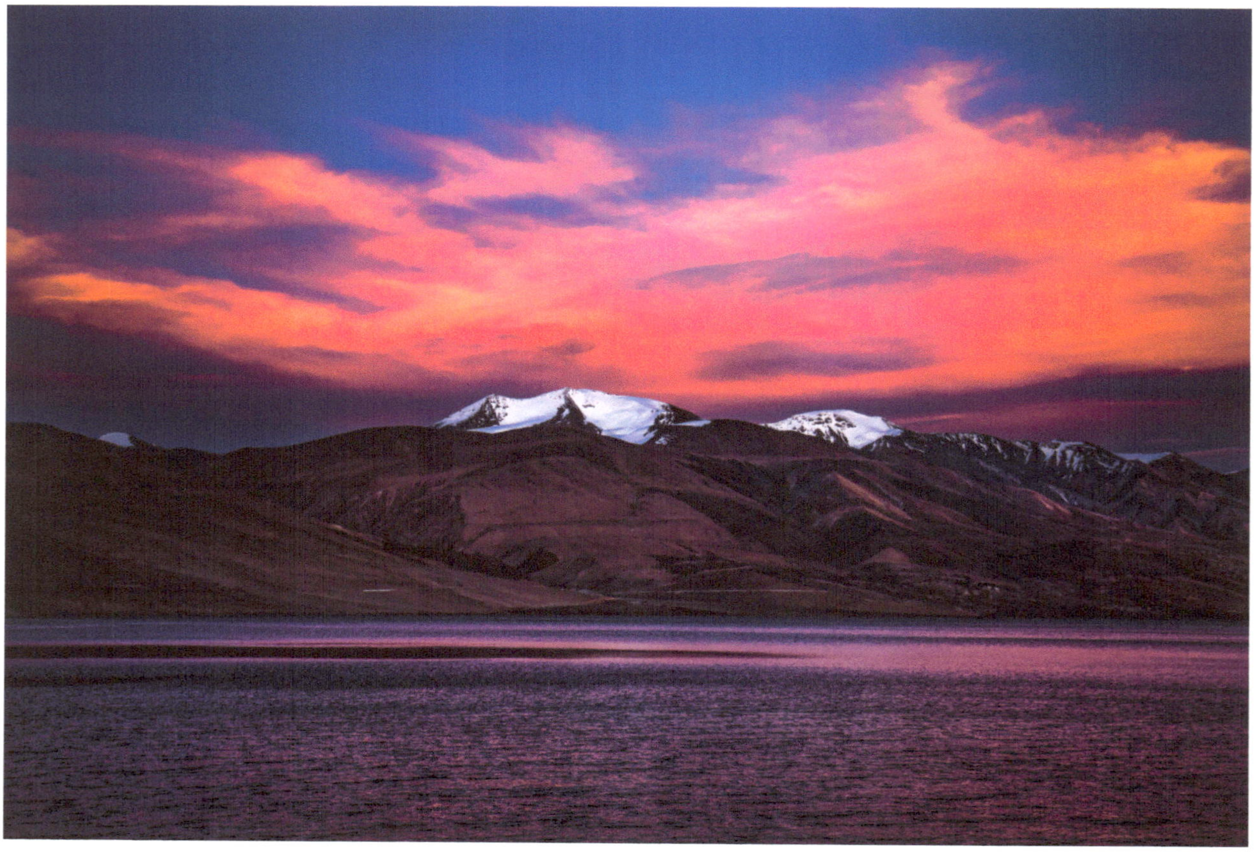

Mount Himalaya
foundation.app/@sujithsudarsan/~/94070
Minted: October 3, 2021

@UjvalKumar
Ujval Kumar, wildlife photographer

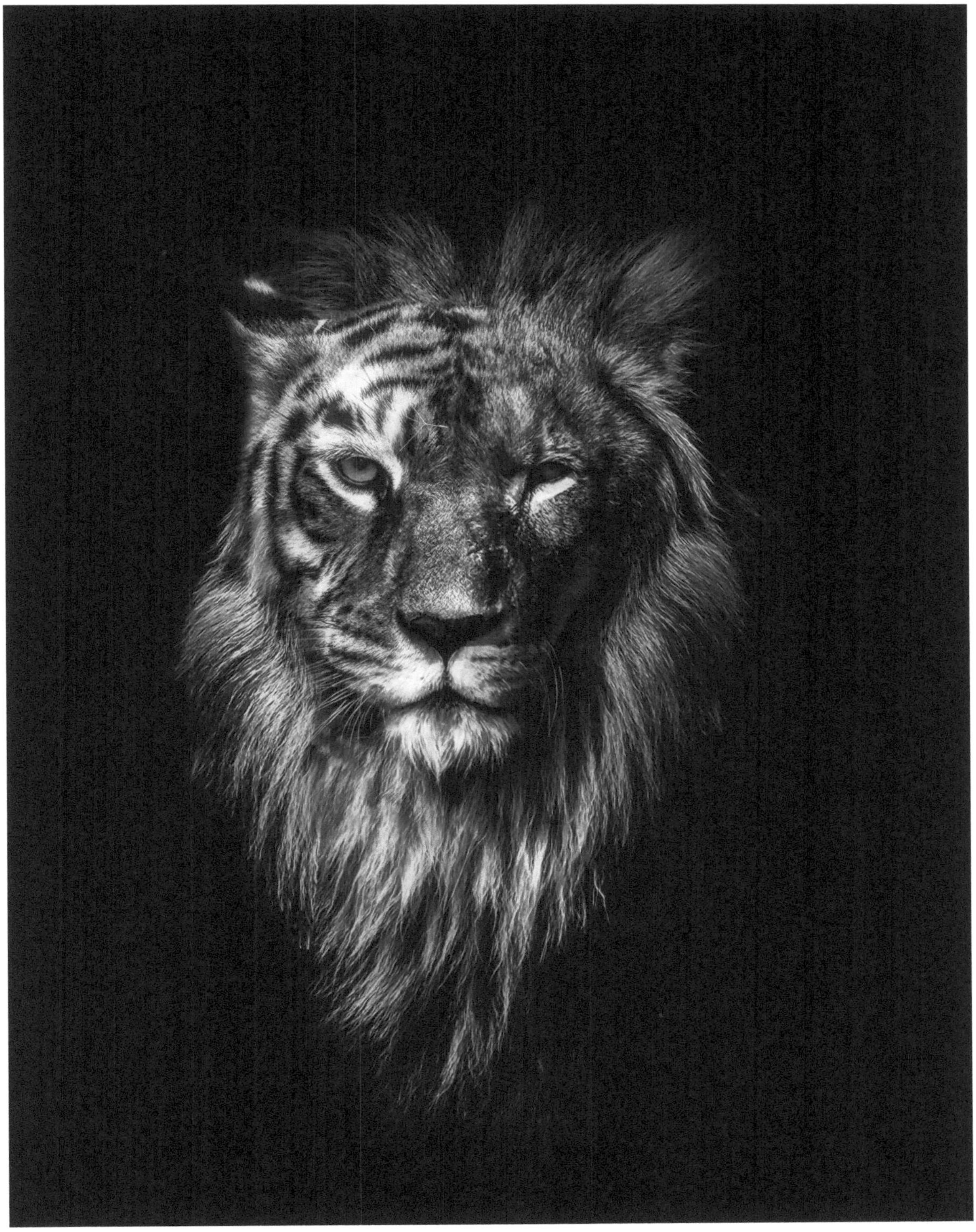

One World

foundation.app/@UjvalPasupuleti/~/61427

Minted: July 19, 2021

PORTRAITURE

Portraiture centers on the human figure as a subject. It's realized by photography, painting, or a combination of media.

@_Soulcraft_

Benjamin Sumner Franke, photographer

"I discovered this beautiful dead juniper in Utah, hidden on the cliff edge of an overlook. It's an example of the joys of creating—collaboration with nature itself."

Alchemy of Alignment collection

Soulcraft describes his artistic approach as a silent dance of alignment. The **Alchemy of Alignment** collection conjures up 45 unions between the female form enveloped in nature. What does that mean in simple terms though? Symmetry, balance, contrast?

If collaboration is the canvas for **Alchemy of Alignment**, magical compositions bring out the best in both. But art isn't supposed to be technical, right? It's about the feels, especially when you're behind the lens.

The Bonneville Salt Flats in Utah is one of many international destinations that Soulcraft has called his artistic home over the last three years. He writes:

*"**Alchemy of Alignment** is a selection of award-winning photos I've captured since I began shooting in the summer of 2018. After years of studying the figure as an art student, I entered the design industry and was completely separated from my roots and passion. In 2018 I left my job as lead concept artist for a circus in Las Vegas, bought a ticket to Iceland and a DSLR camera. That month-long journey began what has been a rediscovery of my passion and galvanized my focus as an artist."*

*"Throughout the journey, I've encountered a repeated experience, a trance-like state and astonishing synchronicity. Much like Cartier-Bresson's **Decisive Moment**, the crux of my art is revealed during moments of what I call Alignment. Nature, the muse, and my artistic choices reach a nexus, a crossroads where the image is born. I call this the **Alchemy of Alignment.**"*

Soulcraft's collectors include @Punk6529 who acquired **Solstice Moonrise** for the 6529 Museum. Each of the models—Vivian Cove, Sienna Benton, and Viribus Femina—playfully jump in formation to create the letters 'gm', which is an abbreviation for 'good morning' among the time-pressed NFT community on Twitter.

"What I find unique about photography is that the desired image already exists as a moment in time. The artist's job is to frame it and capture it in their own way."

Juniper's Song
opensea.io/collection/alchemy-of-alignment
Minted: August 17, 2021

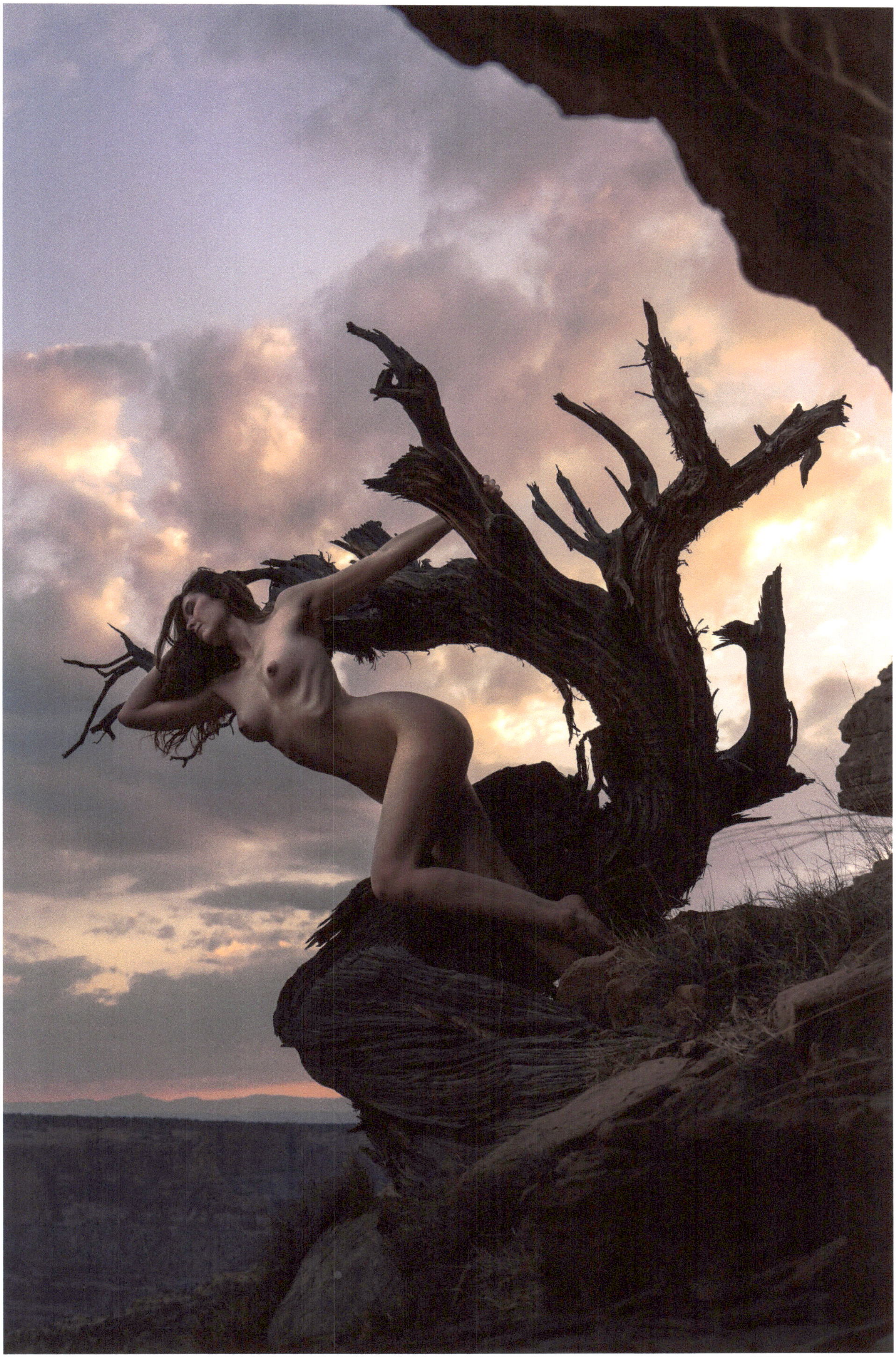

@_Soulcraft_
Benjamin Sumner Franke, photographer

"I've made so many memories, so many friends, and connected deeply with the lands I've explored."

Alchemy of Alignment collection

In **Thunder Egg**, notice the models placement in the bottom third of the photo, grounding the image. The darker contrast in the top third leads our eyes downward and then inwards. Our eyes love odd numbers more than even when it comes to form, and the five craters balance out the vibe. This visual dance between nature and woman is conscious. According to the artist:

"For the last three years I've traveled from California to Iceland, Maui, Oregon, Nevada, Utah, Peru, and Mexico capturing the beauty of the feminine form juxtaposed and mirrored in nature."

What we often forget is that many artists were forced to censor their creativity on Web2.0 social media or risk being de-platformed to appease advertisers. **Thunder Egg** represents the birth of an entirely new era of creativity—free from the shackles of rules built to constrain instead of encourage the human spirit.

Reaching further back in time on the blockchain, there is a collection of 22 minted artworks titled **Revelare** that are yet to be discovered by collectors. Each image gives a glimpse into the first packs of integral film ever shot by Soulcraft. Integral film—which first gained mainstream use under the Polaroid brand name—integrates all the layers to expose, develop, and fix the photo into a plastic envelope and frame. Reflecting on the process, the artist said:

"To witness a captured moment develop on the spot, slowly revealing from the blank frame, remains one of my most cherished experiences in photography."

Thunder Egg
opensea.io/collection/alchemy-of-alignment
Minted: September 23, 2021

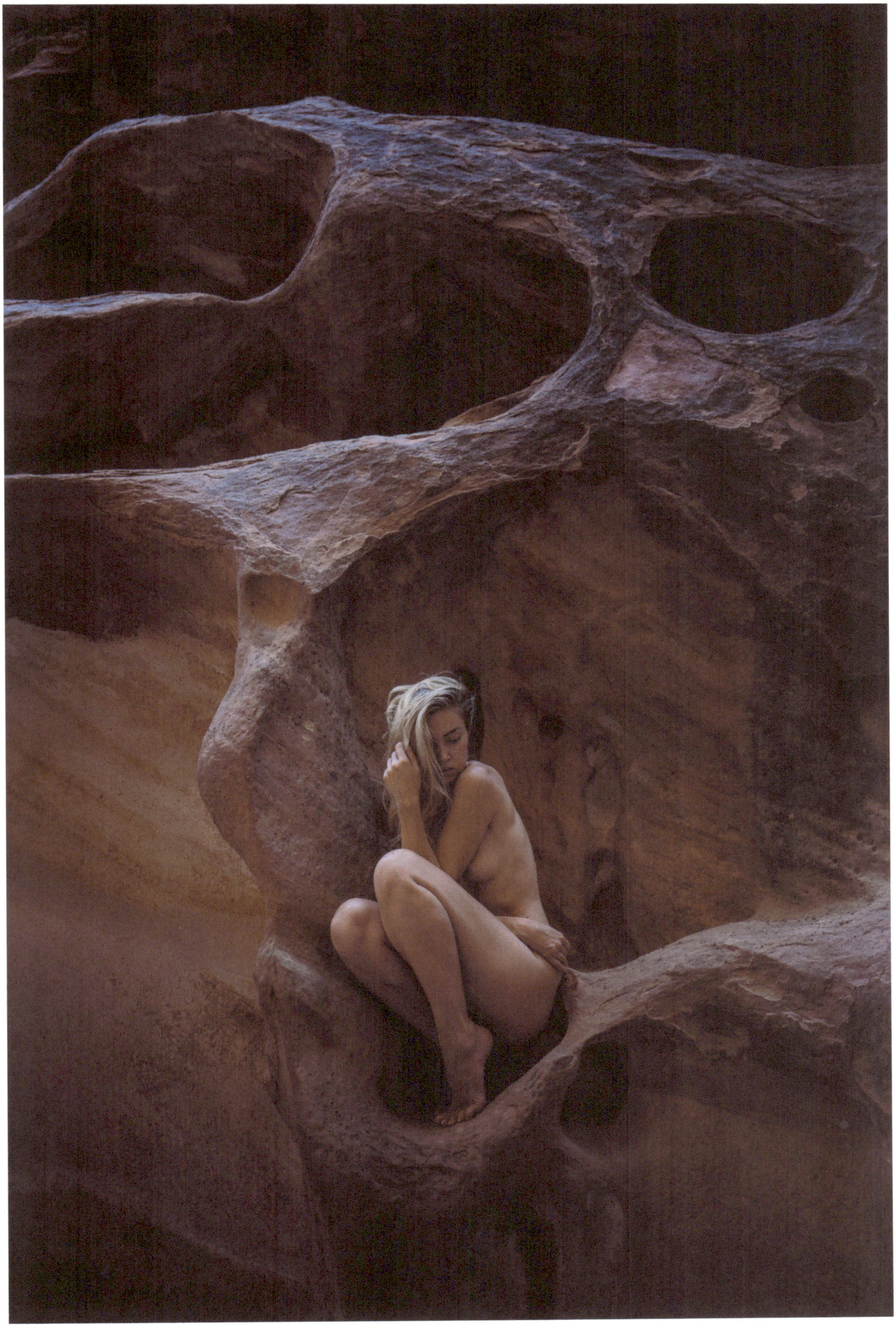

@agnimax

Agnisoonu, photographer

Thousand Shades of Life collection

Wandering the streets can often tell us so much more about humanity than nature does, and nowhere on the planet has street-level energy like India. Whether you're a nature lover or a street photography appreciator, Agni has you covered. Photographs in the **Thousand Shades of Life** collection are the kind worth exploring frame by frame. Each says something about Agni's ability to draw out the fullest expression of the subject. He recounts the story behind the photo here:

"During one of my visits to Kolukkumalai, my Jeep driver Murukan invited me to his village, Pachappulkodi Tribal Colony. Accepting his invitation, I went there. I came across a small school and noticed these children playing. Murukan asked them to pose for me when he saw them. The kids posed for me as if they were taking a class photo. The kids were thrilled when I showed them the picture after the click. They wanted me to take their single portraits. I was more than happy to do that for them."

The photo **Beautiful children in Pachappulkodi tribal colony** embodies the intent of the entire collection. We've all been one of those children lined up in a shortest to tallest arrangement at some time in our lives. We all know the one kid who doesn't look at the camera. Maybe it was you. For Agni, photography is a means of connecting with every individual and actively encountering their uniqueness:

"My interest in wandering streets, observing people, and listening to their stories developed only after I began photographing seriously. Through photography, I was able to communicate with a variety of people. Each person I met with had a unique personality, and their experiences were filled with emotions. All of those stories compelled me to strive to be a better individual."

"The camera is an instrument that teaches people how to see without a camera."

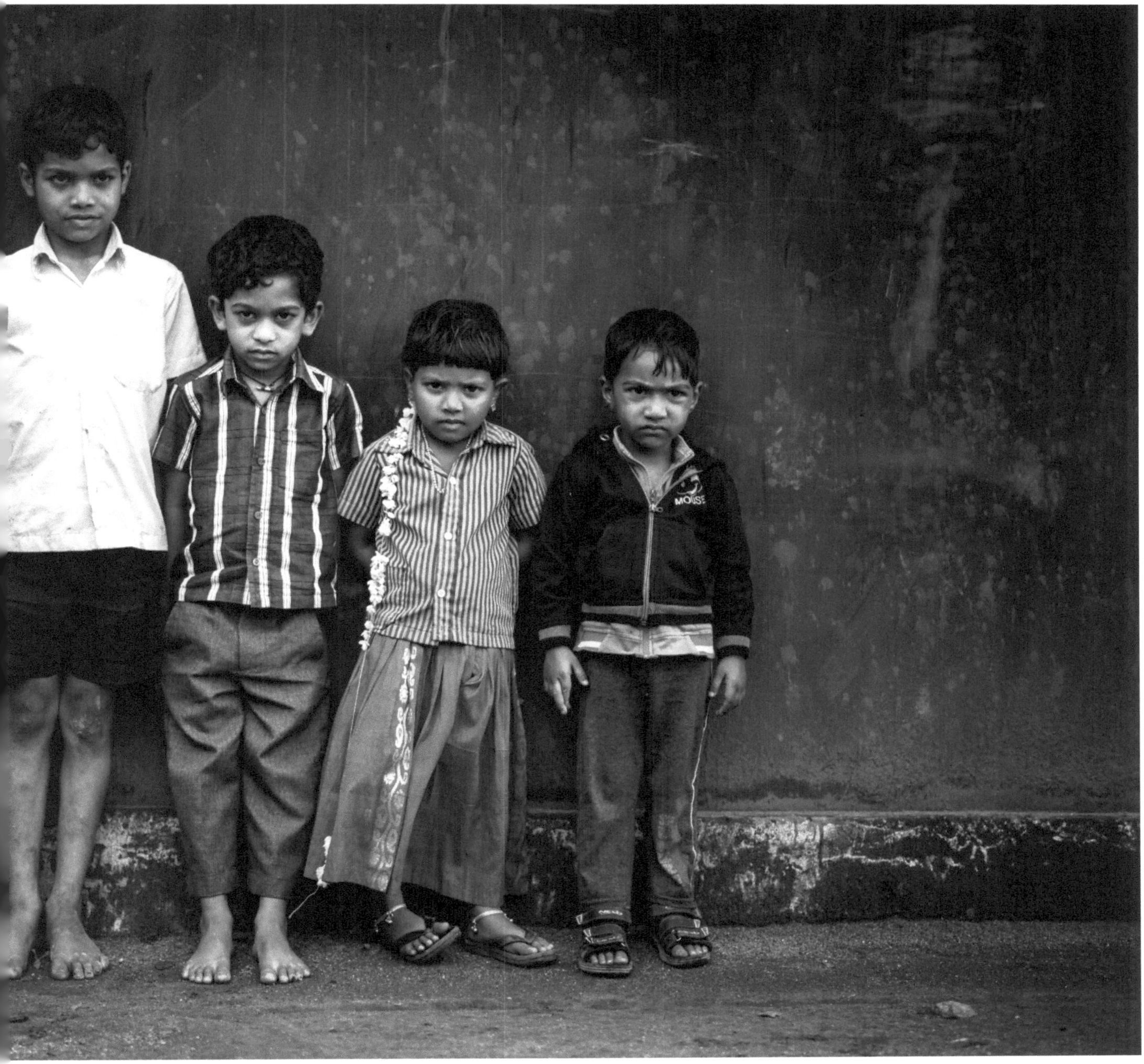

TSL-#009 : Beautiful children in Pachappulkodi tribal colony.

opensea.io/collection/thousand-shades-of-life

Minted: October 18, 2021

@AnaIsabel_Photo
Ana Isabel, fine art portrait photographer

"Inanna is the Sumerian goddess of love, beauty, sex, and justice. She is the personification of emancipation."

Inanna

Ana Isabel saw the potential of minting her fine art portraits way back in March 2021. Each portrait shares her message of empowering women by deftly revealing the magic that sparkles beyond skin deep beauty. **Inanna** was minted on Foundation before the craze of Bored Apes, Hall of Fame Goats, and the Pudgy Penguins.

"I capture people's essence alongside the enchantment of our natural world."

Ana's vision for the place she would help build for women on the blockchain is a place where feminine energy is embraced not exploited. Ana takes inspiration from Gaia, the mother of all life and sees nature as a form of magic.

*"This photographic work is part of my project **Wytches and Seers**, based on ancient goddesses from different mythologies. This is more than a personal project, it is a meaningful and artistic celebration of women and their power."*

With each artwork, Ana acknowledges the contributions of the model, designer, and make-up artist. Co-creators on **Inanna** include Luz Vítrea, Mazz Loxton, and Avalon Saez. Ana also leads a wider movement; she founded the @NFTGoddesses which is dedicated to creating a safe and empowering digital space for women artists. She runs the group with Tina Eisen, Grace Almera, and Priyanka Patel.

Beyond OpenSea there are more gems to be discovered by Ana Isabel including **Queen** minted on KnownOrigin and **Drifting Away** on MakersPlace. The joy of discovering art by artists beyond OpenSea is well worth opening the extra browser tab for.

Inanna
foundation.app/@anaisabel/~/9611
Minted: March 18, 2021

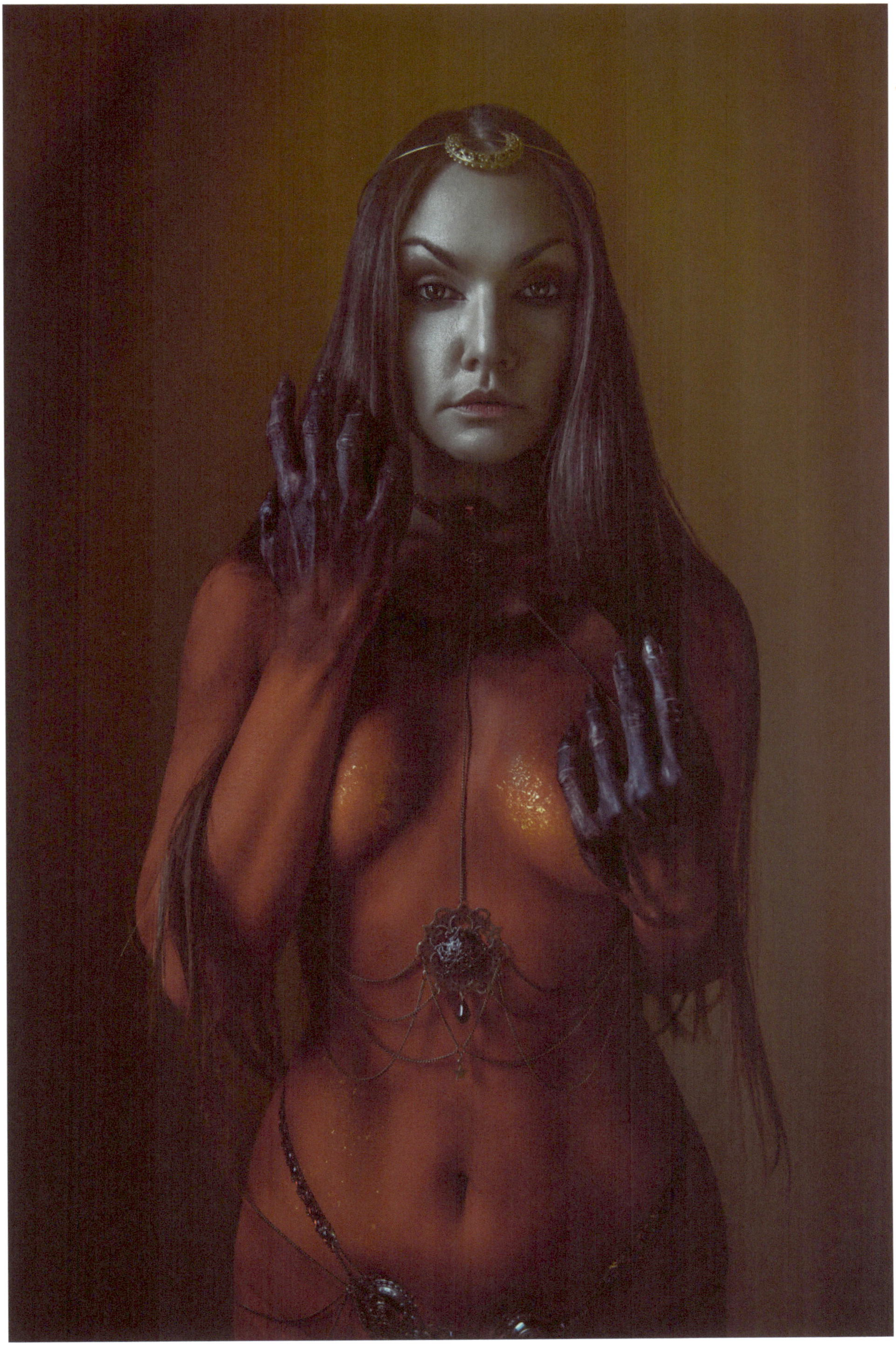

@ArmyDad_eth
Retired Army, husband & daddy of 3

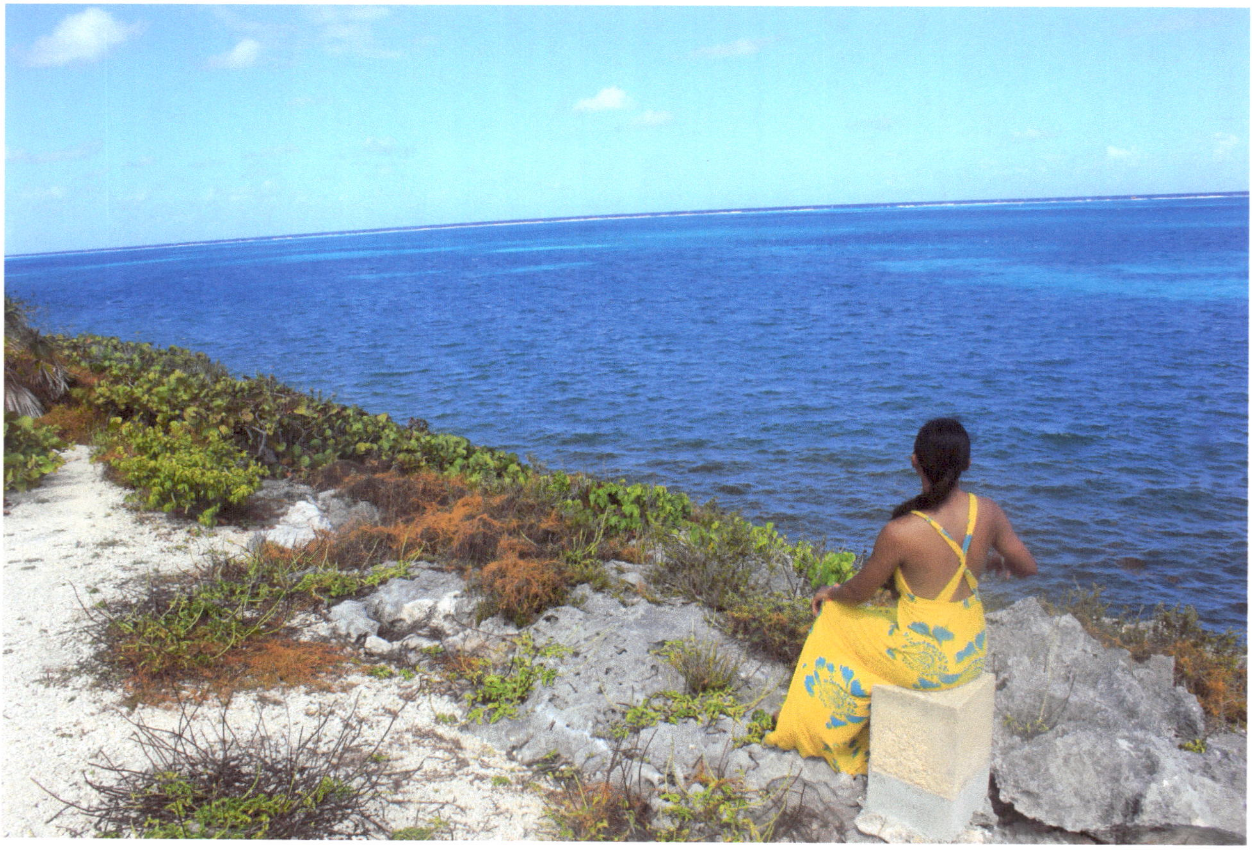

Cayman Queen
opensea.io/collection/limitlessphotography
Minted: January 5, 2022

@ashikjoh
Ashik John Cheeran, street photographer

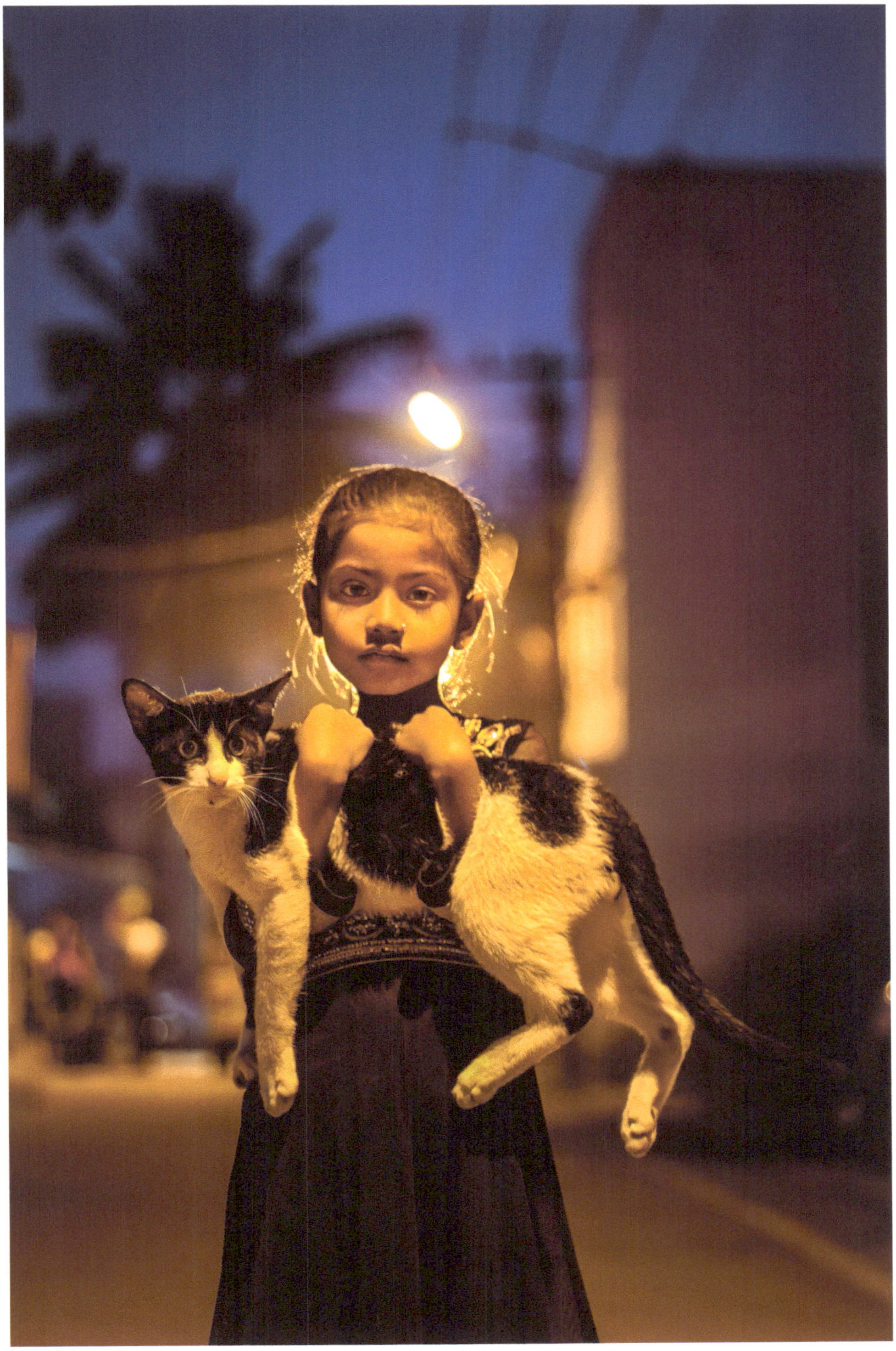

Little Humans #12 - Friendship

opensea.io/collection/little-humans

Minted: September 3, 2021

@ArtBanditzNFT
Claudiu Guraliuc, fine art photographer

ArtBanditz X GC collection

Rembrandt, Caravaggio, and Rubens are master painters that we remember from Art History class. Baroque is a style of painting associated with a set period in time. So how can it also be a type of modern photography? The answer becomes clear when you investigate the painterly world of the artist, known on the blockchain, as GC.

Claudiu Guraliuc is a master photographer from Romania, but he's always held a fascination for the brush techniques of masters from the past. The artist writes:

"Baroque painting has always been close to my soul, especially since I started doing portraiture, I've drooled for the lighting in those painted masterpieces. I got crazy about Chiaroscuro—the colors, the composition, the atmosphere. So I began to obsessively read everything that fell into my hands about the subject, trying to translate this pictorial aesthetic into photography."

Guraliuc holds an Associate distinction with The Master Photographer's Association in the UK, and the distinction of Licentiate of the Royal Photographic Society of Great Britain. He's been awarded numerous international accolades, including receiving the Fine Art Photographer of the Year award in 2020 at the Master Photography Awards Gala in the UK.

The artist has been published by the largest-circulation photography magazines in US (*Popular Photography*) and UK (*Digital Photo Pro*). In 2022, Guraliuc will have art exhibitions at the Katsea Art Gallery in Baltimore in the United States; and at the Brukenthal National Museum in Sibia, Romania. Yet, the current collection represents, in many ways, the highest achievement of his lengthy career:

"I have always done painterly portraiture and loved it, but working on these images, I truly felt that this is what I was always meant to do. As a wonderful bonus, the greatest honor I have been awarded in my photographic career so far was earned with an image as part of this series."

Award Collection #5
https://opensea.io/collection/artbanditznftgc
Minted: September 17, 2021

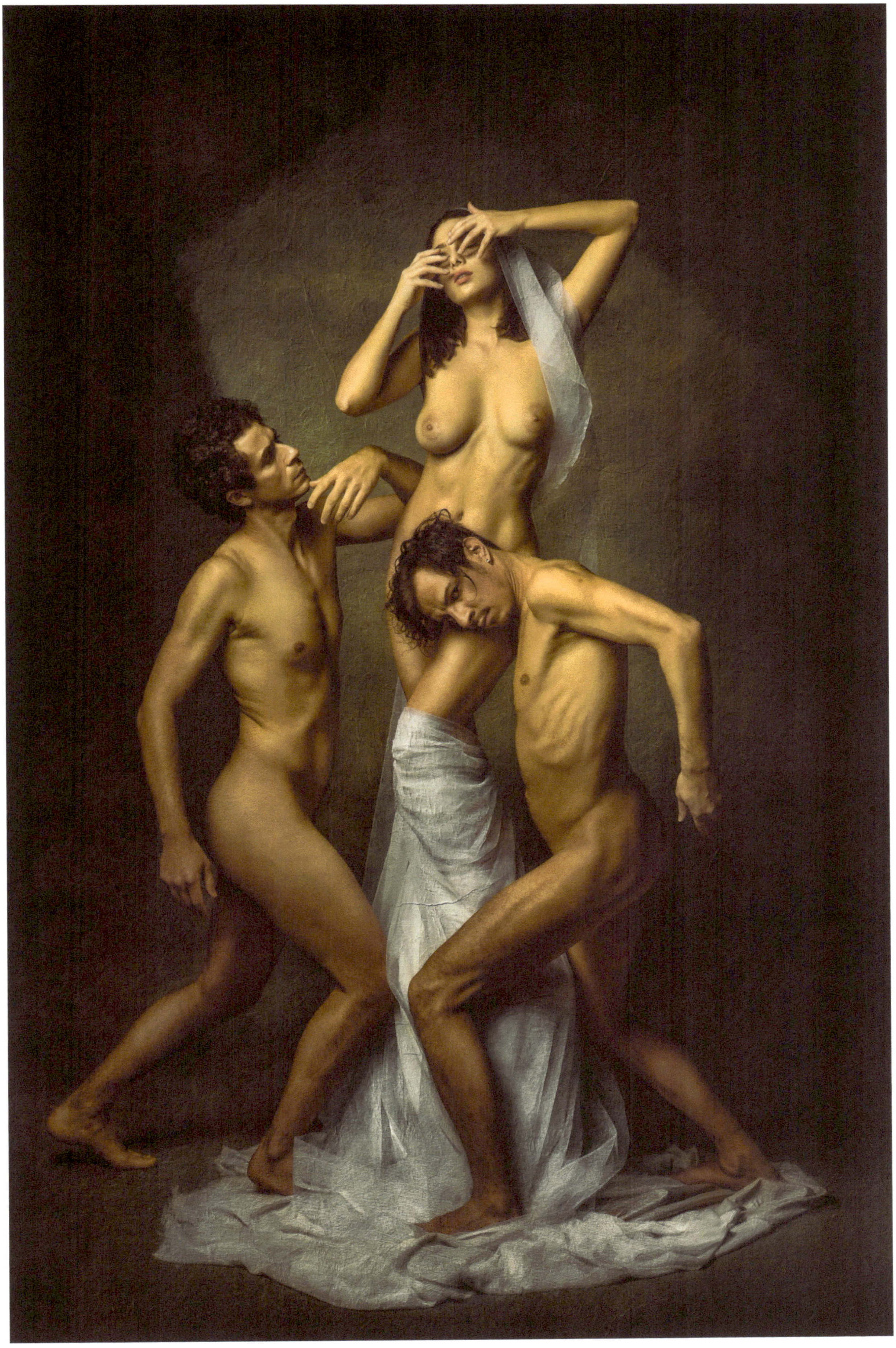

@dearsoftness
Riley Luna, artist & photographer

"You don't need to have high expectations, you just need the will to create despite the fear."

A love letter to you, art, and our kairos

Midnight skies convey a sense of calm as one roams the empty, dimly-lit streets while the city sleeps. That same muted palette of blues, indigo and cobalt, define the work of Riley Luna that she presents across OpenSea, Foundation, and OBJKT.com. The artist writes about her motivation:

"Photography for me is about portraying the mystery and essence of beauty. Subjectivity, impactful thought, and feeling is everywhere. I want you to share the raw and complex human emotion with everyone else who took that extra moment to stop and truly look at art through curious eyes."

"The frontispiece of the collection is a photo titled **a love letter to you, art, and our kairos**. The Greek word *kairos* translates to 'a time when conditions are right for the accomplishment of a crucial action.' It is the most opportune and decisive moment.

In the piece, the artist herself is crowned with a tiara, commonly worn as a symbol of femininity or victory. She is embraced in a heart-shaped patterned blanket holding a trio of flowers near her shoulder. With the artist's face shrouded in shadow, the portrait's symbolism takes centre stage.

A collection by the same name, **a love letter to you, art, and our kairos**, on OpenSea is home to 11 soft blue artworks. Each piece expresses deeply felt emotions, translating what's felt inside for the viewer to feel too. As the artist says poetically:

"Those who've created before me loved me, questioned me, and gave me freedom. It's time to give back."

a love letter to you, art, and our kairos
foundation.app/@rileyluna/~/106060
Minted: November 8, 2021

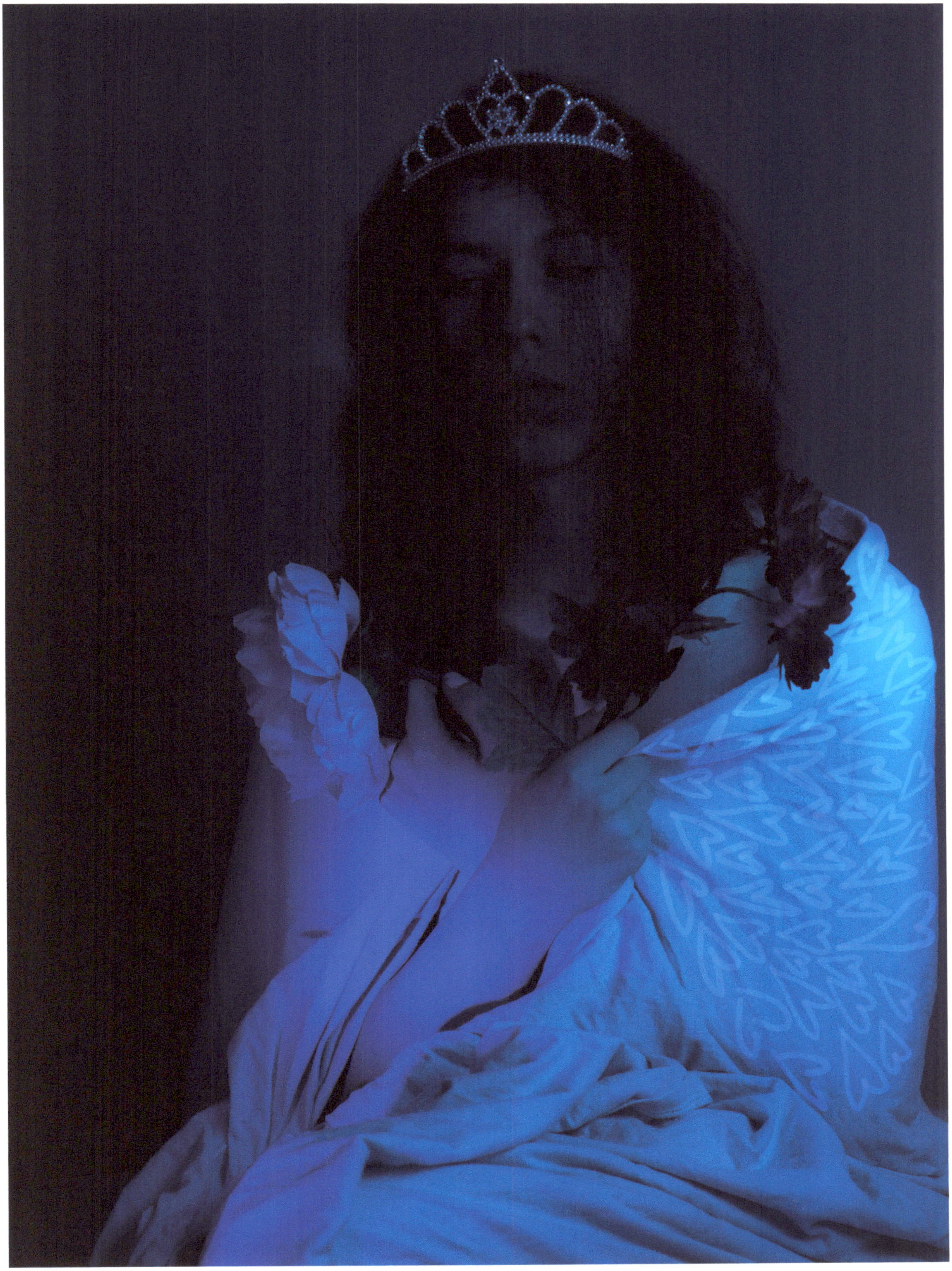

@korbinian_vogt
Korbinian Vogt, photographer

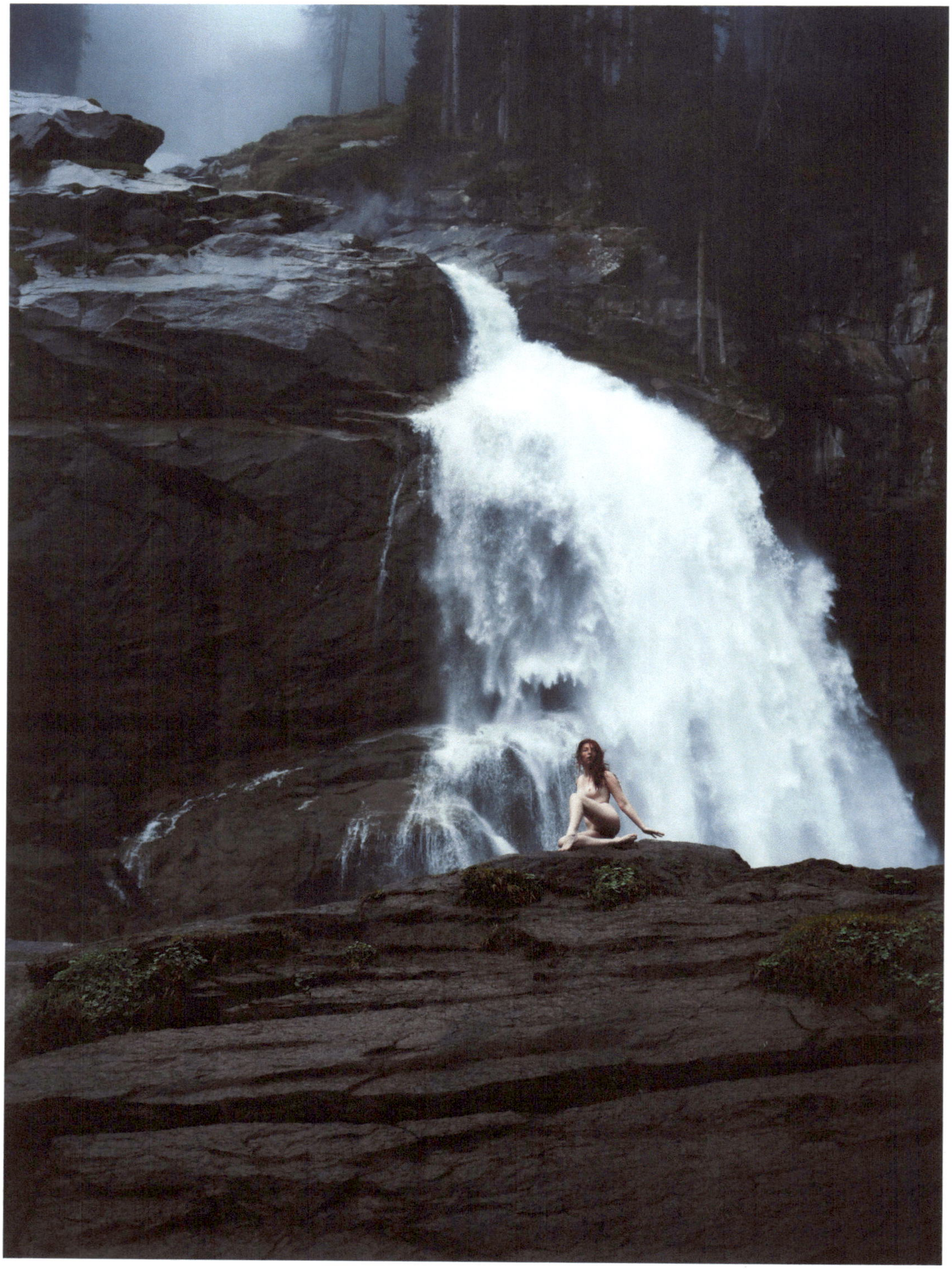

Autumn Waterfall 88/100
opensea.io/collection/korbinian-vogt-editions
Minted: November 15, 2021

@korbinian_vogt
Korbinian Vogt, photographer

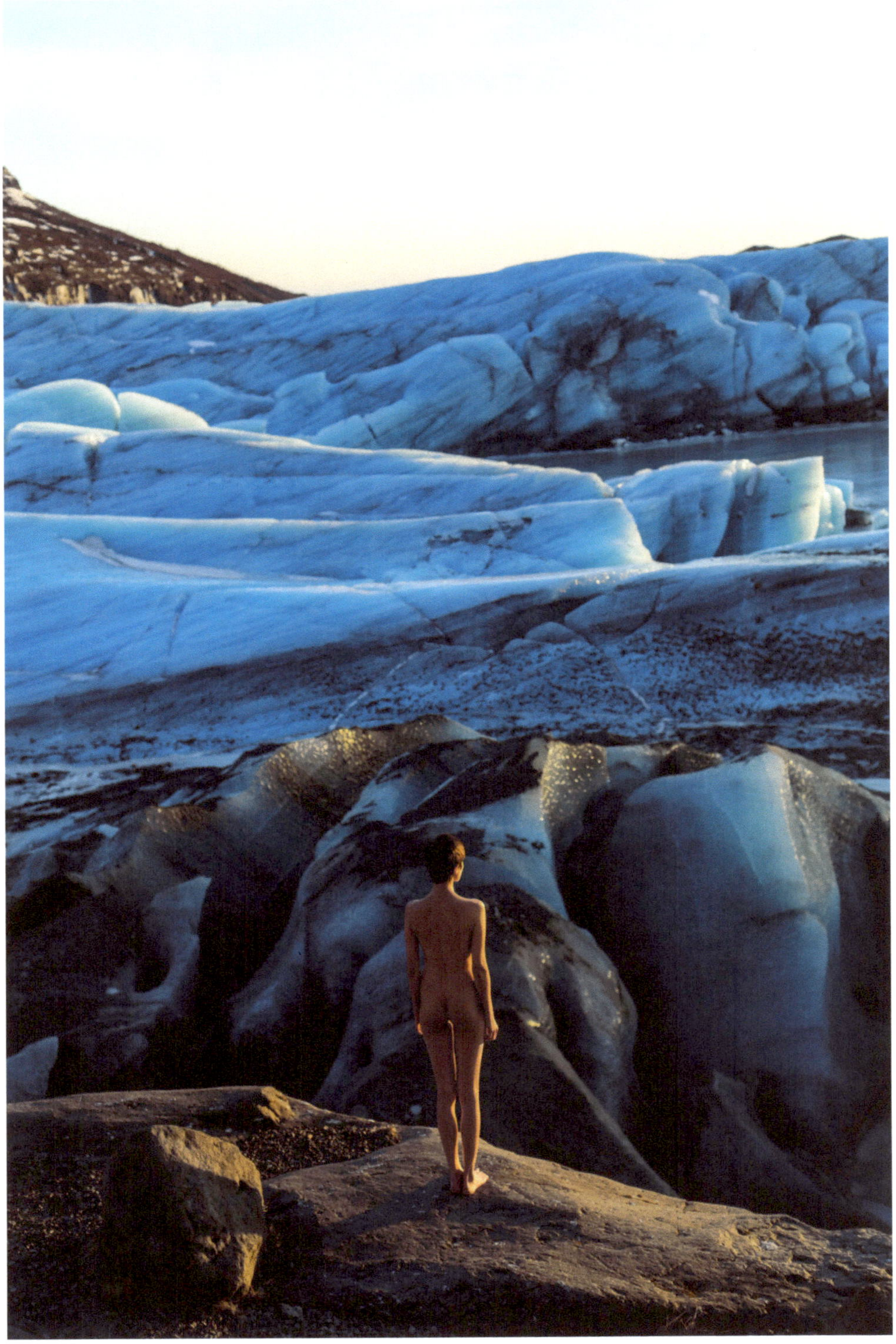

At the glacier

opensea.io/collection/korbinianvogt-unique-works

Minted: September 13, 2021

@lilycallisto
Lily culumus, artist

*“**Cloud Street** is a collection of memories of my immediate family, from two orbits around the sun.”*

Cloud Street collection

Capturing moments of those nearest to us is a practice many families do. It may feel worthy of memorialising because we're moved in some way, or because it's a special time. We hope that by taking a photograph we'll preserve that moment forever. There is another kind of documenting—moments of disruption or transformation. Perhaps the **Cloud Street** collection by artist Lily Callisto is both.

According to Lily, she crafts images in which “you can feel whispers of love and longing.” From her Argyle Street Studio in the northern reaches of New South Wales, Australia, Lily shared a thought by writer Susan Sontag relating to the artist's work:

“All photographs are memento mori. *To take a photograph is to participate in another person's mortality, vulnerability, and mutability. Precisely by slicing out this moment and freezing it, all photographs testify to time's relentless melt.”*

The **Cloud Street** collection feels deeply personal as we are ushered into Lily's private family moments over a two-year period. Lily reflects that those “disquieting years saw drought, fire, flood and pandemic come to our doorstep.” Yet, despite the turmoil of external events outside of her control, each photograph, when viewed as a part of the larger series, transfers the deep love that Lily feels for her family. She writes:

*“**Cumulus #3** is my partner and our daughter. The whole collection is my immediate family. I think this is the oldest photo in the collection. It was taken as the sun set and the full moon rose by the sea.”*

Cloud Street was shot using digital photography as well as 35mm and 120 film. This is fine art as a photo documentary from a remote location where family and belonging are shared in an almost dream-like state, inviting us to experience the moment too.

Cumulus #3
opensea.io/collection/cloudstreet
Minted: October 28, 2021

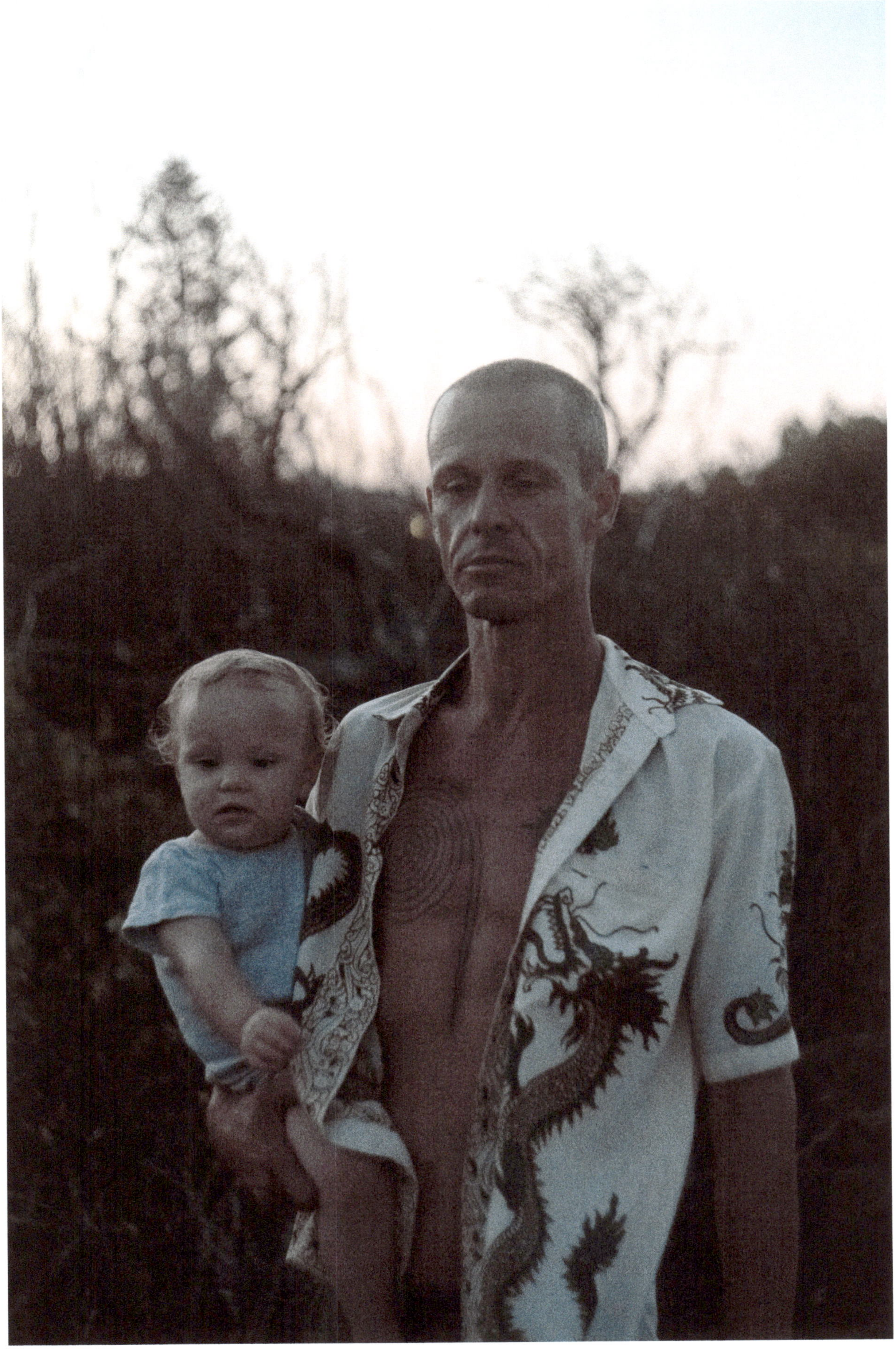

@PrateekSaraf25
Prateek Saraf, photographer

"A turban means pride. He wears pride on his face."

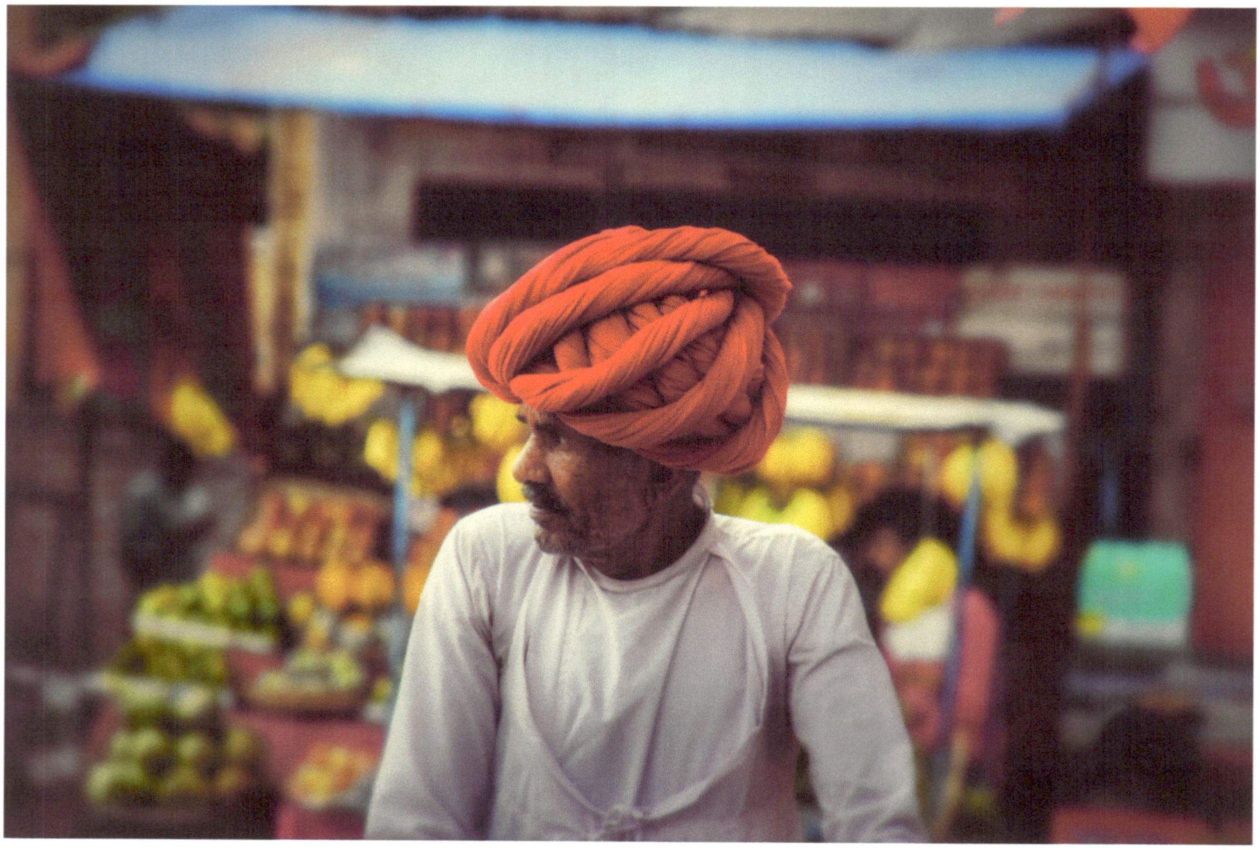

The Turbanator
foundation.app/@prateeksaraf/~/95044
Minted: October 6, 2021

@SREERANJ
Sreeranj Sreedhar, street & documentary photographer

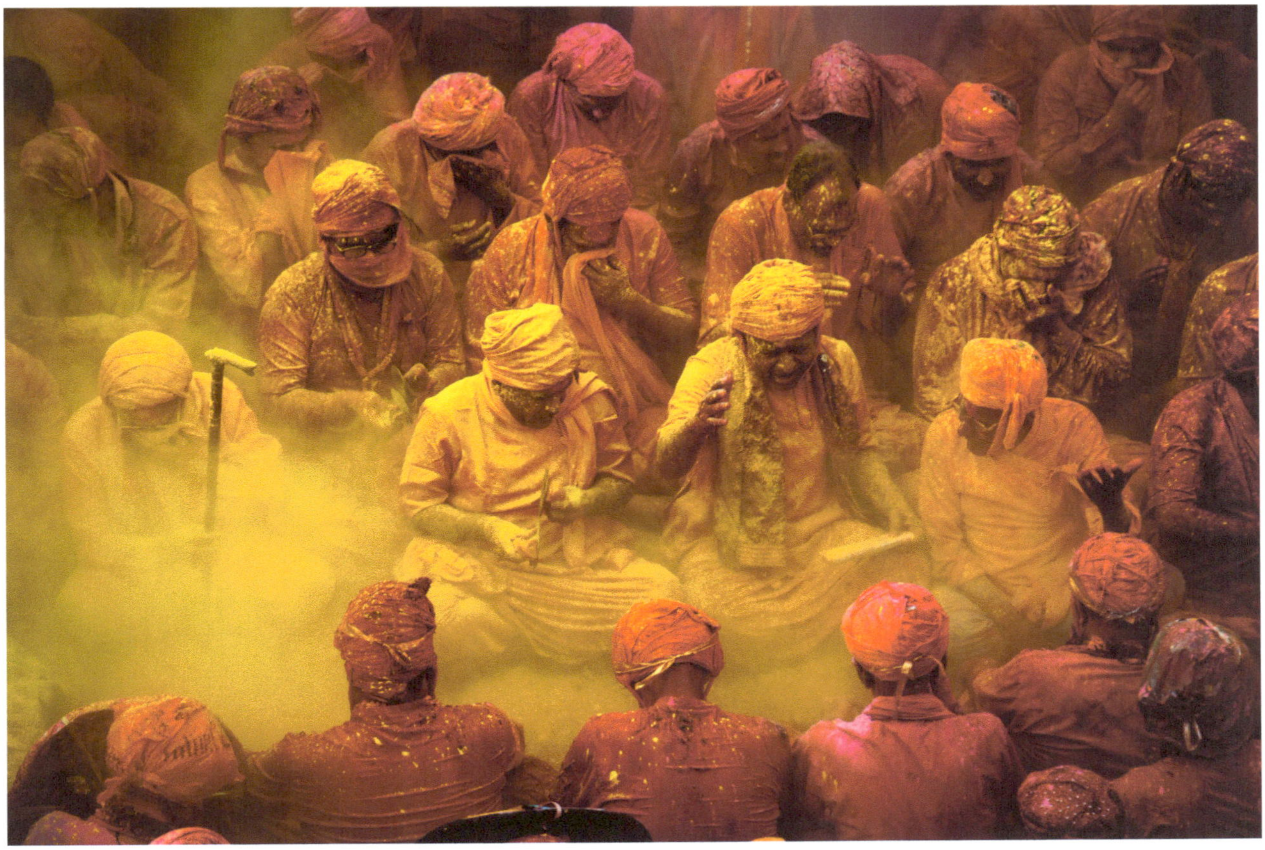

COLOR SPLASH

foundation.app/@sreeranj/~/93382

Minted: October 1, 2021

@The_bohomonk
Bohomonk, editorial photographer

"This image is an effort to paint in light, a deeper emotion, darker in nature."

Lilith

Selecting the first few artworks to mint on Foundation sets an artist's baseline for what collectors might expect. From a back catalog of choice, what to choose? Bohomonk has shown intentionality with the speed of each piece released. All artworks found a desirable collector's home at a leisurely pace. In fact, the latest work **Lilith** (featured here) has already found a collector, @shaun8149.

The subject, **Lilith**, is centered and bathed in red light. She has a pensive stare and a retractive stance with a forearm held up, shielding her face from the gaze of the lens. A cross necklace and earring represent a barely-visible symbol of hope and strength. A poem that the artist placed in the image's description reads:

"The smouldering eyes. The caress so foreign. Her forked tongue drove it all. And she won't let go 'til my soul's stigmatised. She introduced me to her fellow demons; Fancy! They lived inside me."

For this style-framed Foundation genesis piece **The Inception**, Bohomonk selected a right hand pressed against a foggy glass pane. The photographer has sparingly added collection images including **The Epilogue [Prēta]**, followed by **Mirrored**, and **Häzel**.

Beyond Foundation, Bohomonk has shown the same restraint in releasing five street photographs on the Tezos blockchain including **Train of Thought**. The artist writes:

"Every person has a train of thought on which they travel when alone. The dignity and nobility of their life, as well as their happiness depend upon the direction in which that train is going, the baggage it carries and the scenery through which it travels."

Lilith
foundation.app/@the_bohomonk/~/111797
Minted: November 27, 2021

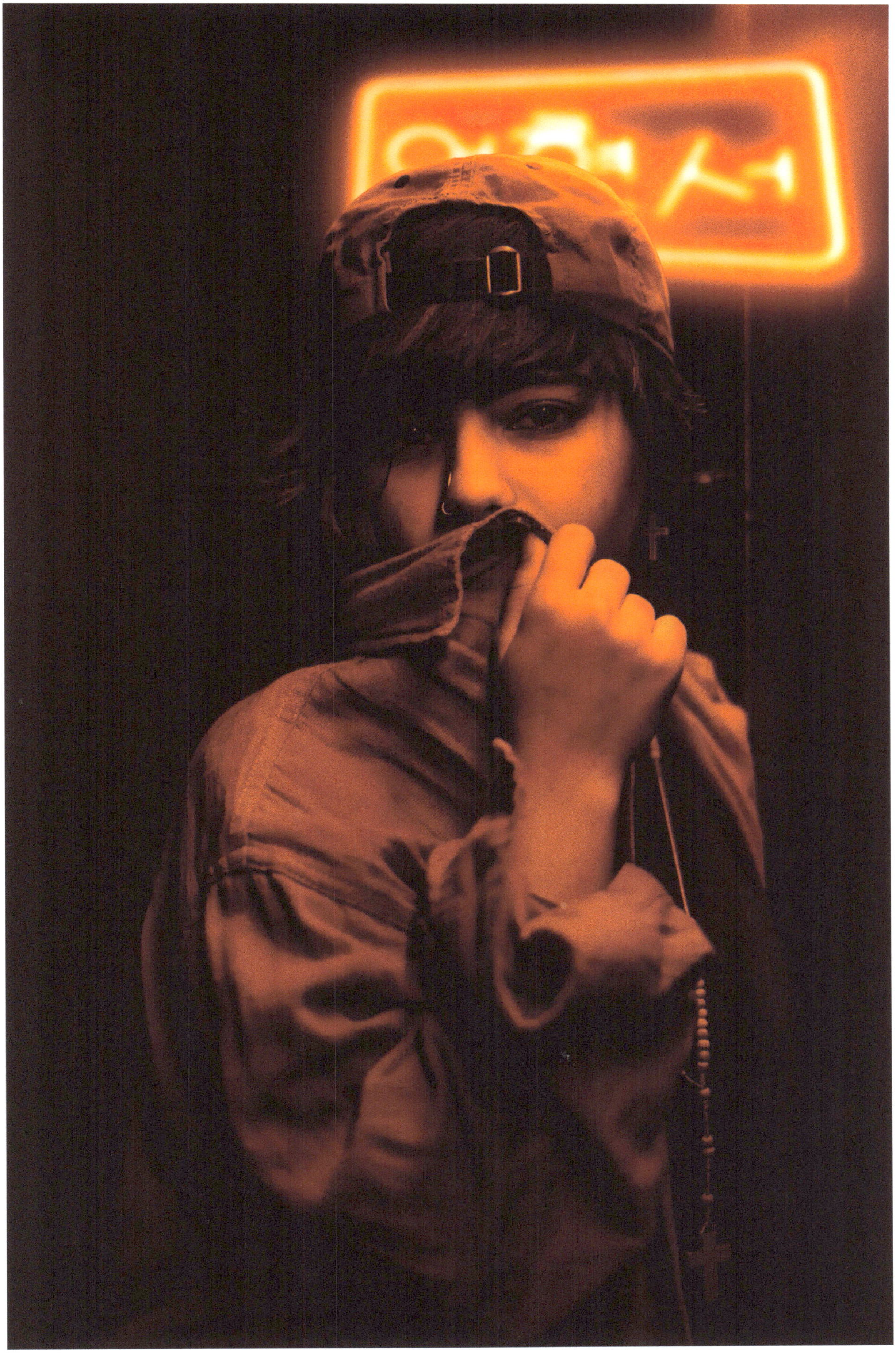

@ThinSlicePhoto
Sean Conte, visual storyteller

Baptism of Light

Playing with light focuses us to understand what's being said in an image. In addition, a restrained color palette is a big part of the work of photographer Sean Conte, who has an innate skill of communicating emotion through light.

Sean's photo **Baptism of Light** is flooded with an ochre glow, setting the scene with a symmetry that centers you right in the middle of a conversation between the two mysterious subjects.

What are they discussing? She's speaking with hand gestures. He's listening intently with a notepad. The beauty of a restrained palette encourages one to inspect the piece closely. Of the soft yellow light beyond the curtains, the photographer writes:

"Somewhere between the eye and the soul, light lives and moves and affects. Its greatest quality is not illumination, but transcendence. It can touch the heart, shift perception, and display the expanse of time."

The best art reaches deep into our own heart and psyche. If you can make someone feel something, you have a unique talent.

Creators who make a living from commercial media off-chain have a dual role, especially if they're able to bridge their style aesthetic from the corporate world to NFTs. Based in Los Angeles, Sean successfully dances on this edge by working as a cinematographer in commercials, films, and music videos for clients such as Nike, Lululemon, LucasFilm, Turkish Airlines, and W Hotels to name a few.

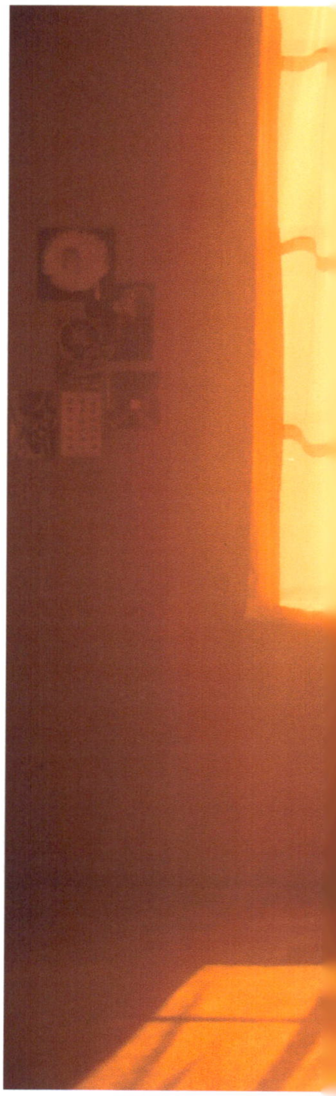

"If you let it, light will tell its own story. Bathe a story in the right light and you won't need to look for a meaning; it will be felt."

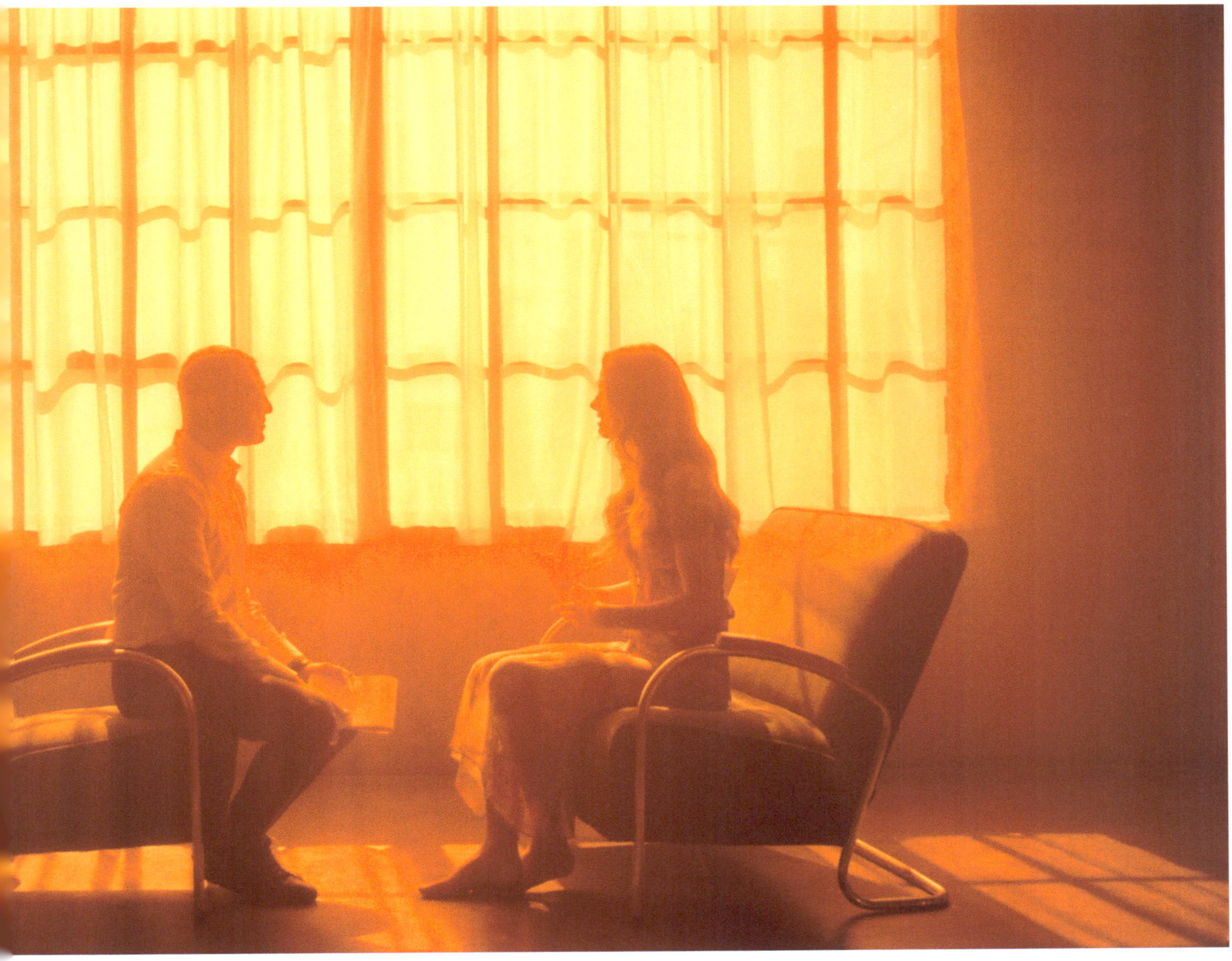

Baptism of Light
foundation.app/@ThinSlicePhoto/~/89949
Minted: September 23, 2021

1/1s

Most NFTs are minted in a limited number of authentic pieces.
The rarest artworks are 1/1s; they are truly one of a kind.

@_r0yart
Roya Ghassemmi, figurative artist

*"She is fragile on her storms,
the storms are fragile on her wings."*

Her wings unfolded

Unfolded wings expand from the subject's skin hollow. If clipped wings symbolise constraint, wings unfolded share an uplifting feeling of limitless possibility. Yet the subject is turned from us—her arms crossed protectively. This guarded optimism is an aspect of the artist herself. She says that:

"My artworks act as a tool of expression, a way for me to visually translate the complex ideas that ran through my mind."

Roya is an Iranian-German artist who expresses her views on freedom and human rights through art. Roya first minted an artwork, **Warrior's Soul**, on the Foundation marketplace in April, 2021. In the time since, she has shared messages of beauty and perseverance through the symbolism in her work.

"I archive my imaginations on papers."

MintFace was drawn to an artwork titled **Eleutheromania**. The meaning of it in the description is captured in the phrase: "an intense and irresistible desire for freedom."

The creation of love is a collection of pure feelings. In it Roya shares a collection of sketches and illustrations that are instantly familiar from her mints on Foundation. Each artwork is like peering into a sketchbook of inspiration—delicate and beautiful.

"I'm trying to showcase a wild liberation. I believe that growth, with all its sufferings, is a very beautiful phenomenon, and human beings are, in their simplest form, their truest natural selves when they are growing."

Her wings unfolded
foundation.app/@r0yart/~/113984
Minted: December 4, 2021

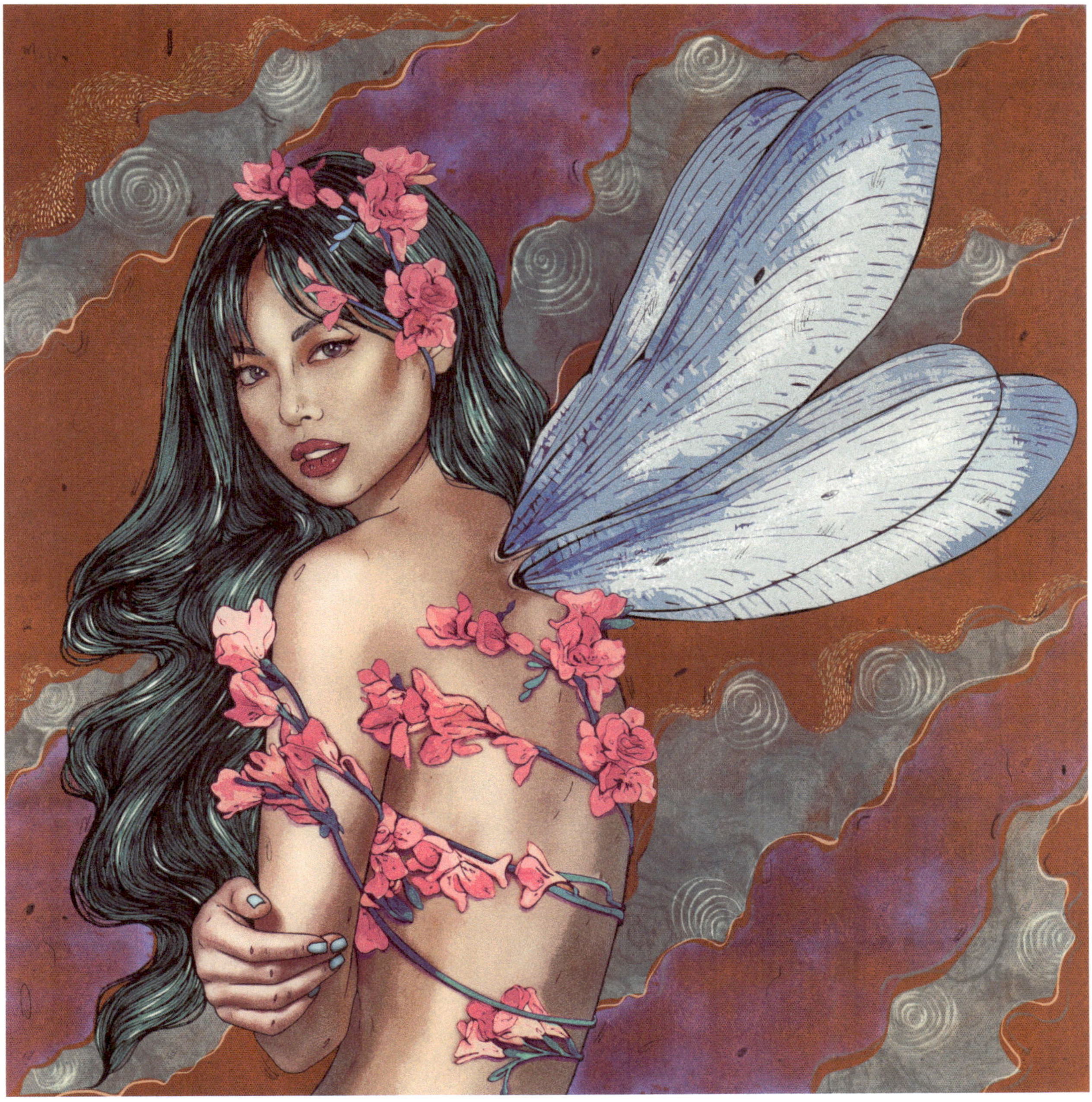

@6529er
The 6529 Designer

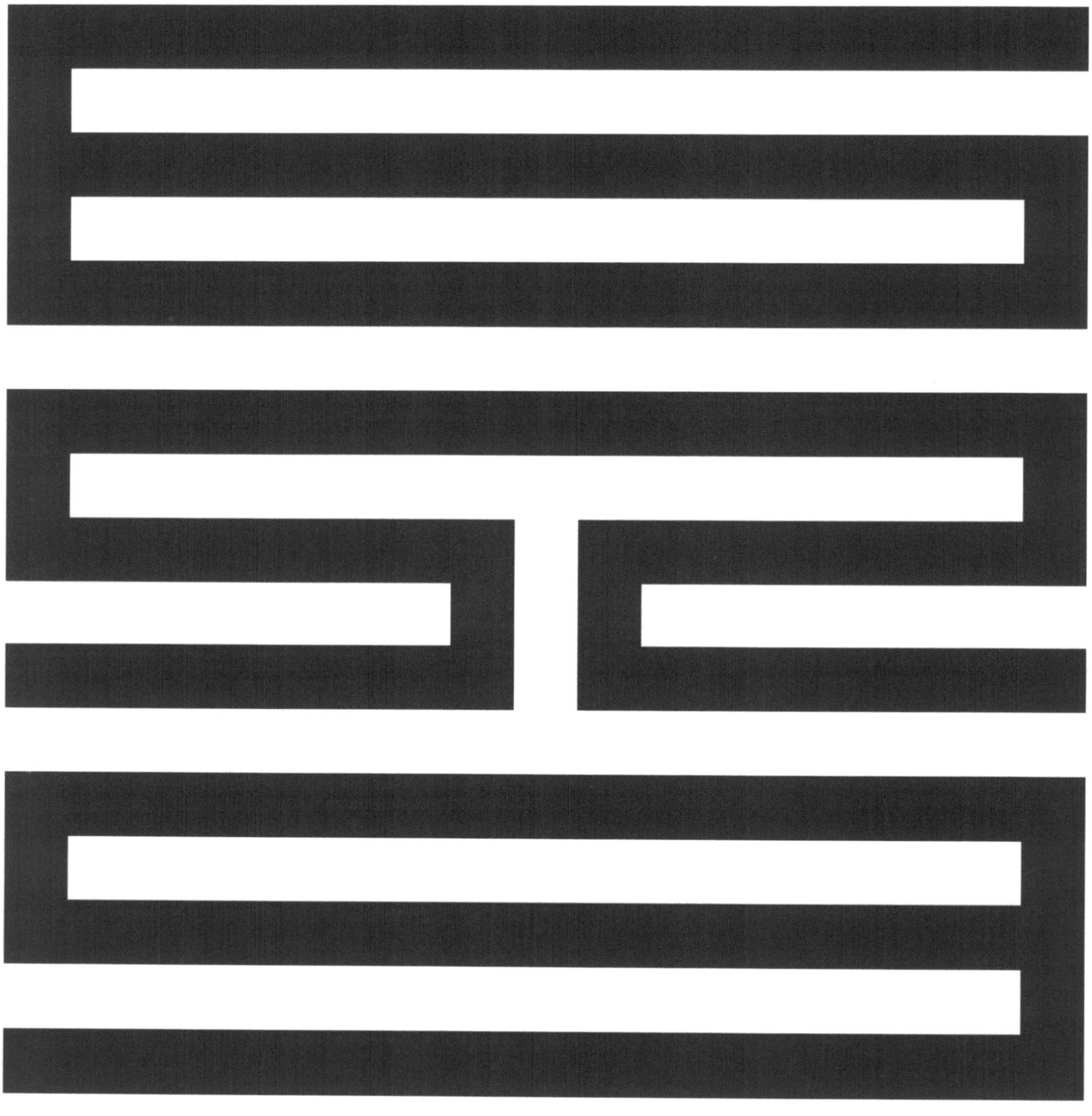

6529 Gradient #21
opensea.io/collection/6529-gradient
Minted: October 5, 2021

@abidaker

Abi Daker, artist & illustrator

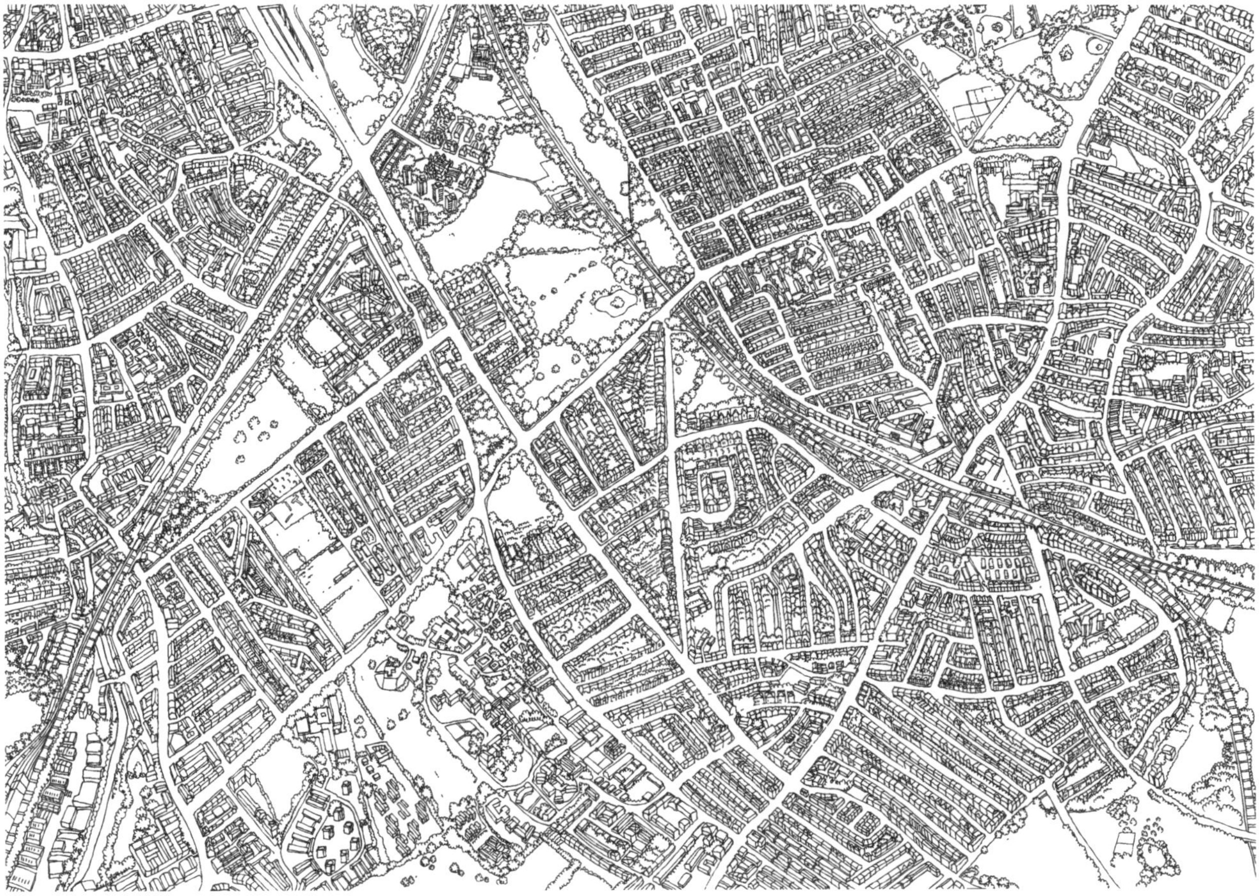

Wandsworth Illustrated Map

opensea.io/collection/illustrated-city-maps

Minted: November 24, 2021

@apocalypticform
Apocalypse Art

"Glowing is an inner activity. The skin is no longer a barrier. The world is no longer objects. The light within and the light around are one."

The Meeings collection

Thirty years of creating art is an immense back catalog of work with which to begin your NFT journey. The art of Apocalypse is about "expressing spiritual truths," according to the artist, and his focus starts with the battle in our minds.

"My artwork is about seeing the unwinnable and ongoing wars, the desperate messes and masses, the endless struggle and striving of humanity. More importantly, it's about winning through love, creativity, and metamorphosis in dark and chaotic times."

Dark stuff. There have been many moments when the lesser aspects of human nature have crested into troops bristling at borders in conflict with others. The 20th Century was full of them. Apocalypse reminds us that such times are not very far removed from our own, and that other wars remain to be fought.

And yet, he seems to say, we can always choose otherwise. Apocalypse juxtaposes the darkness of terror with the light of resilience and faith in humanity's higher potentials—what Steven Pinker called *The Better Angels of Our Nature*.

Artists often communicate an emerging narrative within the culture more clearly than society is able to see. The daily onslaught of breaking news hides deeper currents—an underbelly that Apocalypse wants us to acknowledge, endure, and perhaps transform.

"I've learned that society is like a sculpture—we make it together. It's a projection of our ideas and values. This means we also have the potential to transform society. But will we do it?"

Difficult questions. But there are also bright rays of sunshine in the apocalypse. One came from an unlikely place. XCOPY acquired an earlier artwork edition from the artist titled **Sun Walker** in November, 2021, forever connecting the provenance of XCOPY's OG crypto journey with the up-and-coming Apocalypse. These are the little telltale signs that are a blockchain beauty all of their own.

The artist isn't limited to the digital world. To date, many physical pieces have been shipped to the first NFT owner in their own hand-painted, felt-lined boxes.

"The Apocalypse is already here; it's just unevenly distributed."

Glowing
opensea.io/collection/apocalypse-art-meeings
Minted: October 15, 2021

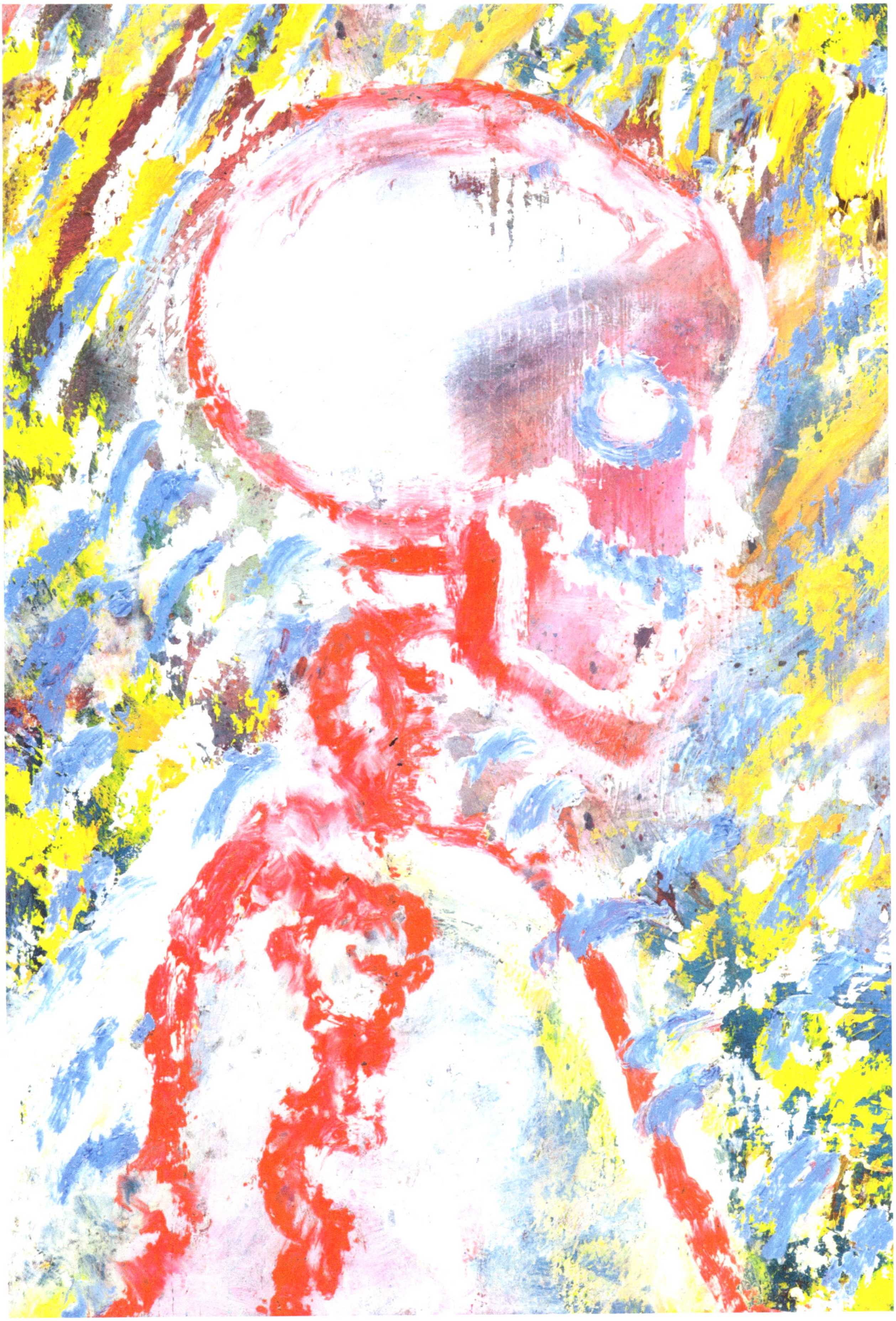

@Crazydoc96

CrazyDoc, doctor & self-taught abstract artist

"Watching sunsets is a way of healing. To be touched by the last warm rays by the end of the day, I choose to move towards a brighter light."

Dr. Abstract collection

Glorious art makes us feel something, even when our brain struggles to make sense of what we are seeing. Our brain deconstructs elements—the colours, lines, and shapes—in an effort to answer the question: 'What does this remind me of?'

When it finds a match in its archives of memories, feelings, and nostalgia, we experience something. That is the gift of abstract art. To that end, the artist known as CrazyDoc has released **Dr. Abstract**—100 digital abstract artworks to tickle our brains. She writes of the collection:

"I made this series comprised of elements based on human experiences expressed in the form of shapes, textures, and gestures put together. The purpose of my artworks is to make the observer feel the art itself with their minds rather than their eyes."

We have been here before thanks to the work of Wassily Kandinsky who was born in 1866. Kandinsky viewed abstract art as the ideal visual mode to express the 'inner necessity' of the artist and to convey universal human emotions and ideas.

Unlike photography or generative art, hand-drawn brushstrokes are literally the signature of the artist. The expressiveness and connectedness of elements within each artwork are made by the hand and felt by the heart. We get to feel some of what CrazyDoc feels through each artwork.

The most human of characteristics is to express our feelings and hold space for others to express their feelings as well. Each of the artworks in the **Dr. Abstract** collection is a gift that rewards both desires.

RIDE ON SUNSET
opensea.io/collection/dr-abstract
Minted: October 25, 2021

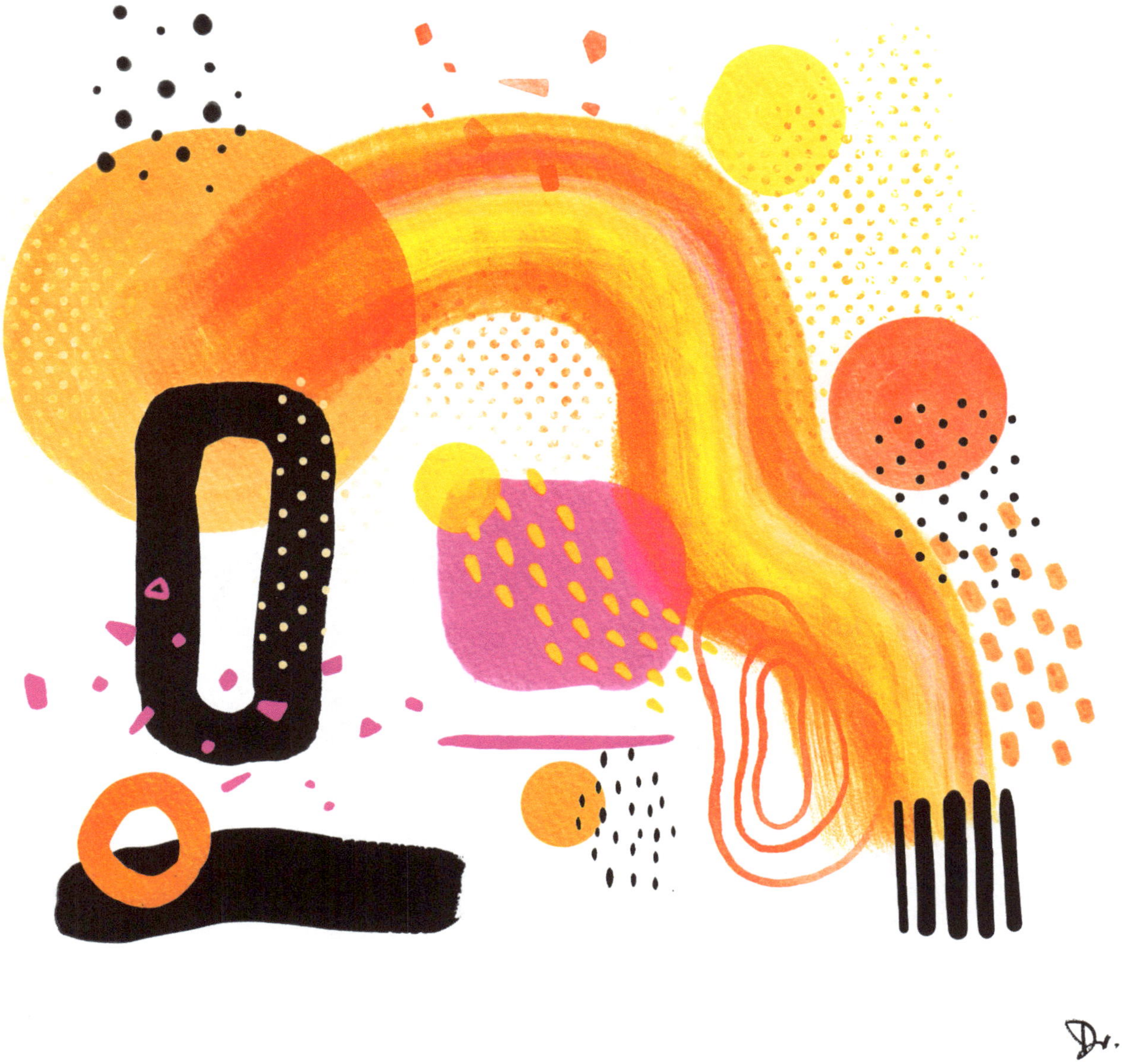

@DomBakerArtist
Dominique Baker, artist

"I love Aotearoa (the Māori name for New Zealand) and my carved paintings aim to exhibit elements of the heritage and cultures that shape me."

Carved Geisha collection

The beauty of art created by indigenous artists is that we all become richer through the sharing of their culturally-important stories. **Carved Geisha** is a genesis collection of hand-painted and carved acrylic paintings on wood by Dominique Baker.

*"**Half-Caste** was my very first Geisha painted and carved on wood frame. My pieces can be recognised as artwork belonging to* Aotearoa *that embody a* wairua *or 'feeling' from the Pacific. My art reflects a connection to Asia, as can be seen in the idealised geisha and samurai warrior. But more importantly, my artwork aims to exhibit my journey of identity through Māori art and culture."*

Dominique has added three more collections to her 2021 minted works, including a selection of 1/1's in the **Tondo Geisha** collection, Koi Tondo fish with markings unique to the Pacific region; and **Flowers, Frocks and Samurai** a small series of 21 artworks.

"My work is informed by street art and exploring a range of methods of making, resulting in visually intricate pieces. It was something about their mysterious yet elegant poses that drew me in. One painting of a Geisha led to another and before I knew it that's all I wanted to paint."

To create each artwork, wooden panel frames are prepared with the use of clear gesso and shellac varnish and then acrylic paint is applied. These mediums subtly represent the colonial influence of Aotearoa's history. The artist writes about her process:

"Japanese steel chisels carve the intricate details, such as kōwhaiwhai *(Māori motif) seen on* tukutuku *panels, flowers, hair highlights, weaving,* taaniko *patterns, and bird feathers. This form of carving or etching, suggests a connection to the Māori art form of* whakairo."

Half Caste
opensea.io/collection/carved-geishas
Minted: October 18, 2021

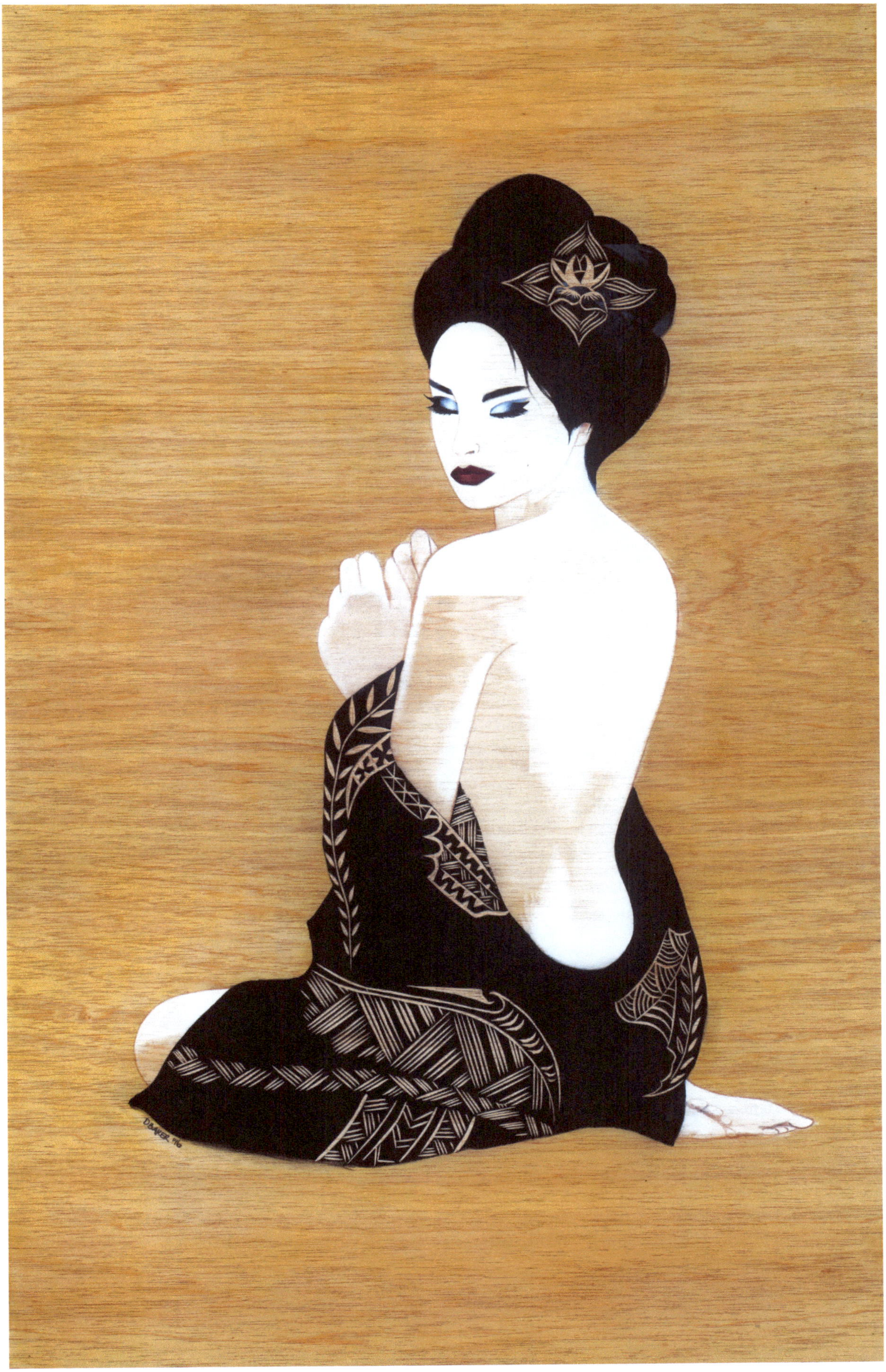
D.BAKER '10

@FirstLadyNFT
First Lady, artist

"The ladies are independent, they are confident, and they have a voice."

500 Ladies collection

500 Ladies is an epic project dreamed up by First Lady to hand-make a collection of doll-like mannikins. Each unique piece was handcrafted into an actual miniature lady, complete with flowing dresses and manufactured head. According to the artist:

"All the ladies are distinct individuals, and can be thought of as representing the huge variety of roles for women in contemporary society—from mothers and doctors to engineers and artists."

In an incredible year-long mission, a whole community of 'little women' was made. Some pieces are made from crafted objects that First Lady has stitched, crocheted, embroidered, and knitted. Others are created from discarded objects such as washers, doorknobs, and printer heads—remnants of our industrial and technological society. These cannibalised parts help to create unique individuals wearing contemporary fashions, so the ladies carry these remnants of past generations into the 21st century.

"The ladies have a shared history or DNA, but hopefully they also elicit fond memories in others. It's great when someone points out one of them, and says 'My grandmother had one of those hour glasses' or 'I had a tea towel like that when I was young'."

The 500 Ladies are presented as NFTs, yet none of them would be out of place on a fashion show catwalk in London, Paris or New York. They exude confidence and style.

There are rares with names like AC/DC, Afro, Electric Girl, **The Artist** and The Collector. You can also sort by the accessory each lady carries such as handbag, belt, necklace, scarf, or the even obscure qualities like feather boa, trousers, or diamond buttons.

"They are part of a community, they are also able to stand on their own and can be themselves. When there were 20 of them there wasn't such an impact, but now that there are 500, it is different. It's not just a small family group, but a whole society."

Lady #000 (The Artist)
opensea.io/collection/500ladies
Minted: October 31, 2021

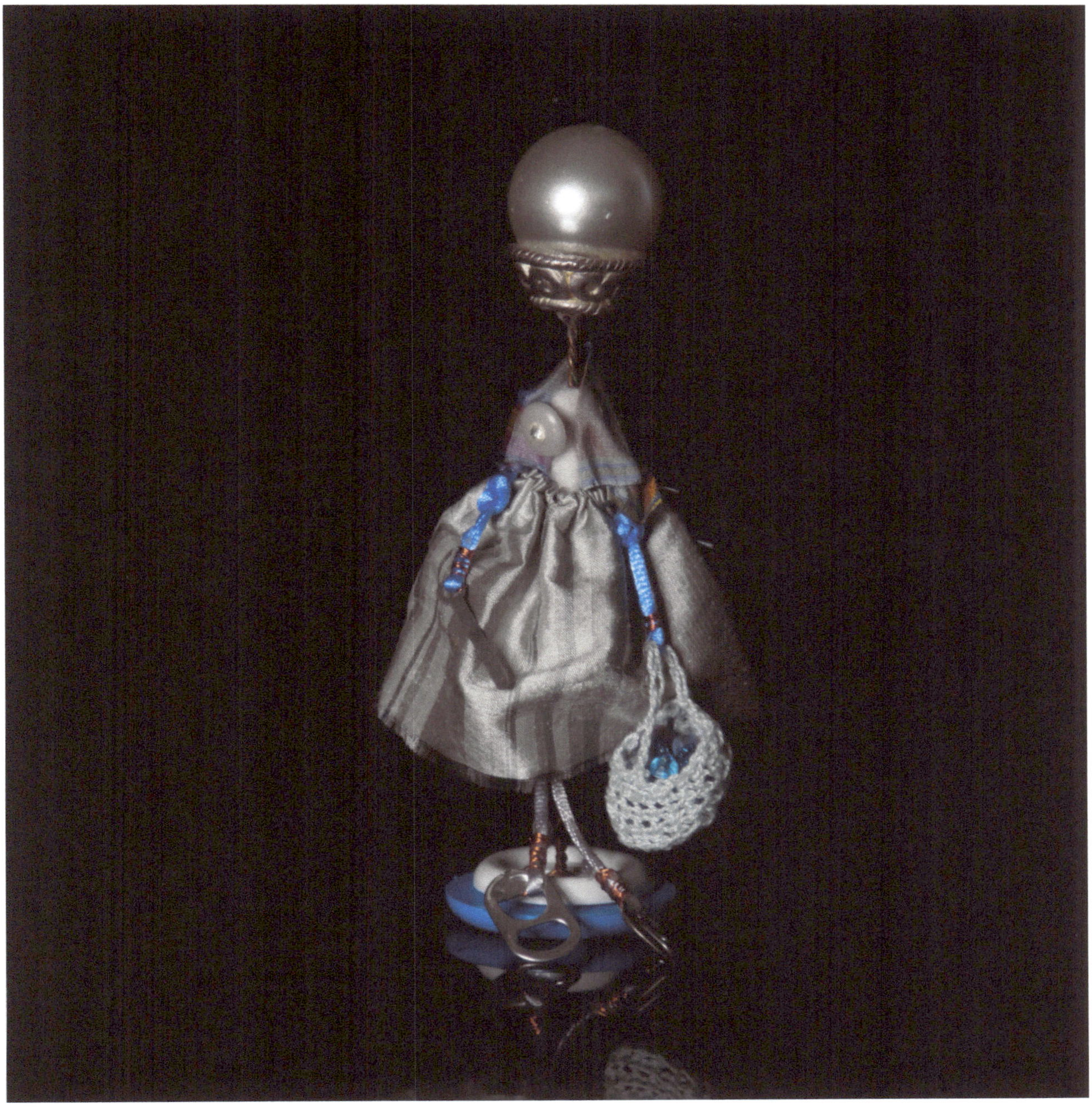

@frey
Jake Frey, artist & entrepreneur

Probably Nothing collection

'Probably nothing' are two words tweeted in irony when understating the significance of an event in the world of Web3.0. Artist Jake Frey has minted the phrase—turning it into an NFT that includes lifetime access and discounts to a new Web3.0 marketplace, Americana Technologies. Probably nothing is probably something.

The ability for an NFT to provide lifetime discounts on a marketplace is in itself ground-breaking. First up, you'll be able to get a sweet deal on NFTs you already own, and now want to bring into the real world with holographic, plated cards linked to their digital provenance.

Crossover technology, that blends the virtual with the real, helps bridge the gap in understanding for those not yet in the Web3.0 world. When we see a CryptoPunk, Cool Cat, or Bored Ape spray-painted onto a wall in Brooklyn or plastered on to a billboard in Times Square, it feels significant.

Americana Technologies is delivering that same crossover technology by retrofitting your NFTs into the trusted collectible card format that 20th Century collectors have enjoyed. Printing your NFTs as collectible cards is just one product of many that the Probably Nothing collection gives you preferential access to.

There's more to this project that makes any NFT into a physical collectible. Jake is also attempting to reverse the polarity of the universe by making any physical object into an NFT. Wait, what? Yup. Put any off-chain asset on-chain thanks to the NFTA Universal Chip. Each chip includes both a GPS sensor for location and a RFID chip that stores the identification information. According to Jake:

"For the first time ever, physical objects can gain the security and benefits that the blockchain offers."

Probably Nothing #1
opensea.io/collection/probablynothingnft
Minted: October 22, 2021

Probably nothing.

@graphitegeorgia
Georgia Robinson, artist

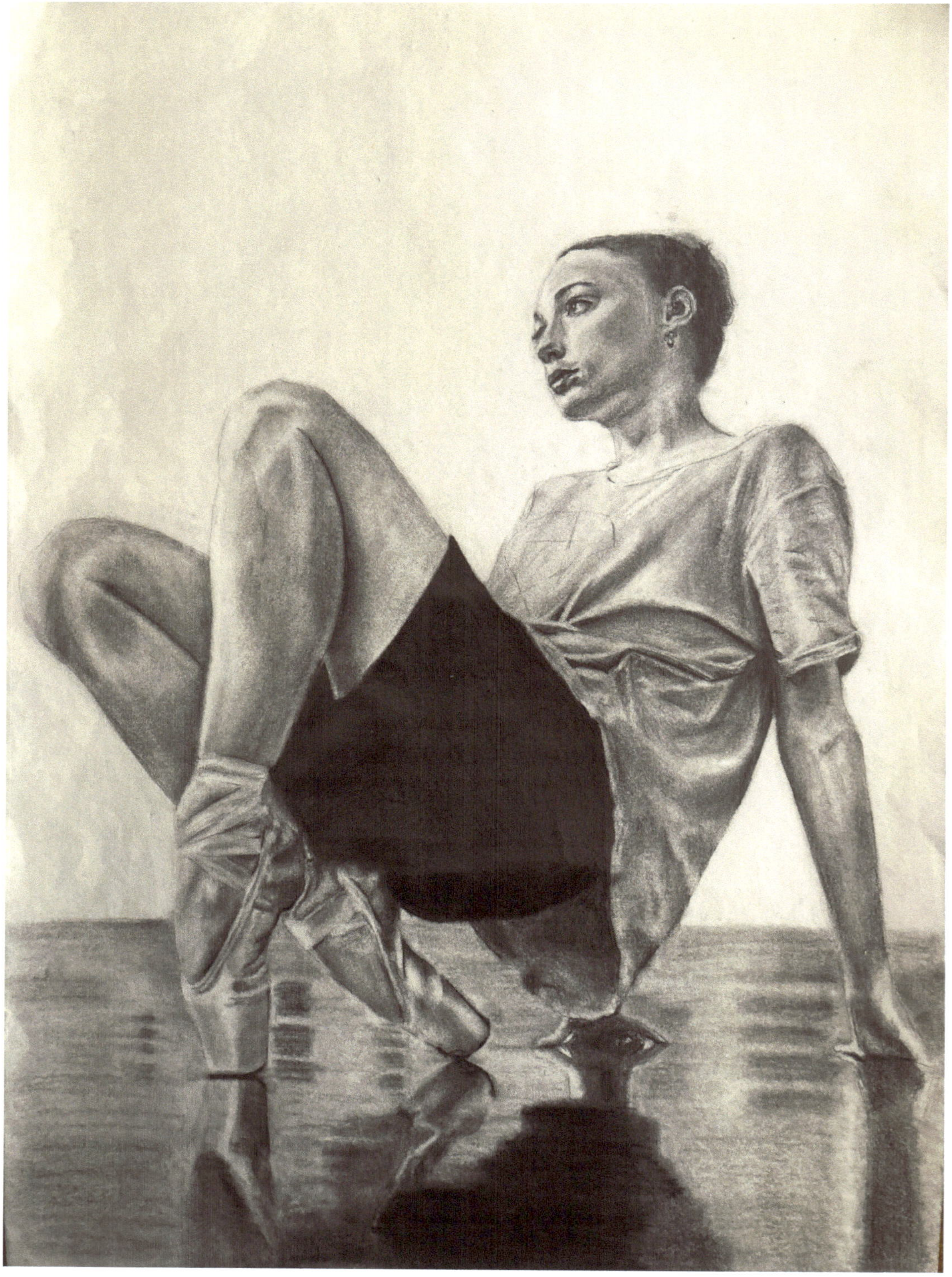

Ballerina
opensea.io/collection/gr0b-collection
Minted: October 19, 2021

@LegoPunks
CryptoPopz, creator

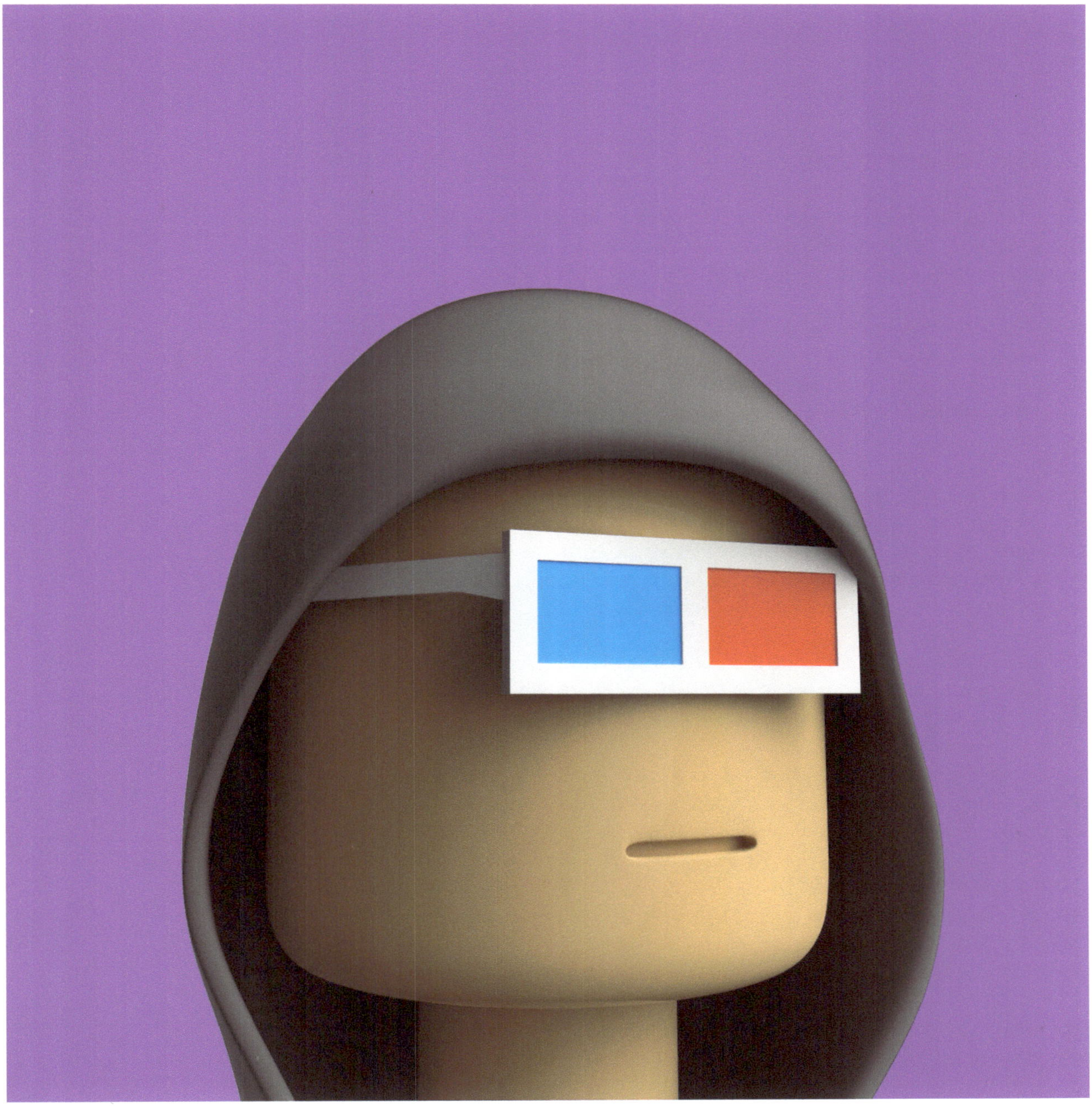

LegoPunk #222

opensea.io/collection/legopunks

Minted: December 4, 2021

@GregHollandJewl
Greg Holland, craftsman of unique fine jewellery

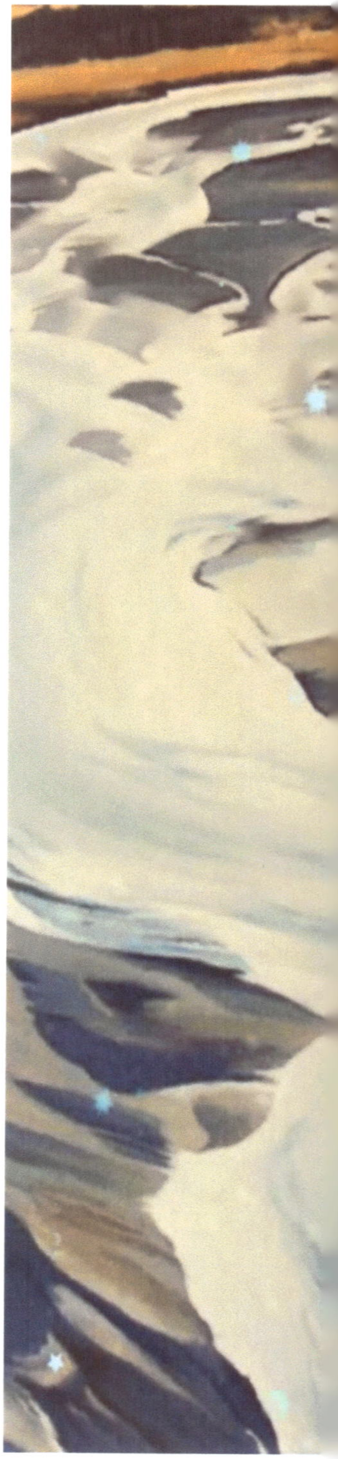

Inspired – Objet d'Art collection

The phrase 'diamond hands' means holding your digital asset forever—or, at the very least, a long time. Back in the regular world, diamonds remain the artifact of wedding proposals, dressing us up to ask the question of a lifetime.

Enter Greg Holland, the first diamond jeweller in New Zealand minting real diamond ice on the blockchain. Why does provenance on the blockchain matter? It gives the buyer more than a signed certificate of authenticity. After all, signatures can be forged and certificates can be reprinted. Of course, there's also the cool factor of having a timestamped piece of jewellery. The talented craftsman speaks of his inspiration:

"The idea for ***Braided Icon*** *came to me back in 2013. It was a moment I will never forget. It was a gloomy day in the Southern Alps of New Zealand. I was standing on a ridge at 1,921 metres, The sky cleared briefly—allowing the sun to reveal a breath-taking vista of snow-capped mountains stretching as far as the eye could see. In a jaw-dropping moment, the search for 'my artistic look' was unexpectedly realised."*

"The Waimakariri River's headwaters lie in the heart of the Southern Alps, a river whose beauty I have spent countless hours enjoying. It possesses an energy and life force of its own and evokes in me a feeling of connection."

New Zealand's iconic 'braided' rivers are unique, natural phenomena of the Canterbury landscape. The seven, slow-moving river plains—Waiau Toa, Waiau Uwha, Hurunui, Waimakariri, Rakaia, Rangitata, and Waitaki weave their unique paths across the land.

New Zealand was the first country in the world to grant a river the same legal rights as a human being. The approach of granting legal personality to a river responds to the view of the Iwi tribe of the Whanganui river, which has long revered Te Awa Tupua as a tangible life force, through its traditions, and deep spiritual connection.

Greg loves the pristine environment of New Zealand and treats his NFT community to some of the views he's been inspired by every day. On purchase, each diamond ring is shipped in a sealed presentation box to any destination in Australasia, Japan, United Kingdom, Europe, USA and Canada with some the proceeds going to support NFT artists and some to the New Zealand 'Make A Wish' Foundation.

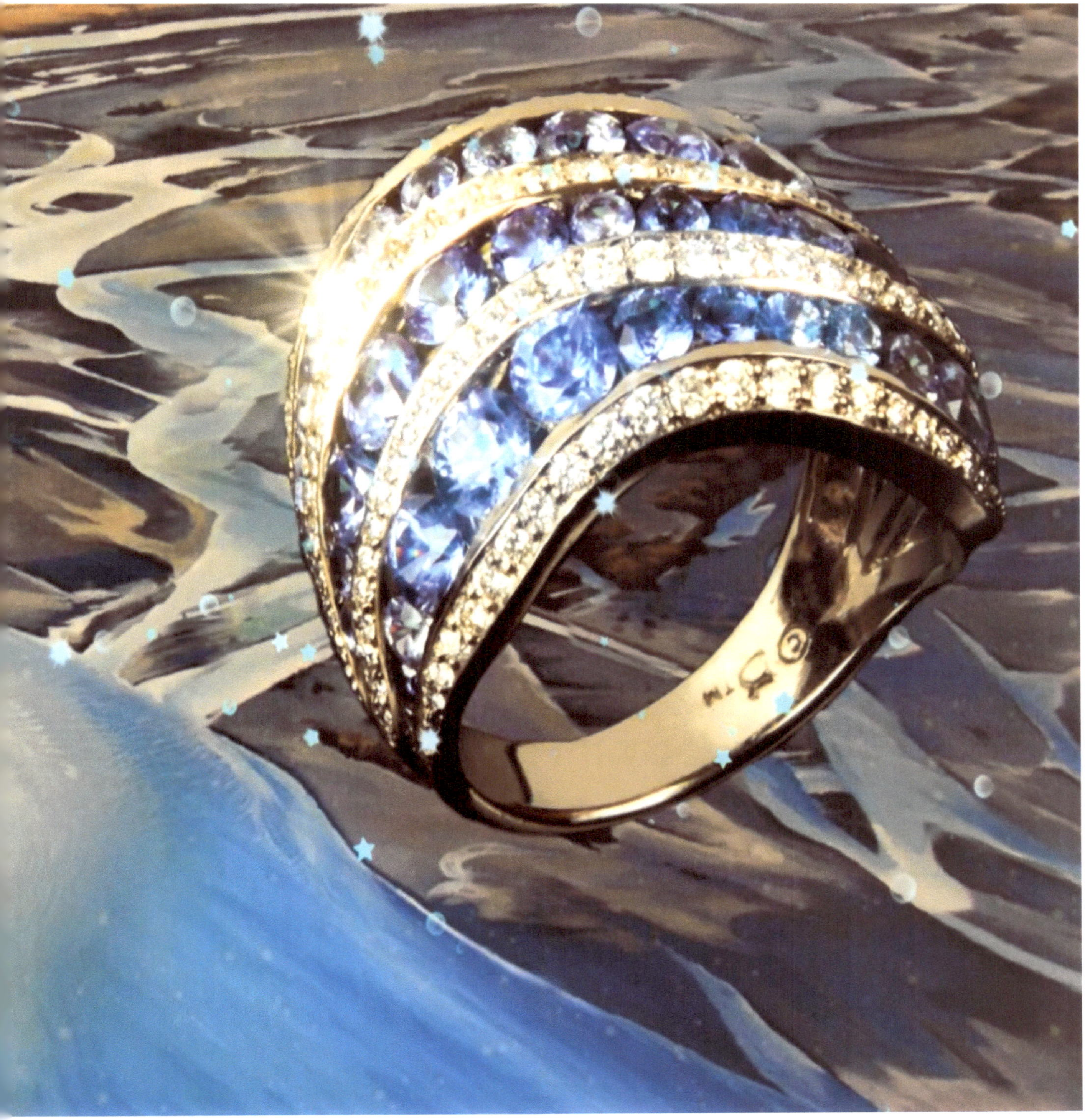

Braided Icon – 'Waimakariri'

opensea.io/collection/objetdart

Minted: November 23, 2021

@hariology

Hariprasad CM, Rubik's Cube artist

"This artwork is a representation of all aspects of womanhood, especially the fierce strength that is often dormant within them as symbolized by the goddess Devi."

The Mighty One!

The conceptual artist Hariology has adopted a children's toy, the Rubik's Cube, as a building block for his artwork. In the process, he's created artwork and portraits with hundreds and sometimes thousands of unique cubes. In fact, **The Mighty One!** was constructed from 600 individual Rubik's Cubes weighing over 70 kilograms.

The Rubik's Cube was invented by Ernő Rubik and within its 36 small facets lie well beyond 43 quintillion possible combinations. The 1980s brought the Rubik's Cube into pop culture with many of us growing up trying to match the colors of all six sides. It's a passion that captivated Hariology as well. He says that, as a child:

"I would play around with each pixel, recolor them, decide if I should add blues or greens or even blacks. Sometimes I'd even keep it as a monochrome version."

Hariology goes beyond what we see in a singular object and shows the potential of what can be created with a collective vision. He is part of the World Cube Association and was one of the artists that built the largest Rubik's Cube mosaics in Asia. But, when it comes to imagining new pieces, he's definitely 'old school.'

"The most engaging stage in the making of a Rubik's mosaic portrait is in its design. That's the stage I enjoy the most. I know a lot of people who randomly generate the design using computer programs. But there is no fun in that. I still do it by hand."

Now Hariology is minting his massive and very physical artworks as NFTs with each Rubik's Cube playing a role in creating the physical 'pixels.' In the past, he has created portraits of artist Salvador Dalí, entrepreneur Gary Vee, footballer Cristiano Ronaldo, and even the entire cast of *F.R.I.E.N.D.S.*—all with Rubik's Cubes.

If you are curious about his actual construction process, each NFT includes a short time-lapse video detailing, row by row, how the sculpture takes shape.

The Mighty One!
foundation.app/@hariology/~/98555
Minted: October 16, 2021

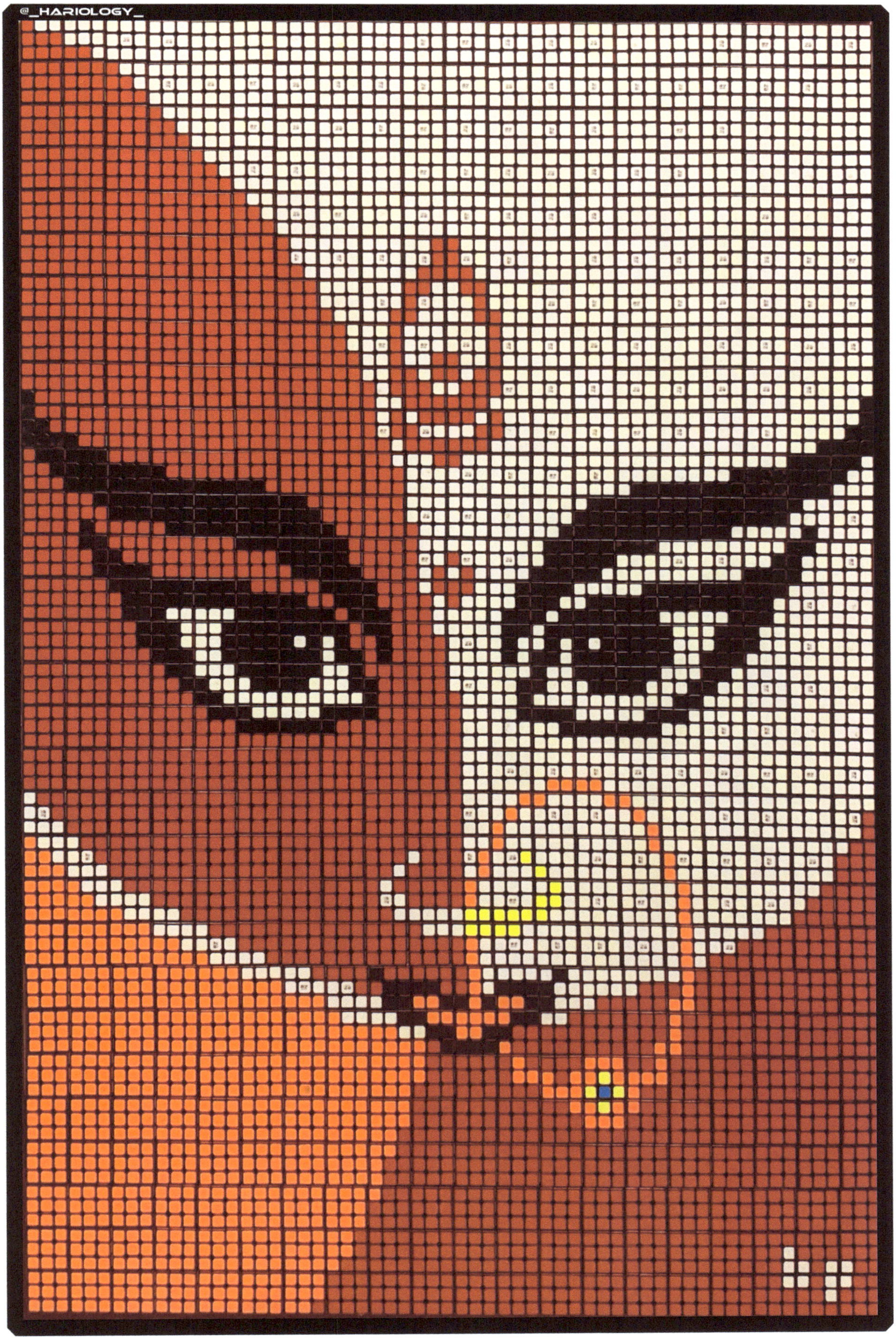
@_HARIOLOGY_

@HugoFaz

Hugo Faz, photographer & performance artist

100 Nude Shoots of Hugo collection

Brazilian Hugo Faz is a leading light for artists in emerging economies, such as many in South America, where the exchange rate with international markets creates a Web3.0 participation hurdle. Faz wants to use the blockchain power of NFTs to correct the imbalance. To this end, he started an incubator, NU NFT, for a range of artists including Rony Hernandes, Luiz Leles, and Jhen Scalco. Of the effort, Hugo says:

"The NFT art space is currently missing the best artists due to global asymmetries. NU NFT is an initiative to help with this. Soon it will become a full-fledged DAO."

Hugo is building a pipeline between art collectors and talent historically cut off from anything beyond the local gallery. Artists selected for the roster are almost exclusively women, BIPOC, and LGBTQ+ artists. Where English is a second language, Hugo lends a hand. Where gas fees for listing are prohibitive, NU NFT foots the bill. If there's an individual that personifies the WAGMI (We Are Gonna Make It) spirit, it's Hugo.

Cutting-edge performance art permeates Hugo's 10-year body of work in film and photography. Whether portraying the many facets of the Brazilian queer art scene or making censorship-defying artistic statements, the artist immerses himself in themes such as the body, identity, the human-machine relationship, necropolitics, and crypto.

The image shown here, **1 - Rebirth, with Rony Hernandes**, is the first in a series called **100 Nude Shoots of Hugo**. Hugo, of course, is the model while the photographer is Rony (as acknowledged in the title) the newly-released collection on Foundation will continue to grow and evolve over time. According to Hugo:

*"**Rebirth** is the first minted interpretation in the blockchain of my work **100 Nude Shoots**—a project that is the epitome of my life-long, open-ended, ongoing artistic research on the portrayal of the human figure. It will sprawl across 100 collaborations with 100 different artists. It will ll end when I can longer make art with my body. All I know about the pathway is I'll make it as original and controversial as I can."*

1 - Rebirth, with Rony Hernandes
foundation.app/@hugofaz/100nudeshoots/1
Minted: December 9, 2021

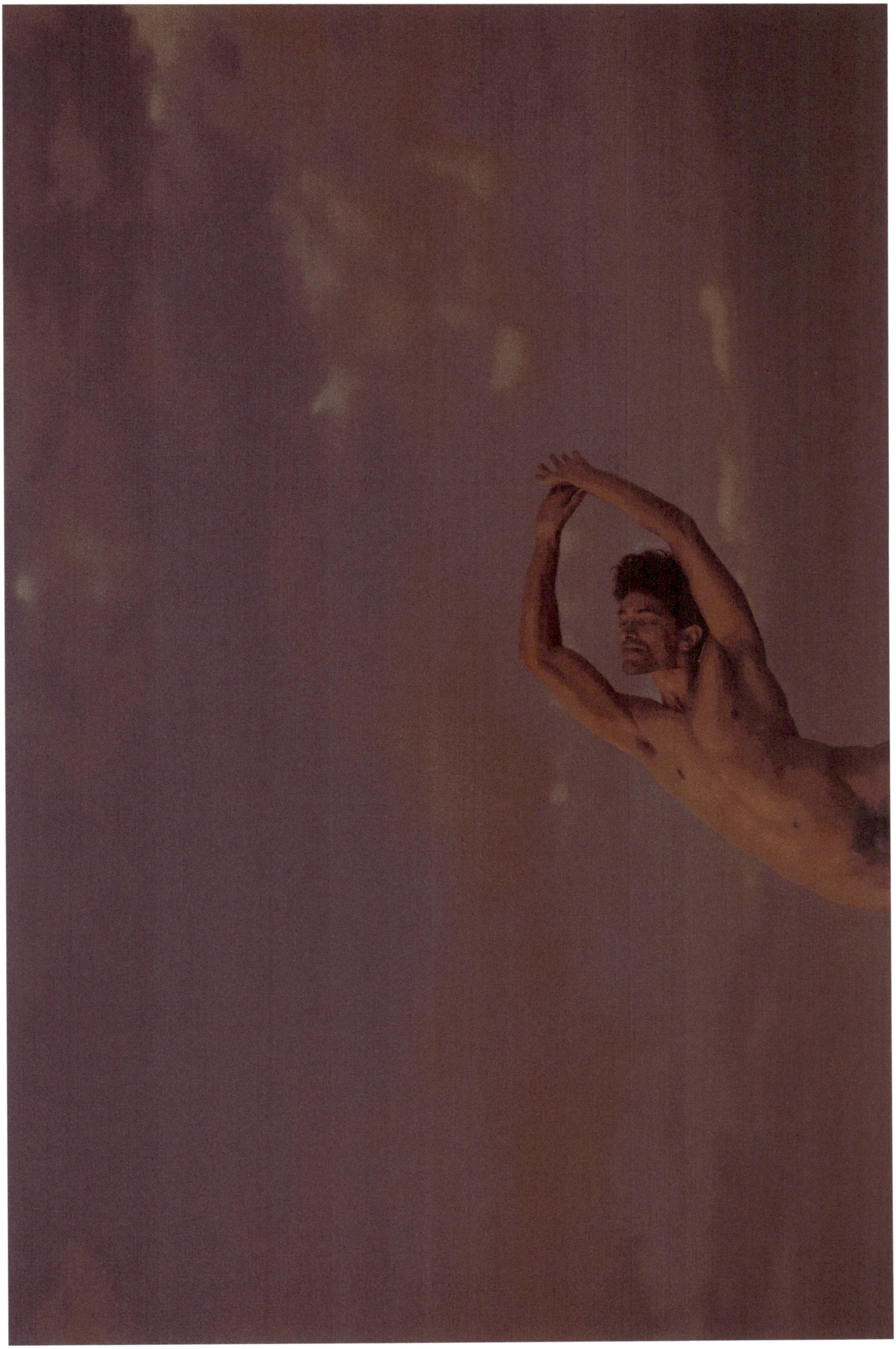

@kitahara_keiko
Keiko Kitahara, artist

"This work was painted with acrylic paints on canvas, using a pipe rather than a brush. After that, I edited it digitally."

Cavel II

The artist Keiko Kitahara has an eye for delightful and engaging abstraction. When you look closely at **Cavel II**, the various colourful shapes act like tiny stained-glass windows, totally devoid of brushstrokes. Each artwork is actually painted with a pipe, which provides a denser application of pigment.

A related work, **Cavel**, was acquired by the well-known digital art collector Bharat Krymo. **Cavel II** came to life a month later, this time minted on OpenSea. The layering and smudging of paint layers of the first **Cavel** gave way to a cleaner palette.

Woven amid the chunks of colour, is a dark stick figure, evidently in motion. The linear presence quietly holds each scene together. There are also works by Keiko that focus simply on each single brushstroke. Their purity is almost like a small bell ringing.

Ever searching for new ideas, Keiko has experimented with interactive artwork minted on the blockchain through the Async marketplace. Her **Pathfinder** NFT shows a new scene every 60 minutes as programmed by her custom smart contract.

The beauty of abstraction is it leaves much for the viewer to decide. It let's us fill in the story with our own memories and thoughts. Kandinsky, Mondrian and Rothko all explored colour in ways previously unimagined.

Art is more than 3D glasses atop an ape or a beanie placed with pixelation on a punk. Art has always rewarded the artists who arrived with their own vision and style.

We may be a collective community establishing our own norms, but we rely on the freshness of approach from artists such as Keiko to keep reminding us that the path is only just emerging for us all.

Cavel II
opensea.io/collection/keikokitahara
Minted: June 20, 2021

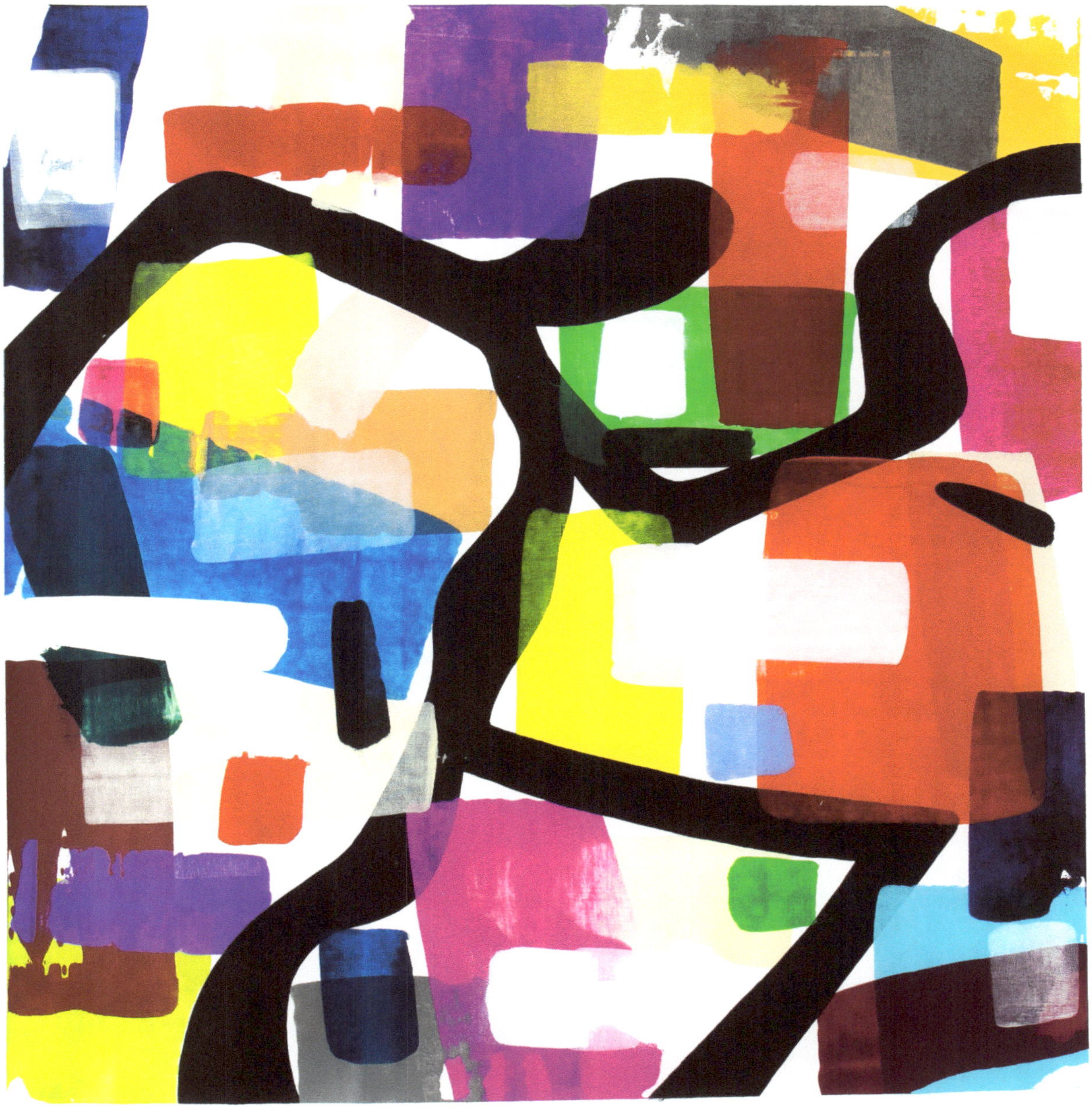

@komodaharu
Haru Komoda, illustrator & founder of HAKABOCHI

"The finite in the infinite. If the place changes, the view changes. What do we see?"

GANMEN collection

A work from the **GANMEN** series called **KOON #3** greets the viewer with a smile, proudly displaying its pearly white teeth and sickly green gums. Dancing around the mouth, where a face should be, are multi-colored globules bookended by floppy ears (or wings). Yet the creature has no eyes. It is blind, floating in its own dark landscape. A bowler hat perched on top brings a sense of formality to the imposing cartoon head.

"Acceleration of imagination."

Art deserves to be free and as expansive as an ocean for collectors, however the OpenSea filter system doesn't immerse us fully in the metaverse. Haru has thought ahead and curated his collection into a few OnCyber virtual galleries titled **Silence**, **Midnight sun**, and **Moon in the middle day**.

Inside the gallery is another character, **GANMEN BADGER**, that may have fallen on its sword according to the Daikanyama Gallery curator: "These are a group of works in which badgers appear to have performed harakiri. This is fitting, since according to Haru, pain and cuteness coexist side-by-side."

Outside of digital art galleries, Haru's artwork **The wind changed direction** was shown in Times Square (New York City) by the art collector Punk6529 during the massive NFT NYC event. This was unimaginable when Haru minted his first NFT in April, 2021.

GANMEN -KOON- #3
opensea.io/collection/harukomoda
Minted: June 1, 2021

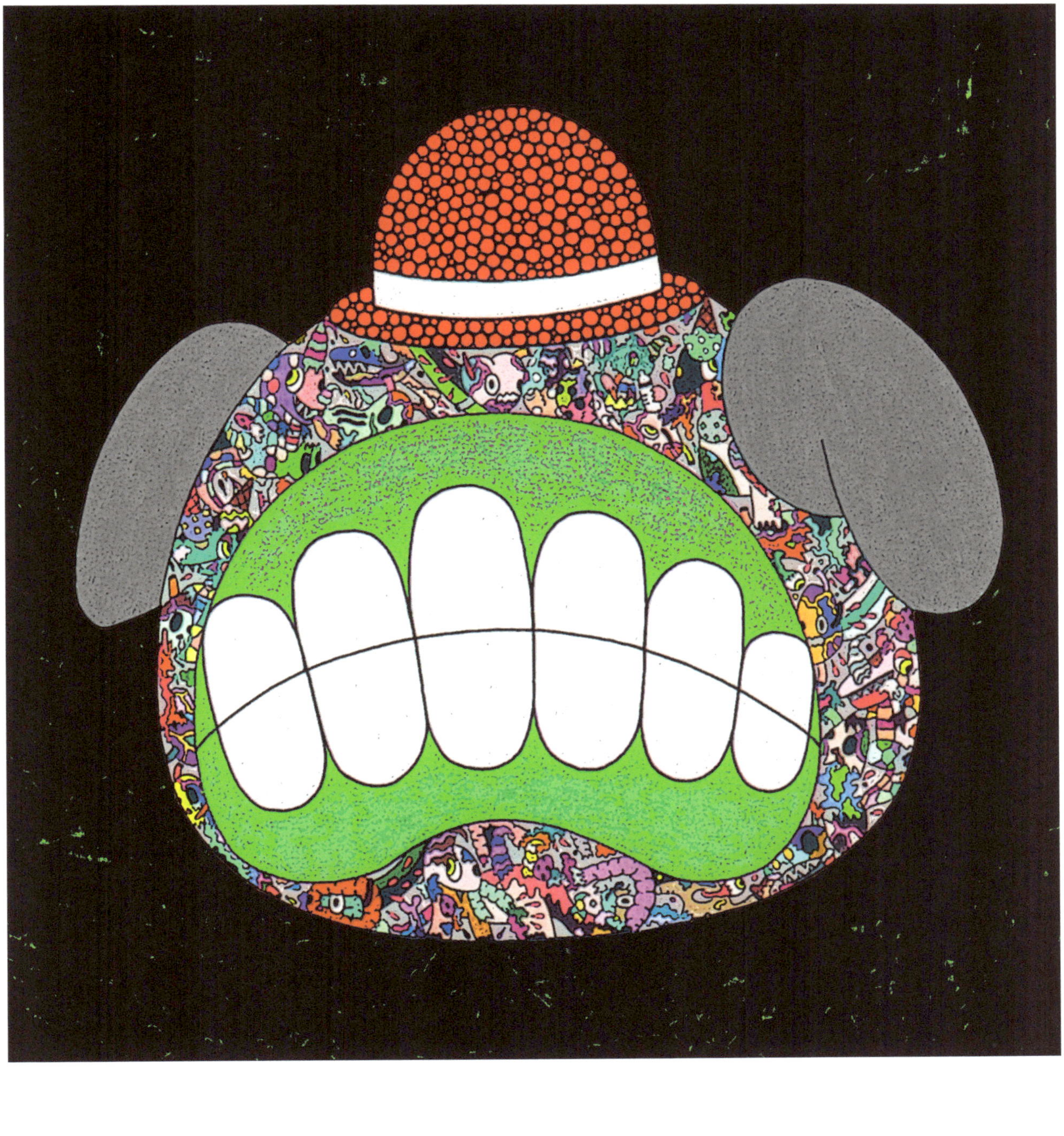

@NFTWannabe
Brandon Walsh, OG crypto-artist

"Everything in your mind. Everything is in your mind. I believe only one thing."

What's the art?

Brandon Walsh joined SuperRare way back in 2019, which anoints him as a legitimate OG crypto-artist. Since then he's shared over 111 creations, making his multi-year lineage even rarer. His first three works **The Lost Marble**, **Infinite Eyethereum** and **Faketoshis Vision** brought him income when he needed it most. Brandon was homeless, without any family or friends for support. In 2021, he moved into his first apartment, thanks to his crypto-art and his new friends (or 'frens').

Why do early mints matter? The collector @2YeahYeah has a thesis on early crypto-artists and a great Twitter thread where he deconstructs why certain SuperRare artists have potentially more upside than they're currently being valued at.

The first 4,434 tokens (SuperRare V1) look like ERC20 tokens as the original version of the ERC721 standard had a similar interface as the ERC20 standard. There will never be more than 4,434 tokens on the original SuperRare contract. Brandon was there minting artwork in these formative moments of blockchain art. The artist recalls:

"When crypto-art was in its formative stages, the art was considerably different than it is today. Those who discovered the genre early were a combination of revolutionary and artist. The appeal of NFTs was as immutable, uncensored vehicles of expression."

"Nobody was 'in it for the money' during that time. The art was remarkably honest, varied, and personal. When the scene went mainstream, the new blood was focused on profit and status. That early spirit—and the art that reflected it—became much harder to find. This piece ***What's the art?*** *and its companion* ***What's the point?*** *were created as a commentary on this shifting dynamic within the NFT ecosystem."*

"I miss the days when I could tell who made every single NFT on SuperRare without even looking at the names. There weren't two styles that were even remotely similar. There was a undeniable uniqueness about everyone's art."

Brandon's latest work shifts towards poetry with titles like **What's the point?** and the piece shown here, **What's the art?** A good question indeed. Is the art the dot? The art can be whatever we wish it to be. The textured background may be the art. Make your own mind up and consider Brandon's perspective on the pure origins of minted art.

What's the art?
superrare.com/artwork-v2/what's-the-art-25768
Minted: June 29, 2021

●

If the point it is not, the art is the dot.

@ObscurePrints
Obscure, artist

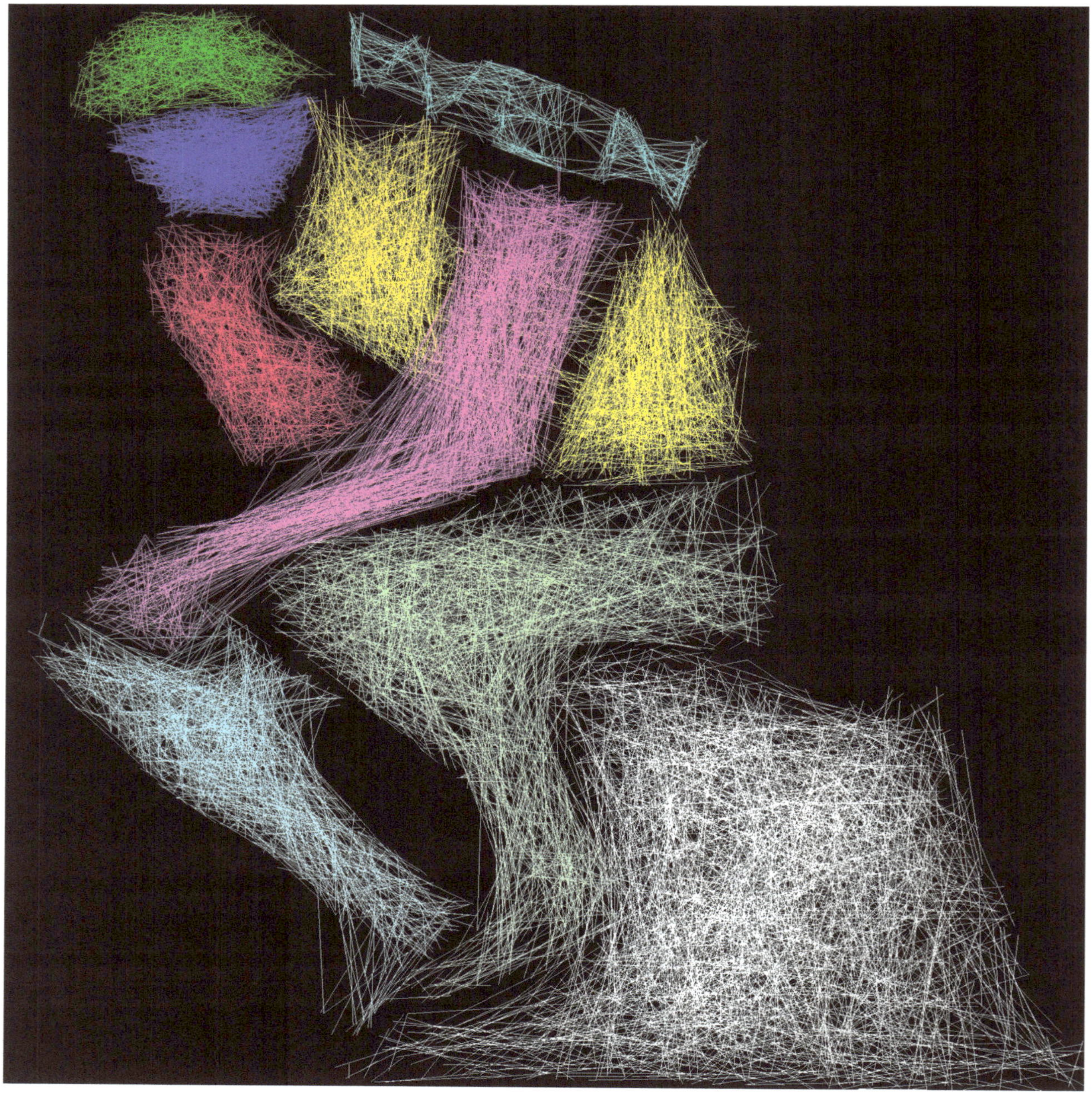

WEN

kollect.me/obscurestatues

Minted: November 1, 2021

@pinkOpalette
Gayathri, artist & designer

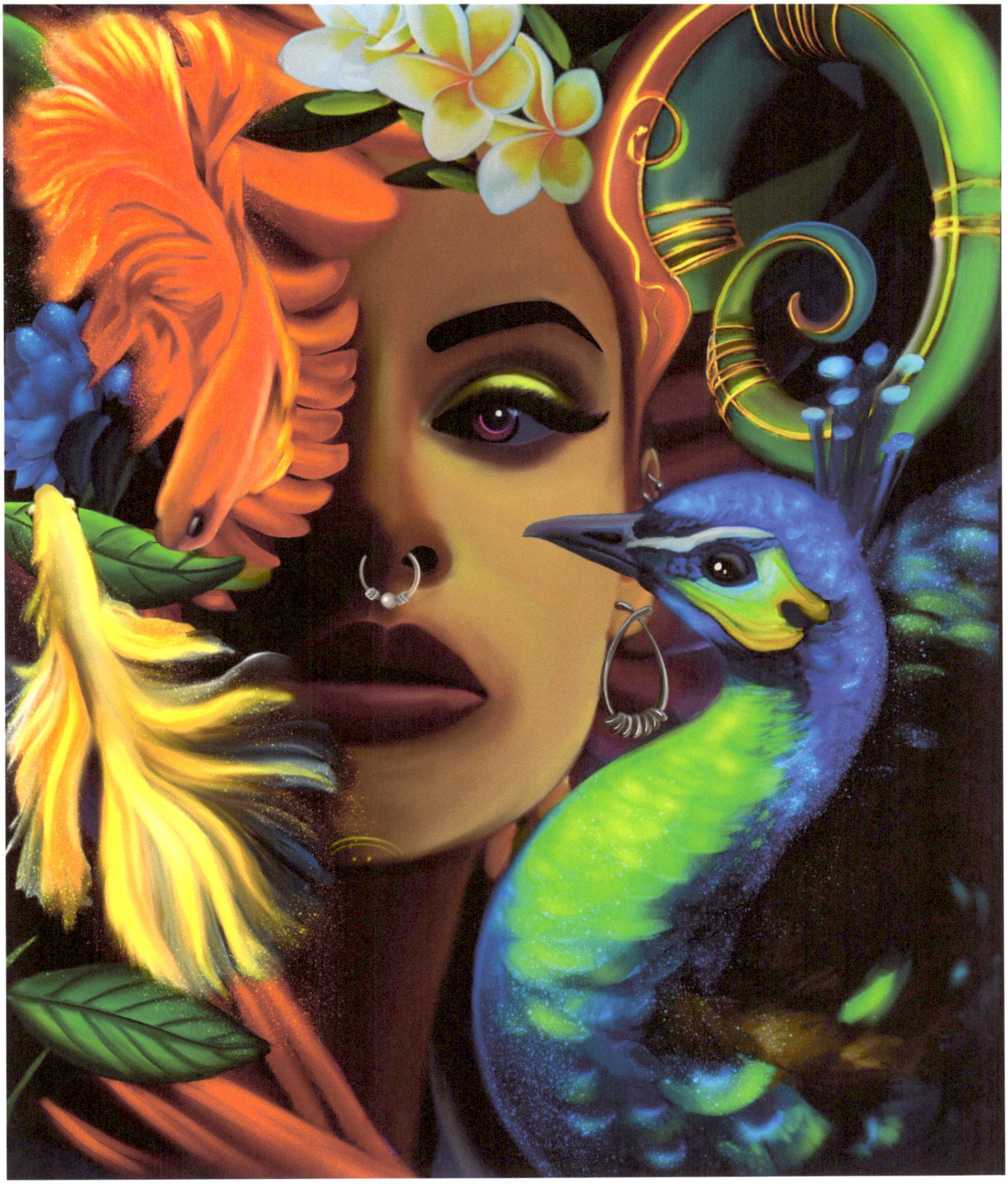

Rediscovering Beauty

foundation.app/@pink0_palette/~/112021

Minted: November 28, 2021

@Pixelfactory_

Ullas Jose, 3D & 2D artist

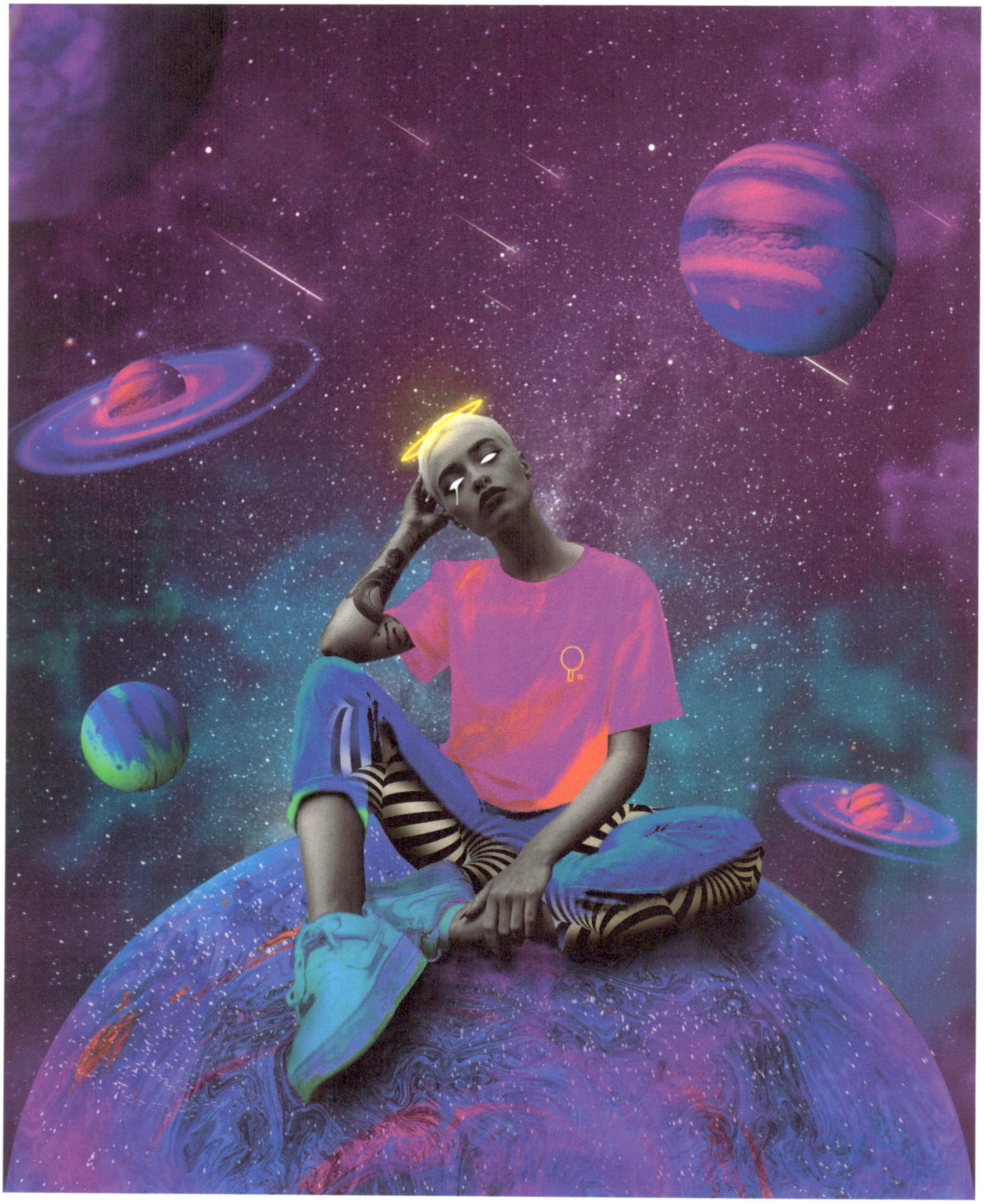

The Epiphany Of Tiamat

foundation.app/@pixelfactory_/~/45285

Minted: June 5, 2021

@Sacredvoo
Sacred Voo, artist

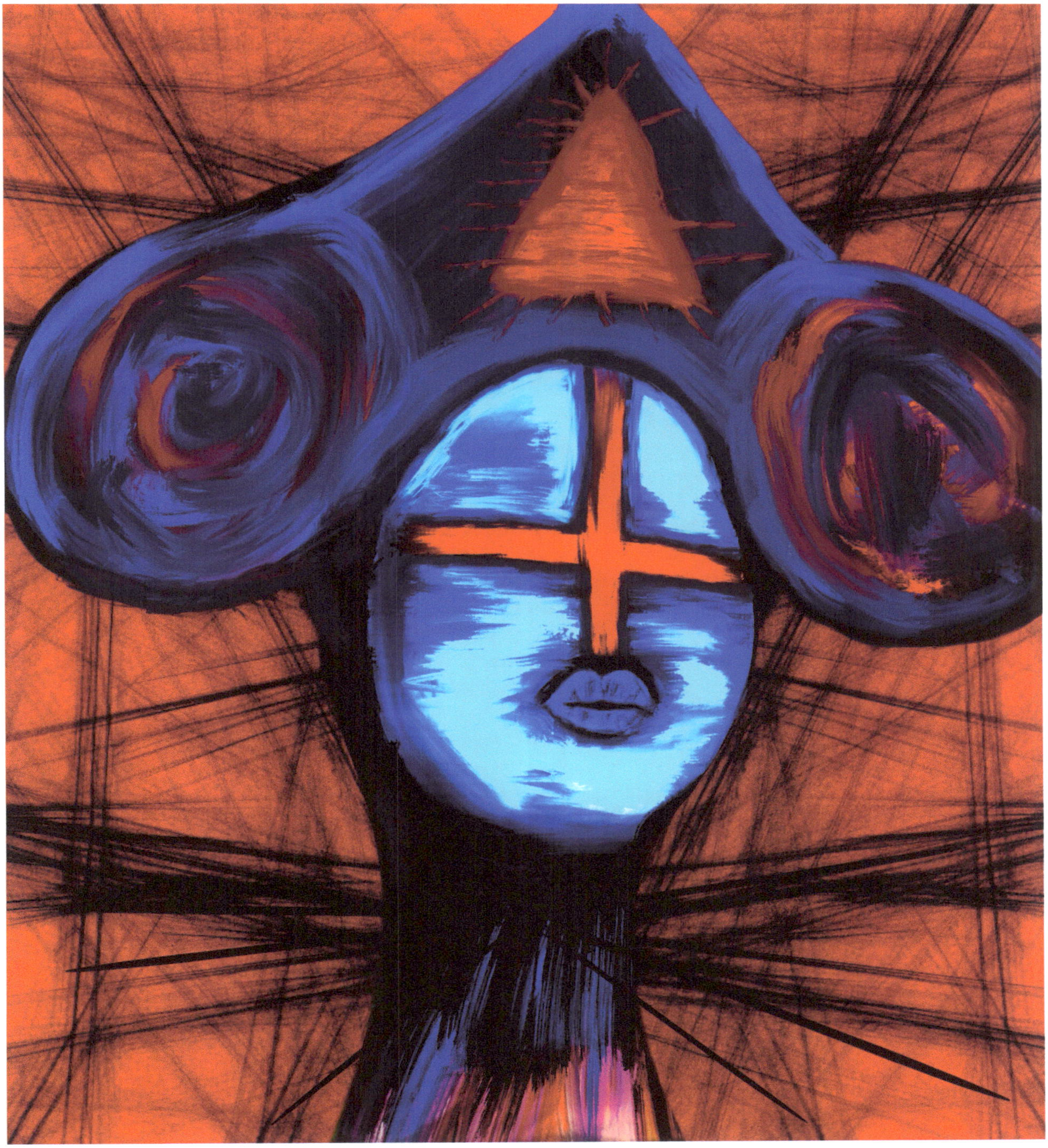

NFT HIGH PRIESTESS #1/1

https://opensea.io/collection/sacred-voo

Minted: August 31, 2021

@SabaMakesNFTs

Saba SW, creator of @fuzziemints

"Leadership is no easy feat, but if you lead by heart and by example, then you got it made."

FuZZieMiNTs collection

FuZZieMiNTs are perhaps the cutest of all the animals bouncing around on the blockchain. Cuteness isn't enough however, when you're offering collectible buyers slight permutations on the same theme. You'll hear the NFT crowd chanting 'we want utility' from the stadium, and if you're the home team and you don't deliver, the art might not be enough.

Saba is the creator of the **FuZZieMiNTs** gaming collectible NFT series that eventually promises a family-friendly game from the game studio Saba founded. It's a fun and fresh direction, and she's happy to point the way with integrity and creativity.

Each **FuZZieMiNTs** includes an AR-ready 3D model so you can walk (I mean, bounce) around in augmented reality. AR meetups will never be the same. **FuZZieMiNTs** is a hybrid generative project which means multiple connected computers lighten the load for the creator doing much of the work. But the idea wasn't a guaranteed hit:

*"When I started 2021, I didn't know that I'd sell over 500 NFTs. This year has been epic. Thank you to everyone who got a **FuZZieMiNT**. The community has changed my life."*

Beyond the cuteness factor, **FuZZieMiNTs** have their own personalities born from a combination of attributes including body color, eye color, and fur color. Every little fluffy creature comes with its own vibe trait so you can choose from such qualities as loyalty, magic, health, love, creativity, intelligence, intuition, empathy, wealth, generosity, compassion, courage, humor, leadership, equality, patience, and honesty. These are the positive vibes that each **FuZZieMiNT** puts out into the metaverse.

Growing from their furry cute heads are rarity items including curved horns, ringed horns, branched horns, and antennae. Some FuZZieMiNTs are rarer than others with the **FuZZie100** being the earliest minted and most sought after. In true play to earn style, all **FuZZieMiNT** holders can also receive coins in the form of $FZBT tokens.

FuZZieMiNTs
opensea.io/collection/fuzziemints
Minted: September 9, 2021

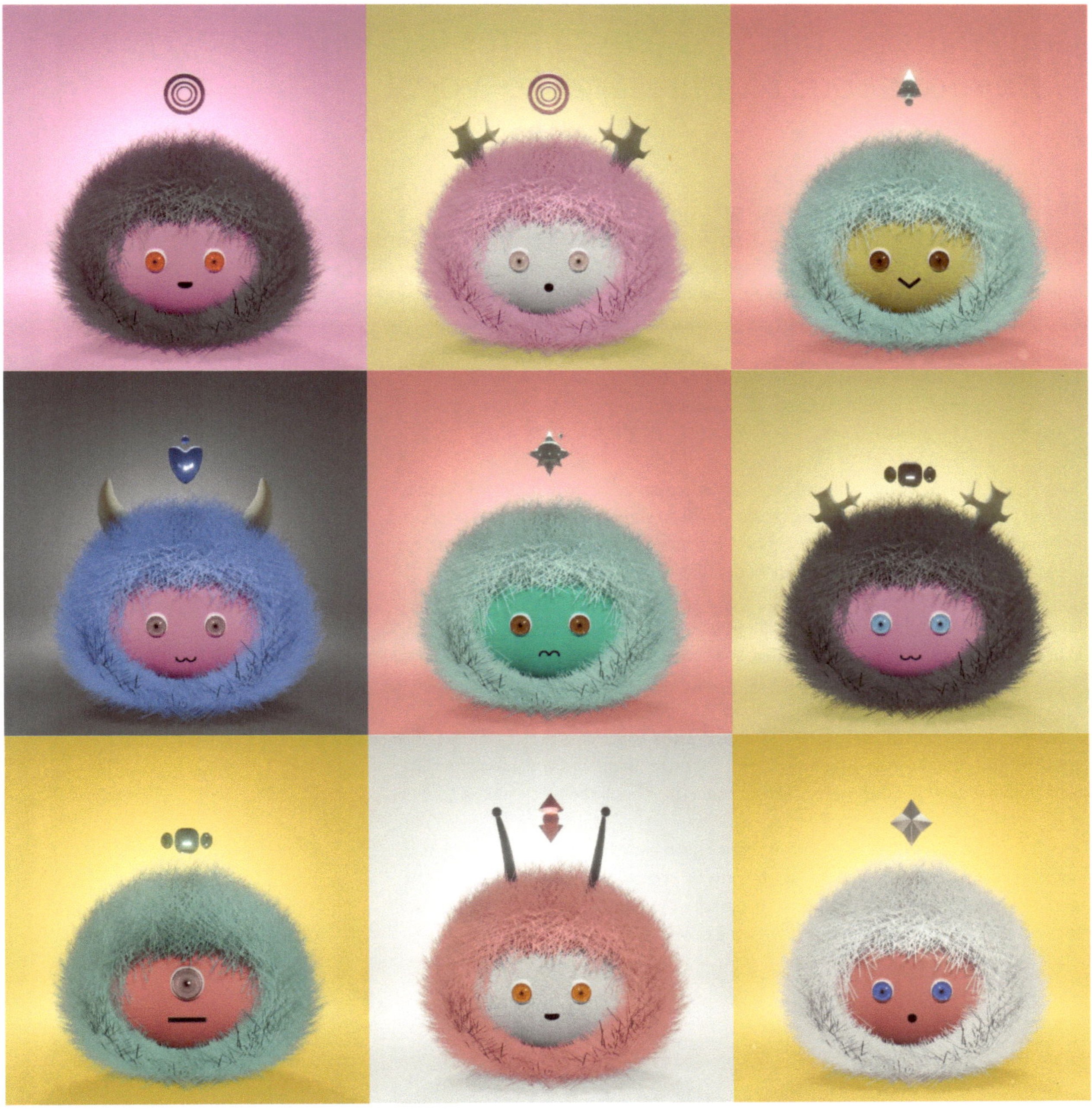

@toadboats
@nft_Vis, artist

"Super Frog is the Horny Toad mascot for Texas Christian University, my alma mater. It seems fitting to have a purple Horny ToadBoat to represent. Go Frogs!"

ToadBoats LaunchPad collection

This irreverent, fun project started from a keyboard mishap while trying to type the word 'bot'—an extra 'a' suddenly created the word 'ToadBoats'. Such a happy accident. A potential amphibian robot was transformed into a smiley boat-faced toad.

The ToadBoats LaunchPad collection will number 68 when completed. According to the artist, the project is an experiment in his own learning journey. Here are the questions that he asked himself.

"Can I teach myself to create digital art? Can I successfully deploy an ERC721 smart contract and mint NFTs that are not on the OpenSea shared contract? Can I develop and manage a community of collectors and interested parties that align with the art or ideas behind it? Can we bring this to our youth?"

It appears that the answer to most of these queries is 'yes.' Though the ToadBoats LaunchPad collection exists on OpenSea, the actual smart contract was created on WeMintArt. In addition, a Discord channel is buzzing with active community members.

The artist known on Twitter as @NFT_Vis has put the ToadBoats project in the public domain with a CC0 licence. That means we can adopt ToadBoats and make them our own, merchandise them, and generally set them free to sail the blockchain.

Why does it matter to create your own smart contract rather than use a platform contract like OpenSea or Foundation? Autonomy. You own your own contract and it can't be cancelled by a marketplace. And, perhaps more importantly, you get control of the code and how people interact with the code.

Super ToadBoat #16
opensea.io/collection/toadboats-launchpad
Minted: November 29, 2021

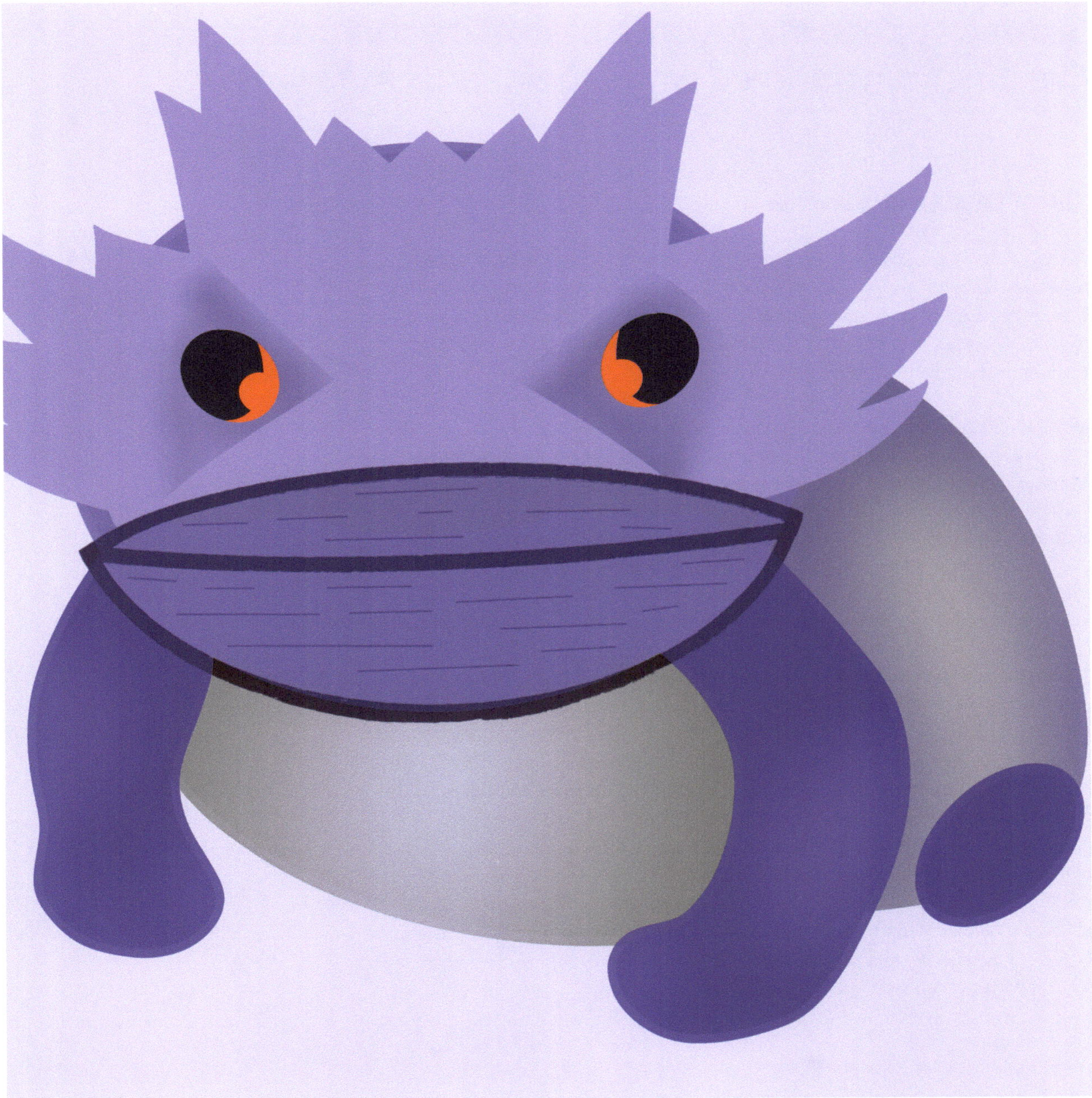

@Xose_Casal

Xose Casal, fine art photographer

"Since I was a child I have had a fixation with Stormtroopers, my favorite Star Wars *characters. I've always wondered what their private life was."*

TROOPERSCAPES collection

Photographer Xose Casal has spent his lifetime learning the intricacies of his craft. He began as a teenager, exploring the ways of chemical photography in black-and-white. Now, as an adult, he's seen his chosen art form transformed by the digital era. Xose has fully embraced all the benefits of the new technology, specializing in landscape and long-exposure photography.

As an NFT artist, Xose has a few collections on Foundation. The one he shares with us here is called **Trooperscapes**. As the title implies, it's a series of landscapes starring the most maligned of sci-fi bad guys—the Stormtroopers in the *Star Wars* franchise.

Here in **Trooperscapes #3. FCK the Empire**, a Stormtrooper stands in a position like Homer Simpson (as if saying a silent "doh" to himself). In the animated image, puffs of smoke emit from his helmet and uniform. Perhaps the internal circuitry of his suit is failing. Perhaps he has no idea why he's standing in the middle of a vast, empty ocean.

*"**Trooperscapes** is my own personal tribute to Stormtroopers—a mixed-media project of scale model photography, long exposure landscape, and digital animation."*

Beyond the charming, tongue-in-cheek humor of this collection, it appears that Xose has constructed a photography career of much accomplishment. He participated in photo competitions, receiving numerous awards both national and international, including a second place in 2013 International Photography Awards and the top prizes of the International Federation of Photographic Art (Blue Pin and Gold Medal FIAP); the Photographic Society America (Gold Medal PSA); the United Photographers International (Gold Medal UPI); the Gold Medal at the prestigious Trierenberg Super Circuit of Austria; as well as Gold Medals of the Spanish Confederation of Photography (CEF) and the Catalan Federation of Photography (FCF).

TROOPERSCAPES #3. FCK the Empire
foundation.app/@xosecasal/~/55426
Minted: July 2, 2021

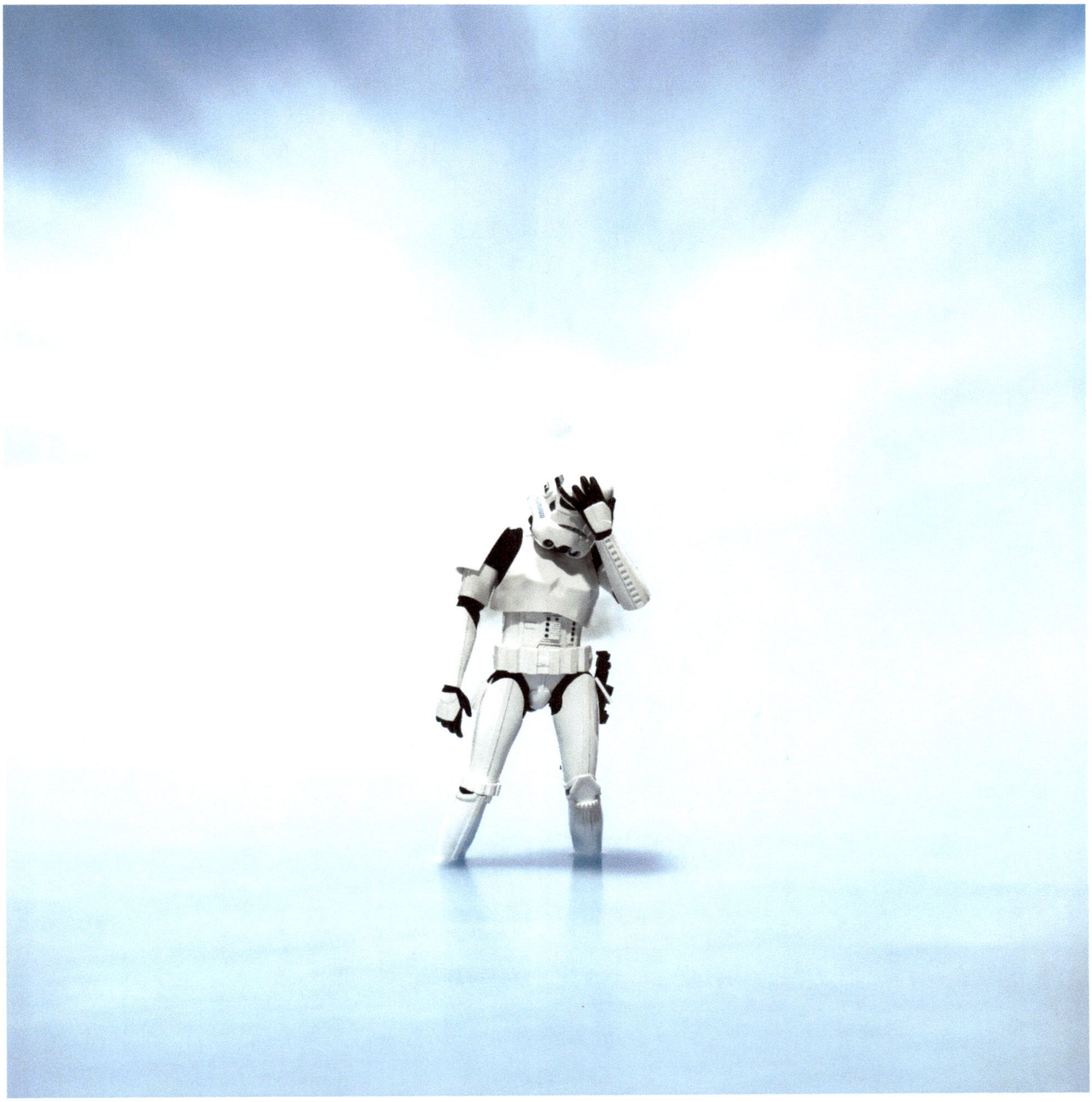

COLLECTORS

Collectors who value provenance acquire art minted on the blockchain, and their collections are enjoyed beyond the confines of physical walls.

@artNFTlove
BYTESOIL, collector

"There was a decision to be made: A CryptoPunk for 0.9 ETH or this nice **Bored Ape Yacht Club** *for 0.54 ETH. The shocking pink primate fit into our SnowCrash CyberPunk mindset with his holo glasses looking into a bright future! So we literally 'aped in.'"*

Bored Ape Yacht Club #6731
Artist: Bored Ape Yacht Club
opensea.io/collection/boredapeyachtclub
Minted: May 1, 2021

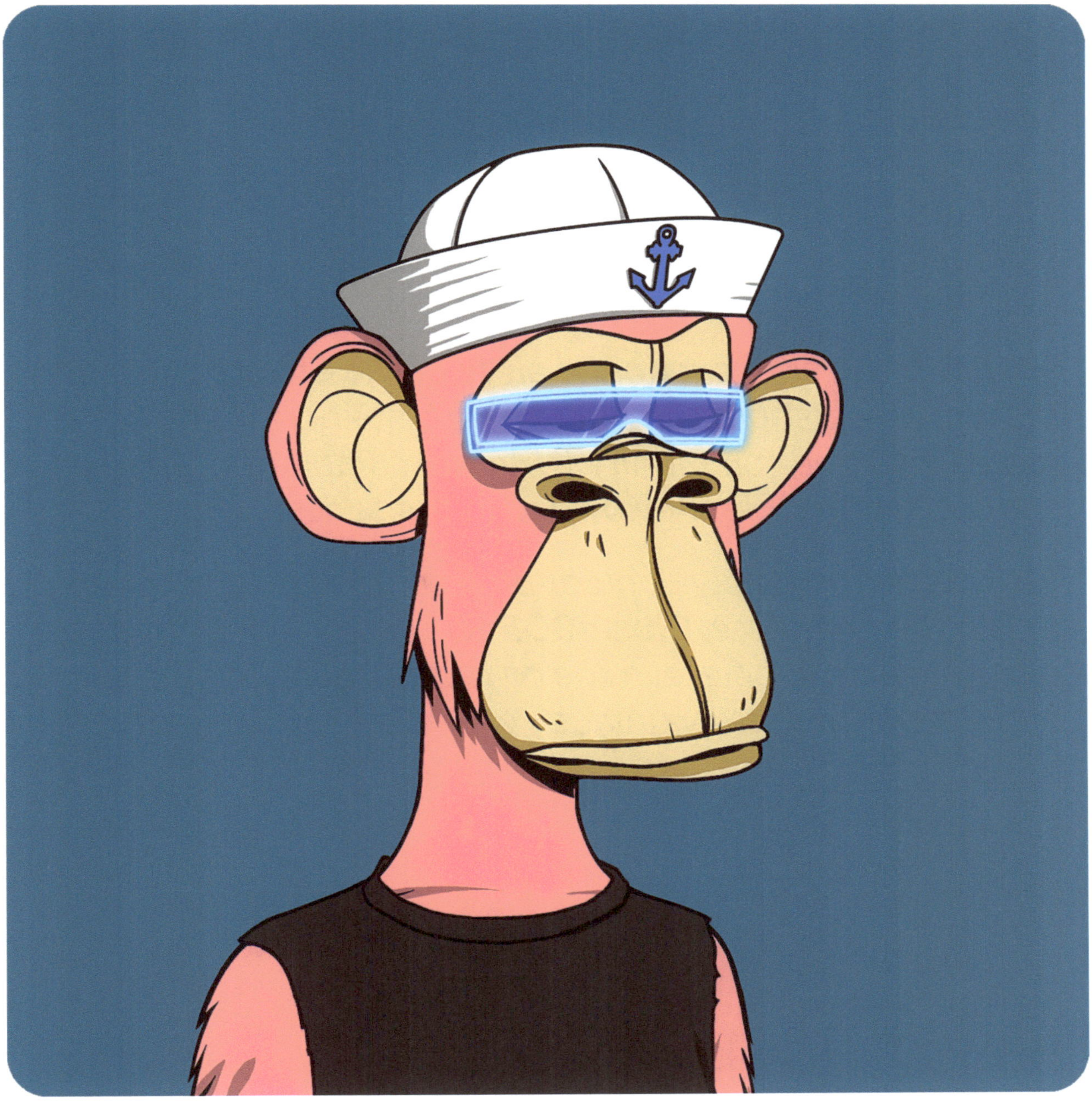

@cryptopathic
Siinamota, collector

*"**Sirxn 0** is the final auctioned piece of the **Ghxsts** collection. This was the first project where an artist—here, GxngYxng—worked with the community to create combinations based on the existing NFTs they owned in the series.*

*This was an incredibly popular project, and I'm lucky enough to own the first piece, **Ghxst 001**. So I became dedicated to capturing the last piece in the collection, allowing me to create something truly unique."*

Sirxn 0 - Bioluminescent Sirxn
Artist: GxngYxng
opensea.io/collection/ghxsts
Minted: August 21, 2021

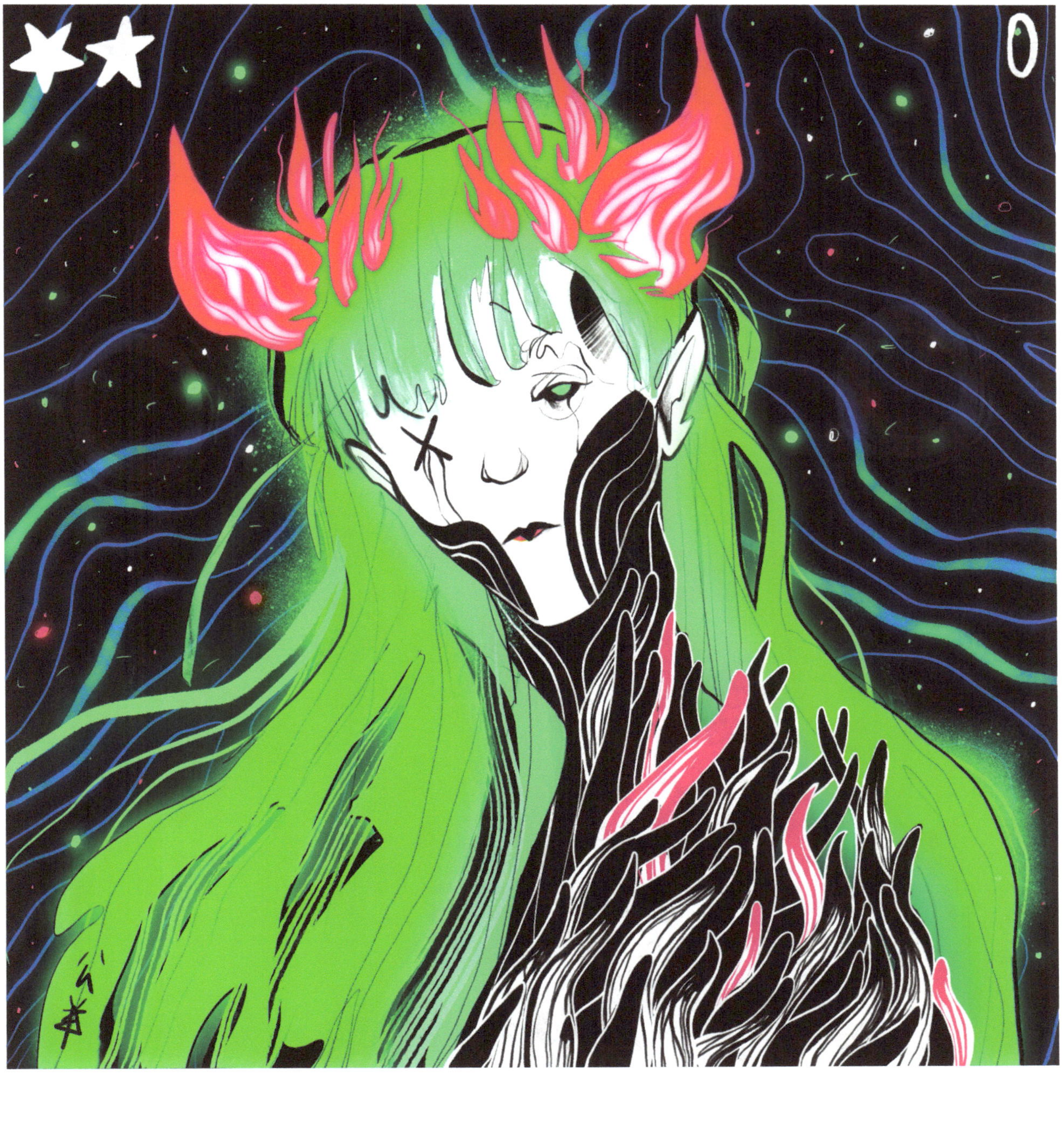

@joshuagalloway
Joshua Galloway, collector

"I'm a big fan of The Hitchhiker's Guide to the Galaxy *by Douglas Adams. In the book, the number '42' is the answer to the ultimate question of life, the universe, and everything else (including, probably, the metaverse).*

I started my career in video games, so collecting in-game currencies and in-game items were not foreign to me. However, I see true art collecting as seeking answers to counter my insatiable quest for knowledge."

Ultimate Answer...?
Artist: Q Yoneda
https://foundation.app/@qyoneda/~/38716
Minted: May 21, 2021

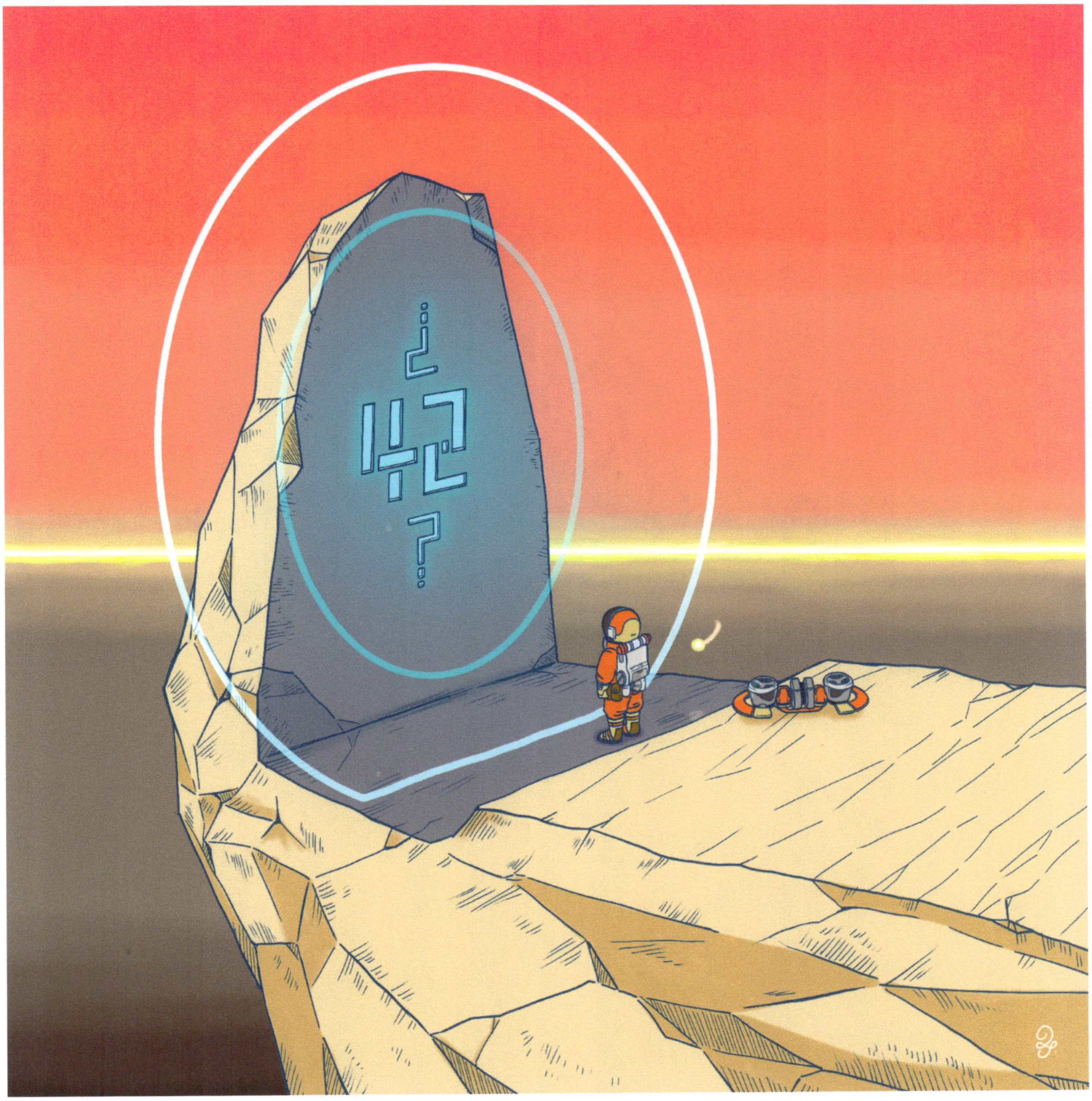

About the Author

@mintfaced (mintface.eth)

Ryan Jennings, inspiring confidence in digital art ownership

I'm the founder of MintFace (mintface.xyz) and the NFT Digital Artist Economy Workshop (digitalartisteconomy.com), onboarding the next 2,000 artists into the digital artist economy.

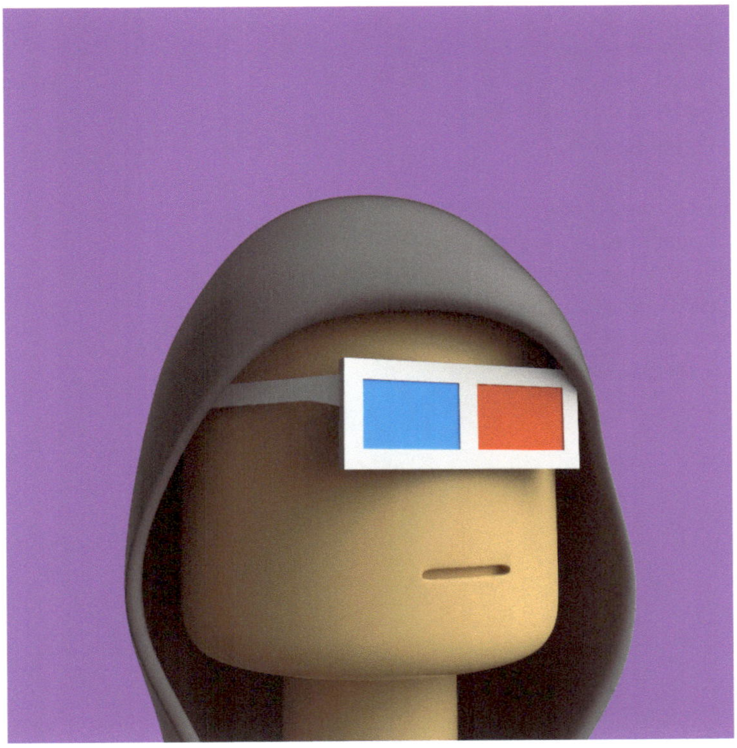

LegoPunk #222

NFT Digital Artist Economy Workshop

The NFT Digital Artist Economy Workshop helps artists launch their first NFT art show on the blockchain, meaning that is eligible to collect commission for life. Artists join a group of digital art pioneers who are forging a new paradigm for all types of creatives. Just as exciting, this workshop helps artists to discover digital art collectors who value provenance as well as creativity. The workshop is deal for three kinds of people:

- Well-known artists who are eager to create a digital art portfolio from their back catalogue, or start afresh with new work to mint on the blockchain.

- Graphic and lens-based artists with a social media following and print buyers who want to deconstruct how to this audience into digital art collectors.

- New artists, without a reputation or following, who want to skip the traditional art barriers by creating direct connections in a thriving digital art community.

The workshop unfolds into a number of sessions, including: how art is minted digitally, how to examine your back catalogue with NFTs in mind, price setting and royalties, navigating copyright, and how to launch your first art show.

Each workshop is hosted in a live, highly-interactive environment, so you'll be creating not watching. In addition, many participants say that the cohort of fellow artists they met was just as important to their growth. Beyond the workshop, they've developed as real-world friends and colleagues, helping to spur each other's growth.

The instructor is MintFace. Prior to offering the workshop, he established a world-first trademark licensing system, protected by AI, for software companies that export globally. He believes that many of the next 10,000 artists who join the digital artist economy will have their lives transformed by the 'commission for life' art movement. MintFace enjoys playing on the edge of business, creativity, and technology and is a leading voices on how digitisation is set to transform our lives through Web3.0.

Artist Index

Acknowledgements

Minted was a decentralized effort where artists stepped forward to be part of the book by contributing art from around the world to bring the book to life. I'd like to thank and give gratitude to the linchpins in the center that brought it all together.

@fredrickhaugen

Thank you to Fredrick Haugen, who with handcrafted-detail designed the book you hold, then edited the text to ensure the voice of the artist was represented. Fredrick is the creator of Seven Good Things, a weekly list of positivity and creativity. His firm, Lindo Labs, is a creative studio that designs, edits, and codes cool stuff for nice folks.

@katherine_roan

A big thank you to Katherine Roan for sourcing high-resolution art, proof reading the print-ready copy and letting me get away with keeping 'buidl' and 'wen' in the final text. Katherine is a top tier ed-tech geek who helps creators make magic. She heads up community management for alumni of the NFT Digital Artist Economy Workshop.

ISBN Hardcover 978-0-473-60817-0

Book designed and edited by Fredrick Haugen

Published by UmPrint Publishing

CryptoArte Painting #4971

Back Cover Artist: Sebastián Brocher

Sebastián hopes that his **CryptoArte Painting** collection, non-fungible token, and decentralized app will help grow the Ethereum community by fostering awareness of blockchain technology in an accessible and fun way. He desires his paintings to provoke thoughtful conversations about the blockchain and make more people aware of what Ethereum is, how it works, and how it can be leveraged.

www.ingramcontent.com/pod-product-compliance
Lightning Source LLC
LaVergne TN
LVHW071242210926
848486LV00007B/324
9780473608170